W9-AXJ-377

THE GEORGE WASHINGTON PAPERS

By Frank Donovan

THE MEDAL
THE TALL FRIGATES
THE EARLY EAGLES
THE UNLUCKY HERO
THE AMERICANISM OF BARRY GOLDWATER
MR. MONROE'S MESSAGE
MR. LINCOLN'S PROCLAMATION

The Papers of the Founding Fathers

THE BENJAMIN FRANKLIN PAPERS
THE THOMAS JEFFERSON PAPERS
THE GEORGE WASHINGTON PAPERS

Juveniles

THE IRONCLADS
THE BRAVE TRAITOR
THE CUTTER
THE MANY WORLDS OF BENJAMIN FRANKLIN
FAMOUS TWENTIETH CENTURY LEADERS
IRONCLADS OF THE CIVIL WAR
THE VIKINGS

Æt. 13.

March 12th 1744/5

Geo Washington

Æt. 17.

Beginning this Eleventh Day of November 1749 —

G Washington

Æt. 25.

I am Sir, Yr Most Obedt Hble Servt

Fort Loudoun
10th Septr 1757 } — Go Washington

Æt. 44.

Yr Most affect Brother,

Go Washington

New York 29th of April 1776.

Four days before his Death. Æt. 67.

Mount Vernon
December 10th
1799 — Go Washington

Facsimiles of George Washington's handwriting, from top to bottom, at ages thirteen, seventeen, twenty-five, forty-four, and sixty-seven, four days before his death.

THE PAPERS OF THE FOUNDING FATHERS

THE GEORGE WASHINGTON PAPERS

Selected, edited and interpreted by

FRANK DONOVAN

ILLUSTRATED

DODD, MEAD & COMPANY

NEW YORK

To Mara and Bob;
and Michael, Steven,
Linda, Douglas,
Patricia and Kim

Library of Congress Catalog Card Number: 64-25772

Printed in the United States of America
by The Cornwall Press, Inc., Cornwall, N. Y.

IN EXPLANATION AND ACKNOWLEDGMENT

George Washington spelled like a gentleman. But the gentlemen of his day, by the standards of this day, were not very good spellers. If judged by present rules of spelling and punctuation, most of the Founding Fathers would have foundered in fifth grade. This is said to explain the extent of the "editorial tampering" with the papers of George Washington in this book.

The very words "editorial tampering" are as a red flag to a bull to some purists, who believe that every dot or comma of the original documents are sacrosanct. This point of view is certainly valid for an edition of historical papers which is designed primarily for reference or research. But this book is meant to be read as well as referred to. So, for ease in reading, punctuation and spelling have been corrected to conform to modern practice wherever this could be done without endangering the meaning of what Washington wrote.

Also, the first Father was frequently rather verbose. To keep these selections from his writings within a volume of reasonable size many of the papers included here have been abridged. A sincere effort has been made not to quote out of context or tamper with the meaning of what he wrote or the ideas which he expressed. Deletions are indicated by an ellipsis (. . .).

In preparing this work the writer has leaned on scholars of the past. It was not necessary to consult original documents, most of which are in some four hundred volumes in the Library of Congress. All of the research for this book was done in the fine library of Yale University, on the shelves of which may be found all of the editions of Washington Papers which have been printed during the past 130 years. The first such edition was published in 1834–1837 by Jared Sparks, President of Harvard. This contained upward of twenty-five hundred letters and documents in twelve volumes.

Dr. Sparks deserves much credit as the earliest editor to attempt to preserve the papers of the Founding Fathers; but he took unforgivable editorial license. Apparently motivated by a desire to create a better literary image for his subject he ruthlessly changed syntax and wording. As an instance, here is a paragraph as Washington wrote it: "Last night was a blowing and Rainy night. Our straw catch'd a Fire yt. we were laying upon and was luckily Preserv'd by one of our Mens awaking when it was in [illegible] we run of four Lots this Day." Sparks made of this: "Our straw, upon which we were lying, took fire, but I was luckily preserved by one of our men awaking when it was in flame. We have run off four lots this day."

Worthington C. Ford's edition of Washington's papers was published, without editorial tampering, in 1889–1893. This was in fourteen volumes which, for commercial reasons, contained less than half of Washington's known writings. The final collection of *The Writings of George Washington* was published in 1931–1940 by authority of Congress under the direction of the United States George Washington Bicentennial Commission. The thirty-seven volumes, which contained all of Washington's essential writings, were edited with meticulous care by John C. Fitzpatrick.

Biographies of George Washington are so numerous that their listing fills a sizable volume of bibliography. Most famous of the early ones is that of the Reverend Mason L. Weems. This little volume was first published in 1800 a few months after Washington's death and has been constantly in print ever since. The most recent edition was published in 1963. It is interesting only as a curiosity, replete with legends and fictional anecdotes designed to create a saintly character that bore little resemblance to the real Washington.

To a lesser extent this was true of all the biographies of the nineteenth and early twentieth centuries. They idolized, rather than depicted, their subject. Then, in 1926, Rupert Hughes wrote the first of the so-called debunking biographies. This presents Washington as a human and very virile character who lost his temper on occasion and sometimes swore mighty oaths. In his effort to humanize his subject Mr. Hughes somewhat belabored minor flaws. His repeated references to drinking and betting seem to indicate that Washington was something of a toper and confirmed gambler. In fact, his indulgence in both of these practices was extremely moderate.

The one biography which stands far above all others is that by Douglas Southall Freeman entitled, simply, *George Washington.* The first six volumes of this work were published between 1948 and 1954. After Mr. Freeman's death the seventh volume was completed, in 1957, by his associates John Alexander Carroll and Mary Wells Ashworth. This comprehensive study presents a true and complete picture of Washington, his times and his contemporaries, in approximately one and a quarter million fascinating, readable words.

CONTENTS

❦

ILLUSTRATIONS

❦

Extended quotations from George Washington and others appear in the larger of the two sizes of type used for the text.

CHAPTER I

THE YOUNG SURVEYOR

❦

WHEN GEORGE WAS about six years old, he was made the wealthy master of a hatchet, of which, like most little boys, he was immoderately fond, and was constantly going about chopping every thing that came in his way. One day, in the garden, where he often amused himself hacking his mother's pea-sticks, he unluckily tried the edge of his hatchet on the body of a beautiful young English cherry tree, which he barked so terribly that I don't believe the tree ever got the better of it. The next morning the old gentleman, finding out what had befallen his tree, which, by the by, was a great favorite, came into the house; and with much warmth asked for the mischievous author, declaring at the time, that he would not have taken five guineas for his tree. Nobody could tell him anything about it. Presently George and his hatchet made their appearance. "George," said his father, "do you know who killed that beautiful little cherry tree yonder in the garden?" This was a tough question; and George staggered under it for a moment; but quickly recovered himself: and looking at his father, with the sweet face of youth brightened with the inexpressible charm of all-conquering truth, he bravely cried, "I can't tell a lie, Pa;

you know I can't tell a lie. I did cut it with my hatchet," "Run to my arms, you dearest boy," cried his father in transports, "run to my arms; glad am I, George, that you killed my tree; for you have paid me for it a thousand fold. Such an act of heroism in my son is more worth than a thousand trees, though blossomed with silver, and their fruits of purest gold!"

So wrote Washington's first biographer, Mason Locke Weems, in 1800, a few months after Washington's death. And in so writing Parson Weems created a legend which marched down the years with much benefit to the candy, bakery and ice cream industries, which still provide goodies in the shape of logs and hatchets to celebrate Washington's natal day. More, with this and other fictitious anecdotes, he created a legendary Washington; an austere and sanctimonious prig.

The truth was not in Weems; but, he believed, he was writing in a good cause—the deification of the father of his country. Throughout the nineteenth and early twentieth centuries others followed in his footsteps to make a cold, superhuman paragon of a great man who is portrayed by his own writings as very human, with a fair share of moderate manly vices. Washington was virile, passionate and at times tempestuous. His stature as statesman and soldier is not lessened by the fact that he drank a little, gambled a little and liked girls. He was ambitious, acquisitive and sometimes obstinate—and when it served his purpose to tell a non-vicious lie, he lied.

The fictitious boyhood which Weems created for Washington may be partially excused by the paucity of facts. Washington left no record of his early years, nor did any of his contemporaries until many years later when his fame encouraged legendary memoirs. When he was President, Washington did write an account of his ancestory in reply to a query from Sir Isaac Heard, Garter Principal King at Arms. He said:

IN THE YEAR 1657, or thereabouts, and during the usurpation of Oliver Cromwell, John and Lawrence Washington, brothers, emigrated from the north of England, and settled at Bridges Creek on Potomac River, in the country of Westmoreland. But from whom they descended, the subscribed is possessed of no document to ascertain.

John Washington [George Washington's great-grandfather] was employed as general against the Indians in Maryland, and as a reward for his services was made a colonel; and the parish wherein he lived was called after him.

Other sources record that John Washington came to America after his father, the Reverend Mr. Lawrence, was ousted from his Anglican living by Cromwell. A book published by Parliament in 1643 listed George Washington's great-great-grandfather among "The First Century of Scandalous, Malignant Priests," libeling him as a "Common frequenter of ale-houses, not only himself sitting daily tippling there, but also encouraging others in that beastly vice, and hath been oft drunk." A defender of the Anglican clergy denied this and claimed that the Reverend Mr. Lawrence was a "worthy, pious very modest, sober person."

Washington's letter to Sir Isaac continued to list the issue of his great-grandfather and grandfather in America, including Augustine, his father, of whom he added:

AUGUSTINE, son of Lawrence and Mildred Washington, married Jane Butler, the daughter of Caleb Butler, of Westmoreland, April 20th, 1715, by whom he had three sons: Butler (who died young), Lawrence, and Augustine, and one daughter, Jane, who died when a child. Jane, wife of Augustine, died Nov. 24th, 1728, and was buried in the family vault at Bridges Creek.

Augustine then married Mary Ball [George Washington's mother] March 6th, 1730, by whom he had issue George, born February 11th [old style], 1732; Betty, born June 20th, 1733; Samuel, born Nov. 16th, 1734; John Augustine, born Jan. 13th, 1735; Charles, May 1st, 1738; and Mildred, June 21st, 1739, who died Oct. 28th, 1740. Augustine departed this life April 12th, 1743, aged forty-nine years, and was interred at Bridges Creek in the vault of his ancestors.

Throughout his life Washington celebrated his birthday on February 11. The calendar which Pope Gregory introduced in 1582 was used throughout Europe, except Russia, but was not adopted in Protestant England and her colonies until 1752. There was a difference of eleven days between the old Julian calendar and the Gregorian, and the start of the new year was changed from March 25 to January 1. Washington should have written the year 1731/2 to conform to current practice.

George lived at his birthplace on Pope's Creek until he was three. The Washingtons then moved to a tract at Little Hunting Creek (present Mount Vernon) and in 1740 to Ferry Farm in Fredericksburg. In 1747 George went to live with his half-brother Lawrence, who had inherited the Hunting Creek property. Lawrence, fourteen years senior to George, had been educated in England and had served under Admiral Vernon on an expedition to Cartegena —hence the name of the house which he built at Hunting Creek, Mount Vernon.

Such formal schooling as young George had—four or five years —ended when he moved to Mount Vernon. There is no positive record of his school days. Later, a minister who knew him said that he had "no other education than reading, writing, and accounts, which he was taught by a convict servant whom his father bought for a schoolmaster." He is also supposed to have gone to a school in Fredericksburg conducted by a Reverend James Marye where he is said to have occupied himself with ciphering while other boys played games, although another legend has him "romping with one of the largest girls. This was so unusual that it excited no little astonishment among the other lads."

The earliest extant writing in Washington's hand is a school copybook of which the first pages are missing. The initial entries are notes on multiplication, decimals and interest. The first full entry is on geometry, of which young George said, "One of the seven sciences, and a very useful and necessary branch of mathematics, whose subject is greatness: for as number is the subject of arithmetic, so that of geometry is magnitude." The copybook exercises then pass through trigonometry into surveying. Mathematics was unquestionably Washington's one good subject.

Another school exercise book contains "Forms of Writings," which includes samples of a promissory note, a bill of exchange, a bail bond, a short will, a servant's indenture. The last ten pages of this book contain the "Rules of Civility" of which much has been made by doting biographers. These comprise 110 rules for mannerly conduct which may have been composed in part by thirteen-year-old George but which were more probably copied from translations of French or Latin works on the subject. A few typical rules which George wrote or copied are:

EVERY ACTION done in company ought to be with some sign of respect to those that are present.

Sleep not when others speak. Sit not when others stand.

Speak not when you should hold your peace.

At play and at fire it's good manners to give place to the last comer.

Come not near the books or writings of another so as to read them unless desired or give your opinion of them unasked.

Let your countenance be pleasant but in serious matters somewhat grave.

Reproach none for the infirmities of nature.

Show not yourself glad at the misfortune of another though he were your enemy.

When you meet with one of greater quality than yourself, stop, and . . . give way for him to pass.

Let your discourse with men of business be short and comprehensive.

In writing or speaking, give to every person his due title according to his degree and the custom of the place.

Strive not with your superiors in argument, but always submit your judgment to others with modesty.

Undertake not to teach your equal in the art himself professes; it savors arrogancy.

In your apparel be modest and endeavor to accommodate nature, rather than to procure admiration.

Associate yourself with men of good quality if you esteem your own reputation; for 'tis better to be alone than in bad company.

Let your conversation be without malice or envy. . . . And in all causes of passion admit reason to govern.

Be not apt to relate news if you know not the truth thereof.

Undertake not what you cannot perform but be careful to keep your promise.

Speak not evil of the absent for it is unjust.

Be not tedious in discourse.

When you speak of God or his attributes, let it be seriously and with reverence.

Let your recreations be manful not sinful.

Labor to keep alive in your breast that little spark of Celestial fire called conscience.

George was fortunate in his brother Lawrence, who stood as a father to him during his teens. He was equally fortunate in his next door neighbors at Mount Vernon, the Fairfaxes. Lord Fairfax was the proprietor of some six million acres in Virginia embracing much of the Shenandoah Valley. William Fairfax, His Lordship's cousin and agent, owned the house next door, Belvoir. Lawrence married his daughter Anne. William's son George William was seven years older than George Washington and was his companion on his first surveying trip. A description of the adolescent Washington is contained in a letter which Lord Fairfax wrote to the boy's mother, who had apparently asked his opinion on sending her son to school in England. After advising against this his Lordship continued:

HE IS STRONG and hardy, and as good a master of a horse as any could desire. His education might have been bettered, but what he has is accurate and inclines him to much life out of doors. He is very grave for one of his age, and reserved in his intercourse; not a great talker at any time. His mind appears to me to act slowly, but, on the whole, to reach just conclusions, and he has an ardent wish to see the right of questions—what my friend Mr. Addison was pleased to call "the intellectual conscience." Method and exactness seem to be natural to George. He is, I suspect, beginning to feel the sap rising, being in the spring of life, and is getting ready to be the prey of your sex, wherefore may the Lord help him and deliver him from the nets those spiders, called women, will cast for his ruin. I presume him to be truthful because he is exact. I wish I could say that he governs his temper. He is subject to attacks of anger on provocation, and sometimes without just cause; but as he is a reasonable person time will cure him of this vice of nature, and in fact he is, in my judgment, a man who will go to school all his life and profit thereby.

When George was fourteen Lawrence proposed to get him a midshipman's commission in the British Navy. His mother would have none of it. George's own teen-age interest was in another direction. His inheritance from his father had been relatively meager. Land and speculation in land offered a way to ultimate wealth, and the surveying of land provided a good, quick income. It is not clear where George learned surveying. His father owned surveying instruments, and George had practiced with them before he was fifteen. Lord Fairfax's small kingdom beyond the Blue

Ridge needed to be surveyed. In 1748 sixteen-year-old George, together with George William Fairfax, joined a surveying party to chart His Lordship's domain. Contrary to legend, Washington was not the surveyor. This was an older man, James Genn. Chainmen and helpers were hired on the frontier. The two Georges were gentlemen adventurers, although young Washington did get to help with the surveying and even to lay out some lots himself.

The record of this survey trip, titled "A Journal of my Journey over the Mountains began Friday the 11th of March, 1747/8," is the initial entry in the earliest of the diaries which Washington kept throughout his life. During the first four days of the trip, in which they traveled to the scene of operations, Washington wrote that "nothing remarkable happened." On the fifth day he recorded:

WE SET OUT EARLY with intent to run round the said land, but being taken in a rain and it increasing very fast obliged us to return. It clearing about one o'clock and our time being too precious to lose we a second time ventured out and worked hard till night and then returned to Pennington's. We got our supper and was lighted into a room, and I, not being so good a woodsman as the rest of my company, stripped myself very orderly and went into the bed as they called it, when to my surprise I found it to be nothing but a little straw, matted together without sheets or anything else, but only one thread-bare blanket with double its weight of vermin, such as lice, fleas, etc. I was glad to get up (as soon as the light was carried from us); I put on my clothes and lay as my companions. Had we not been very tired I am sure we should not have slept much that night. I made a promise not to sleep so from that time forward, choosing rather to sleep in the open air before a fire, as will appear hereafter.

The next day they worked and then

traveled up to Frederick town where our baggage came to us. We cleaned ourselves (to get rid of the game we had caught the night before) and took a review of the town and thence returned to our lodgings where we had a good dinner prepared for us; wine and rum punch in plenty and a good feather bed with clean sheets, which was a very agreeable regale.

For another week they worked, traveled, forded swollen streams and cursed the almost constant rain. On March 23 Washington recorded:

RAINED till about two o'clock and cleared, when we were agreeably surprised at the sight of thirty-odd Indians coming from war with only one scalp. We had some liquor with us of which we gave them part. It, elevating their spirits, put them in the humor of dancing, of whom we had a war dance. Their manner of dancing is as follows: They clear a large circle and make a great fire in the middle, then seat themselves about it. The speaker makes a grand speech, telling them in what manner they are to dance. After he had finished, the best dancer jumps up as one awaked out of a sleep and runs and jumps about the ring in a most comical manner. He is followed by the rest. Then begin their musicians to play. The music is a pot half [full] of water with a deerskin stretched over it as tight as it can and a gourd with shot in it to rattle and a piece of horse's tail tied to it to make it look fine. The one keeps rattling and the other drumming all the while the others are dancing.

The days followed uneventfully and the journal records work, weather and minor hardships. Young Washington at that time was no frontiersman. He was a young gentleman who was used to certain comforts and niceties, and while he did not exactly complain, he did not fail to comment on their absence on the frontier. When they dined at the home of a justice of the peace, Washington seemed surprised that "there was neither a cloth upon the table nor a knife to eat with." He reported that on one night "we had our tent carried off with the wind and was obliged to lie the latter part of the night without covering." On another night, "our straw catched a fire that we were laying upon and was luckily preserved by one of our men awaking when it was in [a blaze]."

The next day while they worked they were "attended by a great company of people; men, women and children that attended us through the woods, as we went, showing their antic tricks. I really think they seemed to be as ignorant a set of people as the Indians. They would never speak English but when spoken to they speak all Dutch." These were undoubtedly Germans who had come down from Pennsylvania to take squatter's rights on Lord Fairfax's land.

After almost a month, roughing it must have started to pale. April 7 was "the first night I slept in a house since I came to the branch," but the next night they were back in a tent, with every man his own cook; "our spits was forked sticks; our plates was a large chip as for dishes we had none." On the following day they "set the surveyor to work whilst Mr. Fairfax and myself stayed at the tent. Our provisions being all exhausted and the person that was to bring us a recruit [more provisions] disappointing us we were obliged to go without until we could get some from the neighbors; which was not till about four or five o'clock in the evening. We then took our leave of the rest of our company [and] rode down to John Colins in order to set off next day homewards."

"Wednesday the 13th of April, 1748, Mr. Fairfax got safe home and I myself safe to my brother's, which concludes my journal."

The teen-age Washington spent much time in the congenial Virginia practice of visiting. Somehow, he seems to have become proficient at billiards, and the account book which he started to keep in his sixteenth year shows him winning 1s 3d from a Thomas Turner, clerk of the court. In later times such proficiency has been considered a sign of a misspent youth. There are also entries for sums that he won at cards. The inclusion of a razor in a list of articles which he took on a visit indicates that he was shaving at sixteen, and the wardrobe which he carried is that of a very well dressed young gentleman. Another account book entry may indicate that he took dancing lessons at this time "to cash paid per music master for my entrance, 3s 9d." Since he neither sang nor played an instrument, this music master may have run a dancing school.

In the back of Washington's copybook are some evidences of adolescent love affairs—or perhaps "crushes" is a better description of his relations with, seemingly, several girls. First is a poem which he either did not complete or of which the last four lines are lost. The acrostic indicates that it was addressed to Frances Alexander, a neighbor.

*F*rom your bright sparkling eyes I was undone;
*R*ays you have; more transparent than the sun,
*A*midst its glory in the rising day
*N*one can you equal in your bright array;
*C*onstant in your calm and unspotted mind;
*E*qual to all, but will to none prove kind
*S*o knowing, seldom one so young, you'll find.

*A*h, woe's me, that I should love and conceal
*L*ong have I wish'd, but never dare reveal,
*E*ven though severely love's pains I feel;
*X*erxes that great, was't free from Cupid's dart,
*A*nd all the greatest heroes, felt the smart.

More mysterious is his affair with the Lowland Beauty who is mentioned in copies of three very similar letters which are in the back of the copybook. One of these, to Robin Washington, contains an expression of his juvenile ardor and incipient fickleness in this long, meandering sentence:

MY PLACE of residence is at present at His Lordship's where I might, was my heart disengaged, pass my time very pleasantly as there's a very agreeable young lady lives in the same house [Colonel George Fairfax's wife's sister] but as that's only adding fuel to fire it makes me the more uneasy for by often and unavoidably being in company with her revives my former passion for your Lowland Beauty; whereas was I to live more retired from young women I might in some measure alleviate my sorrows by burying that chaste and troublesome passion in the grave of oblivion or eternal forgetfulness; for as I am very well assured that's the only antidote or remedy that I shall be relieved by or only recess that can administer any cure or help to me, as I am well convinced was I ever to attempt anything I should only get a denial which would be only adding grief to uneasiness.

George Fairfax had married Sally Cary, and it was her sister Mary to whom Washington referred as the girl who might console him. There is ample evidence that, later, he loved Sally, two years his senior; but there is no indication of any improper relationship with his neighbor's wife. Nobody knows the identity of the Lowland Beauty. To this day there are half a dozen F.F.V.'s who claim her among their ancestors. One intriguing possibility is that she was Lucy Grymes, who later married Henry Lee and became the mother of Lighthorse Harry Lee, one of Washington's generals, and the grandmother of Robert E. Lee, who married the daughter of Washington's adopted son.

For three years after his survey trip for Lord Fairfax, George worked as a professional surveyor. He surveyed the site of the present town of Alexandria, Virginia, and was appointed surveyor of Culpeper County. He undertook another trip to the frontier for Fairfax; this time as the surveyor. Although he was now more at home in the wilderness, he still considered its hardships worthy of comment in a letter which he wrote an unknown Richard:

SINCE YOU RECEIVED my letter in October last I have not slept above three nights or four in a bed but after walking a good deal all the day lay down before the fire upon a little hay, straw, fodder or bearskin, whichever is to be had; with man, wife and children like a parcel of dogs or cats—and happy is he that gets the berth nearest the fire. There's nothing would make it pass off tolerably but a good reward. A doubloon is my constant gain every day that the weather will permit my going out—and sometime six pistoles.

Eighteen-year-old George was seriously interested in pistoles, doubloons and pounds and was making out quite well financially. Surveying gave him opportunities to pick up choice parcels of land for himself, and he invested some of his money in Shenandoah property, without stinting himself on his mounts, his horse furnishings or his wardrobe.

When he was nineteen Washington made the only sea voyage of his life, to Barbados. Brother Lawrence had tuberculosis, and it was hoped that the tropical climate would help. His stepbrother accompanied him and kept a journal of the trip. It is largely a record of stormy or calm days at sea and pleasant but hot days on the island, visiting new friends in the evening or early morning, "by the first dawn of the day, for by the time the sun is half an hour high it is as hot as any time in the day."

On Barbados George saw his first play, "George Barnwell, a Tragedy" and recorded that "the character of Barnwell and several others was said to be well performed." He saw his first fort, which he considered "pretty strongly fortified and mounts about thirty-six guns within its fortifications." And he contracted smallpox. It was a piece of good fortune that he went through the common disease under such favorable conditions and was ever after immune to it in field and camp. Like most of his diary entries his comment on his bout with the pox was terse: "Was strongly attacked with the smallpox: sent for Dr. Lanahan whose attendance was very constant till my recovery and going out which was not 'till Thursday the 12th of December."

Late in December 1751 Lawrence, whose health was not improving, decided to go to Bermuda, and as the surveying season was approaching, George sailed for home. On this voyage he summarized his impressions of Barbados, principally in terms of the economics of its agriculture.

THE EARTH IN MOST PARTS is extremely rich and as black as our richest marsh mould. . . . There was many acres last year that turned out from £140 to £170 as I was informed by credible authority. . . . How wonderful that such people should be in debt and not be able to indulge themselves in all the luxuries as well as necessaries of life. Yet so it happens estates are often alienated for the debts. . . . Their dung they are very careful in saving, and curious in making; which they do by throwing up large heaps of earth and a number of stakes drove therein sufficient for sixteen head of cattle to stand separately tied, to which they are three months together trampling . . . and then it's fit to manure the ground.

Shortly after his return from Barbados another girl briefly appears in George's life in a single letter. This was sixteen-year-old Betty Fauntleroy. Apparently he had proposed to her, been refused and then wrote to her father:

I SHOULD HAVE BEEN down long before this but my business in Frederick detained me somewhat longer than I expected, and immediately on my return from thence I was taken with a violent pleurisy, which has reduced me very low; but purpose, as soon as I recover my strength, to wait on Miss Betsy in hopes of a revocation of the former cruel sentence, and see if I can meet with any alteration in my favor. I have enclosed a letter to her, which should be much obliged to you for the delivery of it.

Either papa Fauntleroy did not deliver the letter or Betsy again said No. Washington never mentioned her again.

Lawrence returned from Bermuda in June 1752 and died a month later. He left a life interest in Mount Vernon to his wife with the provision that, if she died without issue, it was to go to George. Lawrence's infant daughter died a few months later, and when Sally Washington remarried, George bought out her life interest.

As his twentieth birthday neared George was already a man of substance. He had bought two thousand acres in the Shenandoah, and this, with the land that he had inherited, brought his holdings close to five thousand acres. His job as county surveyor paid a hundred pounds per year, and he made much more from private surveys. In the fall of that year he joined a new lodge of Masons. As he approached manhood there are two things that distinguish him from all of the other Founding Fathers at a similar age. In none of his writings is there a single reference to public affairs; and only one diary entry mentions reading. At age sixteen he had recorded, "Read to the reign of King J. In the Spectator read to 143." Washington was a young man of action, neither a scholar nor an intellectual. And his sole contact with military affairs had been his view of a fort in Barbados.

This was about to change. Lawrence had been adjutant of the colony, a position that involved supervising the equipment and drill of the militia and which paid one hundred pounds per year. It was decided to divide the colony into districts and appoint four adjutants. Washington wrote Governor Dinwiddie saying that if he were appointed to one of the posts he "should take the greatest pleasure in punctually obeying from time to time your Honor's commands, and by a strict observance of my duty render myself worthy of your trust reposed in me; I am sensible my best endeavors will not be wanting, and doubt not, but [by] a constant application to fit myself for the office, could I presume your Honor had not in view a more deserving person." George received the appointment and, twenty-one days before his twenty-first birthday, became Major Washington.

In 1753 both France and England were claiming the watershed of the Ohio. The French in Canada had sent troops into what Governor Dinwiddie considered the western part of Virginia. Dinwiddie decided to warn the French off before taking action. Washington volunteered to carry the warning and, despite his youth, was selected for the job because he combined the gentlemanly manners necessary for diplomacy with experience on the frontier. Upon his return from a thousand-mile round trip to near Lake Erie he wrote a long and, for him, detailed report. He started:

WEDNESDAY, 31ST. [of October, 1753] I was commissioned and appointed by the Honorable Robert Dinwiddie, Esq; Governor, etc., of Virginia, to visit and deliver a letter to the commandant of the French forces on the Ohio, and set out on the intended journey the same day. The next I arrived at Fredericksburg, and engaged Mr. Jacob van Braam to be my French interpreter; and proceeded with him to Alexandria, where we provided necessaries. From thence we went to Winchester, and got baggage, horses, etc., and from thence we pursued the new road to Wills Creek [Cumberland, Maryland] where we arrived the 14th of November.

Here I engaged Mr. Gist to pilot us and also hired four others as servitors, Barnaby Currin and John MacQuire, Indian traders, Henry Steward and William Jenkins; and in company with those persons left the inhabitants [the settlements] the day following.

Gist was an experienced fur trader and woodsman, Van Braam a Hollander who spoke French, after a fashion. When questioning some French-speaking Indians he reported that they came from the "Black Islands." Illinois sounded like *Isle Noir*. From Cumberland, Washington led his party across the mountains to the bank of the Monongahela. Here he sent his horses ahead and secured canoes to float down to the junction of that stream with the Allegheny where, he recorded:

AS I GOT DOWN before [from?] the canoe I spent some time in viewing the rivers, and the land in the fork; which I think extremely well situated for a fort, as it has the absolute command of both rivers. The land at the point is twenty or twenty-five feet above the common surface of the water; and a considerable bottom of flat, well-timbered land all around it, very convenient for building; the rivers are each a quarter of a mile or more across, and run here very near at right angles. . . .

Nature has well contrived this lower place for water defense; but the hill whereon it must stand being about a quarter of a mile in length, and then descending gradually on the land side, will render it difficult and very expensive to make a sufficient fortification there, the whole flat upon the hill must be taken in, the side next the descent made extremely high, or else the hill itself cut away; otherwise the enemy may raise batteries within that distance without being exposed to a single shot from the fort.

The land which Washington described in his first treatise on military engineering is now the Golden Triangle of downtown Pittsburgh.

Next stop was Logstown, headquarters of the Seneca chief Half King, a friend of the British. Half King was away at his hunting cabin and Washington met with Oneida chief Monadatoocha "and informed him by John Davison, my Indian interpreter, that I was sent a messenger to the French general; and was ordered to call upon the Sachems of the Six Nations to acquaint them with it. I gave him a string of wampum, and a twist of tobacco, and desired him to send for the Half King (which he promised to do by a runner in the morning) and for other Sachems."

Next day there was some excitement when there "came to town four or ten Frenchmen who had deserted." Washington probably meant to write four or five. He cross-examined these through Van Braam, learned that the main French forces had turned back to winter quarters, and dutifully recorded the details of armament and garrisons at four French forts between New Orleans and Lake Erie which the deserters described.

When Half King returned, Washington addressed the assembled chiefs in the Long House:

BROTHERS, I have called you together in council, by order of your brother, the Governor of Virginia, to acquaint you that I am sent, with all possible dispatch, to visit and deliver a letter to the French commandant, of very great importance to your brothers, the English; and, I dare say, to you their friends and allies.

I was desired, brothers, by your brother the Governor, to call upon you, the Sachems of the Nations, to inform you of it, and to ask your advice and assistance to proceed to the nearest and best road to the French. You see, brothers, I have gotten thus far on my journey.

His honor likewise desired me to apply to you for some of your young men, to conduct and provide provisions for us on our way, and be a safeguard against those French Indians who have taken up the hatchet against us. I have spoken thus particularly to you brothers, because his Honor our Governor treats you as good friends and allies; and holds you in great esteem. To confirm what I have said, I give you this string of wampum.

Half King agreed to go with the white men and provide an escort, but the others hung back. Finally, with Half King and two other Indians, Washington set out for Venango (now Franklin, Pennsylvania). When they arrived five days later he reported:

WE FOUND THE FRENCH colors hoisted at a house from which they had driven Mr. John Frazier, an English subject. I immediately repaired to it, to know where the commander resided. There were three officers, one of whom, Capt. Joncaire, informed me that he had the command of the Ohio; but that there was a general officer at the near fort, where he advised me to apply for an answer. He invited us to sup with them; and treated us with the greatest complaisance. The wine, as they dosed themselves pretty plentifully with it, soon banished the restraint which at first appeared in their conversation; and gave a license to the tongues to reveal their sentiments more freely. They told me that it was their absolute design to take possession of the Ohio and by G— they would do it; for that although they were sensible the English could raise two men for their one, yet they knew their motions were too slow and dilatory to prevent any undertaking of theirs. They pretended to have an undoubted right to the river, from a discovery made by one La Salle sixty years ago.

Washington rode on to Fort LeBoeuf, near the shore of Lake Erie, and presented Dinwiddie's demand to the French commander. While he awaited an answer he made careful notes on the fort. What he had already learned indicated that the French were about to move into the Ohio Valley country in force. He was anxious to get this vital information to Williamsburg with all dispatch. The Indians were a problem. The French were trying to get them drunk, separate them from the English and seduce them to the French side.

While he waited Washington sent three members of his party back with his weakened horses and accepted an offer of two canoes from the French. Finally on December 15, he noted:

THE COMMANDANT ordered a plentiful store of liquor, provision, etc., to be put on board our canoe; and appeared to be extremely complaisant, though he was exerting every artifice which he could invent to set our own Indians at variance with us, to prevent their going until after our departure. Presents, rewards and everything which could be suggested by him or his officers—I can't say that ever in my life I suffered so much anxiety as I did in this affair. I saw that every stratagem which the most fruitful brain could invent was practiced to win the Half King to their interest; and that leaving him here was giving them the opportunity they aimed at.

Washington waited another day for the Indians to collect presents which the French had promised. Then, he wrote:

THE FRENCH were not slack in their inventions to keep the Indians this day also. But as they were obligated, according to promise, to give the present they then endeavored to try the power of liquor; which I doubt not would have prevailed at any other time than this. But I urged and insisted with the King so closely upon his word that he refrained, and set off with us as he had engaged.

For seven days they paddled down the winding river, portaging around frozen sections, and caught up to their horses at Venango. Here they parted with the Indians and set off with the horses. Washington wrote:

I PUT MYSELF in Indian walking dress and continued with them three days, till I found there was no probability of their getting home in any reasonable time. The horses grew less able to travel every day; the cold increased very fast, and the roads were becoming much worse by a deep snow, continually freezing. Therefore, as I was uneasy to get back to make my report of my proceedings to his Honor the Governor, I determined to prosecute my journey the nearest way through the woods, on foot. . . .

I took my necessary papers, pulled off my clothes, and tied myself up in a matchcoat. Then with gun in hand and pack at my back, in which were my papers and provisions, I set out with Mr. Gist, fitted in the same manner, on Wednesday the 26th.

The day following, just after we had passed a place called the Murdering Town . . . we fell in with a party of French Indians, who had lain in wait for us. One of them fired at Mr. Gist or me, not fifteen steps off, but fortunately missed. We took this fellow into custody, and kept him till about nine o'clock at night, then let him go, and walked all the remaining part of the night without making any stop that we might get the start, so far, as to be out of the reach of their pursuit the next day, since we were well assured they would follow our track as soon as it was light.

Gist tells a somewhat different story of the Indian attack in a much more detailed journal which he kept. According to this version there was but one Indian, who pretended to be friendly, offered to guide them and carried Washington's pack. When the major started to tire—walking was a rather unfamiliar exercise to a Virginia gentleman—the Indian offered to carry his rifle too, but

Courtesy of Washington and Lee University—Frick Art Reference Library

"The Virginia Colonel Portrait" painted from life at Mount Vernon by C. W. Peale in 1772. The first authentic portrait of George Washington, it is now owned by Washington and Lee University and hangs in Lee Chapel on the university campus at Lexington, Virginia.

Washington wisely refused this assistance. After a few miles Gist became suspicious of the direction the Indian was taking and questioned him about it. The brave insisted that they would come to his cabin shortly. They pressed on until the Indian suddenly whirled and fired. The white men jumped him before he could reload, and Washington had difficulty in restraining Gist from killing the redskin out of hand. Instead they pretended to accept his explanation that his musket had gone off by accident and sent him on ahead, saying that they needed to rest. After he was gone they walked all night and the following day to reach the Allegheny. There were tracks of unfriendly Ottawas in the vicinity. These may account for Washington's reference to an ambush.

Crossing the Allegheny provided the final adventure of the trip:

THERE WAS no way for getting over but on a raft, which we set about with but one poor hatchet and finished just after sunsetting. This was a whole day's work. Then set off but before we were halfway over we were jammed in the ice in such a manner that we expected every moment our raft to sink and ourselves to perish. I put out my setting pole to try to stop the raft, that the ice might pass by, when the rapidity of the stream threw it with so much violence against the pole that it jerked me out into ten feet water; but I fortunately saved myself by catching hold of one of the raft logs. Notwithstanding all our efforts we could not get the raft to either shore; but were obliged as we were near an island to quit our raft and make to it.

The cold was so extremely severe that Mr. Gist had all his fingers and some of his toes frozen; but the water was shut up so hard [frozen] that we found no difficulty in getting off the island, on the ice, in the morning, and went to Mr. Frazier's. We met here about twenty warriors who were going to the southward to war, but coming to a place upon the head of the great Kunnaway, where they found seven people killed and scalped (all but one woman with very light hair), they turned about and ran back for fear the inhabitants should rise and take them as the authors of the murder. They report that the bodies were lying about the house, and some of them much torn and eaten by hogs. By the marks which were left, they say they were French Indians of the Ottawas Nation, etc., who did it.

As we intended to take horses here, and it required some time to find them, I went up about three miles to the mouth of Youghiogheny to visit Queen Aliquippa, who had expressed great concern that we passed her in going to the fort. I made her a present of a matchcoat and a bottle of rum; which latter was thought much the best present of the two.

After eleven days of uneventful riding Washington reached Belvoir, where he rested a day and thrilled the friendly Fairfaxes with his news of coming war. Then six more days to Williamsburg to lay the French answer before the governor—a polite answer which intimated that the Ohio Valley was French land and they had no intention of leaving it. At Dinwiddie's request Washington wrote the account of his trip, ending with "I hope what has been said will be sufficient to make your Honor satisfied with my conduct; for that was my aim in undertaking the journey, and chief study throughout the prosecution of it."

CHAPTER II

THE YOUNG SOLDIER

❦

ON THE 31ST MARCH (1754) I received from his Honor a lieutenant colonel's commission of the Virginia regiment where of Joshua Fry, Esquire, was colonel . . . with orders to take the troops, which were at that time quartered at Alexandria, under my command and to march with them toward the Ohio, there to aid Captain Trent in building forts and in defending the possessions of His Majesty against the attempts and hostilities of the French.

April the 2nd. Everything being ready, we began our march according to our orders, . . . with two companies of foot, commanded by Captain Peter Hog and Lieutenant Jacob van Braam."

So Washington began his account of his first military command. The words may not be exactly those which he used because the original of this journal was captured by the French at the end of Braddocks expedition and published in France to prove that the English colonists were the aggressors in the French and Indian War. It was retranslated in America, and the only surviving record of what he wrote is from this retranslation. Washington complained vehemently that his notes were misinterpreted in translation, "certainly and strangely metamorphosed; with some parts left out, and many things added that were never thought of." Despite his protest, comparison of the text with letters that he wrote to Dinwiddie, covering much of the same ground, discloses no important discrepancies.

When he received the report of Washington's trip to Fort LeBoeuf, Dinwiddie was avid for action against the French. The Burgesses were not so enthusiastic. They were suspicious that Washington was exaggerating the danger from the French to gain aid for the Ohio Company, of which brother Lawrence had been a founder. Washington indignantly wrote that some considered his report "a fiction and a scheme to promote the interest of a private company."

The governor ordered Indian trader William Trent to raise a hundred men and build a fort at the Forks. He ordered Major Washington to raise a like number. This was more easily said than done. Washington later wrote, "you may, with almost equal success, attempt to raise the dead to life again as the force of this country." He was able to secure twenty-five recruits who, he wrote Dinwiddie,

> . . . are of those loose, idle persons that are quite destitute of house and home and, I may truly say, many of them of clothes; which last renders them very incapable of the necessary service, as they must unavoidably be exposed to inclement weather in their marches, etc. . . . they are as illy provided as can well be conceived, but I really believe every man of them, for their own credit's sake, is willing to be clothed at their own expense. They are perpetually teasing me to have it done, but I am not able to advance the money provided there was no risk in it, which there certainly is, and too great for me to run.

This was the first of many, many appeals for military necessities that Washington would write during his lifetime. And it touches on another point—Washington's interest in money. The Washington of the schoolbooks is far too noble to be concerned with remuneration or public acclaim. The Washington of real life, in his early years, demanded what he considered his due not only in money but, more important, in honors and recognition.

Washington had secured his lieutenant-colonel's commission through an appeal to family friend Richard Corbin, a member of the governor's council, to whom he wrote that he hoped

. . . for a commission above that of major, and to be ranked among the chief officers of this expedition. The command of the whole forces is what I neither look for, expect, nor desire; for I must be impartial enough to confess it is a charge too great for my youth and inexperience to be entrusted with. Knowing this, I have too sincere a love for my country to undertake that which may tend to the prejudice of it. But if I could entertain hopes that you thought me worthy of the post of lieutenant-colonel and would favor me so far as to mention it at the appointment of officers, I could not but entertain a true sense of the kindness.

Colonel Joshua Fry, Washington's immediate superior, never took the field, so the young lieutenant-colonel was in actual command.

Dinwiddie had promised Washington 15s a day. When the lieutenant-colonel learned that his actual stipend was to be but 12s 6d he threatened to resign and wrote the governor:

LET ME SERVE voluntarily; then I will, with the greatest pleasure in life, devote my services to the expedition without any other reward than the satisfaction of serving my country; but to be slaving dangerously for the shadow of pay, through woods, rocks, mountains—I would rather prefer the great toil of a day laborer, and dig for a maintenance . . . than serve upon such ignoble terms; for I really do not see why the lives of His Majesty's subjects in Virginia should be of less value than of those in other parts of his American dominions, expecially when it is well known that we must undergo double their hardship. . . .

I hope what I have said will not be taken amiss; for I really believe . . . we should be treated as gentlemen and officers, and not have annexed to the most trifling pay that ever was given to English officers, the glorious allowance of soldier's diet—a pound of pork, with bread in proportion, every day.

Dinwiddie answered that his "ill-timed complaints" were unreasonable, and Washington wrote another long objection to the officer's pay scale, which was less than half that of the British, complaining that "our pay will not be sufficient to discharge our first expenses." However, he concluded by writing, "The motives that lead me here were pure and noble. I had no view of acquisition but that of honor, by serving faithfully my King and Country."

When Washington moved out of Alexandria his meager force had increased to 120 men. En route to Wills Creek he was reinforced with a company that brought his command to 159. Wagons and pack animals were as scarce as recruits; the entire transport of the "army" was two vehicles. From Wills Creek the young commander sent Half King a belt of wampum and a speech appealing for aid in which he said, "Our hearts burn with love and affection toward you in gratitude for your steadfast attachment to us, as also your friendly speech and wise counsels." He explained that his small force was clearing the roads for "a great number of our warriors . . . with our great guns. We know the character of the treacherous French. . . . I desire with greatest earnestness that you . . . should come as soon as possible to meet us on the road, and to assist us in council. Your Friend and Brother, Go. Washington Conotocarious.

Conotocarious—"Destroyer of Villages"—was the name the Indians had given, for good cause, to Washington's Indian fighter grandfather John.

At Wills Creek he met bad news. The French had arrived at the Forks with a thousand men, Trent's forty-one men had surrendered, and the French were finishing the fort the Virginians had started, which they called Fort Du Quesne—until the British renamed it Fort Pitt and the Americans Pittsburgh.

Washington started to build a road to carry forward the artillery he hoped to receive. This was interrupted by a message from Half King saying that he had discovered a party of about fifty French in a "low, obscure place" about five miles from Washington's camp. Washington wrote Dinwiddie an account of the subsequent action:

I SET OUT with forty men before ten, and was from that time till near sunrise before we reached the Indian's camp, having marched in small path, a heavy rain, and night as dark as it is possible to conceive; we were frequently tumbling one over another, and often so lost that fifteen or twenty minutes search would not find the path again.

When we came to the Half King, I counciled with him, and got his assent to go hand in hand and strike the French. Accordingly, himself, Monocatoocha and a few other Indians set out with us, and when we came to the place where the tracks were, the Half King sent two Indians to follow their track and discover their lodgment, which they did about half a mile from the road, in a very obscure place surrounded with rocks. I thereupon, in conjunction with the Half King and Monocatoocha, formed a disposition to attack them on all sides, which we accordingly did, and after an engagement of about fifteen minutes, we killed ten, wounded one and took twenty-one prisoners. Amongst those that were killed was Monsieur de Jumonville, the commander: Principal officers taken are Monsieur Druillorn and Monsieur La Force, who your Honor has often heard me speak of as a bold enterprising man, and a person of great subtlety and cunning; with these are two cadets.

These officers pretend they were coming on an embassy, but the absurdity of this pretext is too glaring as Your Honor will see by the instructions enclosed. These instructions were to reconnoiter the country, roads, creeks, etc., to Potomac which they were about to do. . . . this, with several other reasons, induced all the officers to believe firmly that they were sent as spies rather than anything else, and has occasioned my sending them as prisoners, although they expected or at least had some hope of being continued as ambassadors.

They finding where we were encamped, instead of coming up in a public manner, sought out one of the most secret retirements, fitter for a deserter than an ambassador to encamp in, stayed there two or three days, sent spies to reconnoiter our camp, as we are told, although they deny it. . . .

I shall expect every hour to be attacked and by unequal numbers, which I must withstand, if there is five to one, or else I fear the consequence will be we shall lose the Indians if we suffer ourselves to be drove back. . . .

Your Honor may depend I will not be surprised, let them come what hour they will. . . . I doubt not but if you hear I am beaten, but you will at the same hear that we have done our duty in fighting as long [as] there was a possibility of hope. . . .

But he was not entirely pessimistic. He added, "If the whole detachment of the French behave with no more resolution than this chosen party did, I flatter myself we shall have no great trouble in driving them to the devil."

To a letter to brother Augustine describing the action Washington added a postscript: "P.S. I fortunately escaped without any wound, for the right wing, where I stood, was exposed to and received all the enemy's fire, and it was the part where the man was killed, and the rest wounded. I heard the bullets whistle, and, believe me, there is something charming in the sound." In another letter to Dinwiddie he admitted that the half-dozen Indians who were with him "served to knock the poor, unhappy wounded in the head and relieved them of their scalps."

At the time of his first encounter with the French, Washington was at Great Meadows where, he reported, "I have just finished a small palisaded fort, in which, with my small numbers, I shall not fear the attack of 500 men." He had referred to the "natural entrenchments" of the site and labeled it a "charming field for an encounter." Actually, the spot where he built Fort Necessity—

which was not finished—was not a good defensive site. His force was brought up to about four hundred men by reinforcements of Virginia volunteers and an independent company of British regulars from South Carolina under Captain James MacKay, who promptly announced that he did not intend to take orders from a colonial lieutenant-colonel.

During June 1754 Washington pushed forward to about thirty-seven miles from Fort Duquesne. He held a three-day council with the chiefs of the Six Nations, Delaware and Shawnee. To the Six Nations he proclaimed:

THE ENGLISH DO NOT intend to hurt you, or any of your allies; . . . they . . . sent an army to maintain your rights; to put you again in possession of your lands, and to take care of your wives and children, to dispossess the French, to maintain your rights and to secure the whole country for you; for these very ends are the English arms now employed; it is for the safety of your wives and your children that we are fighting; and as this is the only motive of our conduct we cannot reasonably doubt of being joined by the rest of your forces to oppose the common enemy. Those who will not join us shall be answerable for whatever may be the consequence; we only desire your brethren to choose the side which seems most acceptable to them; . . . as we have drawn the sword in your cause and in your defense, hesitate no longer, delay not a moment, but put all your wives and children under our protection, and they shall find plenty of provisions; in the meanwhile set your young men and your warriors to sharpening their hatchets, to join and unite with us vigorously in our battles. The present, my brethren, which I offer you is not so considerable as I could wish, but I expect in a short time, a quantity of goods.

The Indians agreed to support the English, but except for a few of Half King's followers no braves joined their forces. Food was getting short. When Indian scouts brought word that the French were about to advance with eight hundred men Washington decided to fall back on Fort Necessity, where the French attacked him with approximately double the English force.

Washington's report to Dinwiddie of this action did not survive, but Dinwiddie's report to the Lords of Trade is almost certainly based on it. The governor wrote:

ON THE THIRD of this month they had intelligence that the French were . . . in full march with 900 men to attack our small camp, which consisted of few more than 300 men besides officers. . . . Immediately they appeared in sight of our camp, and fired at our people at a great distance, which did no harm. Our small forces were drawn up in good order to receive them before their entrenchments, but did not return their first fire, reserving it till they came nigher.

The enemy advanced irregularly within sixty yards of our forces, and then made a second discharge. Observing they did not intend to attack them in open field they [the Virginians] retired within their trenches and reserved their fire—thinking, from their numbers, they would force their trenches. Finding they made no attempt of this kind, the colonel gave orders to our people to fire on the enemy, which they did with great briskness, and the officers declare the engagement continued from eleven o'clock till eight o'clock at night, they being without shelter, rainy weather, and their trenches to the knee in water, whereas the French were sheltered all around our camp by trees; from thence they galled our people all the time as above.

About eight o'clock at night the French called out to parley. Our people, mistrusting their sincerity . . . refused it. At last they desired [us] to send an officer who could speak French, and they gave their parole for his safe return . . . on which the commander sent two officers, to whom they gave their proposals. . . . From our few numbers and our bad situation, they [our forces] were glad to accept of them. Otherwise, [they] were determined to lose their lives rather than be taken prisoners.

The next morning a party from the French came and took

possession of our encampment, and our people marched off with colors flying and beat of drum. But there appeared a fresh party of 100 Indians to join the French, who galled our people much and with difficulty were restrained from attacking them. However they pilfered our people's baggage, and at the beginning of the engagement the French killed all the horses, cattle and live creatures they saw, so that our forces were obliged to carry off the wounded men on their backs to some distance from the place of engagement, where they left them with a guard. The scarcity of provisions made them make quick marches to get among the inhabitants, which was about sixty miles of bad road.

The future commander-in-chief was not censured when he returned to civilization. His mistakes were attributed to youthful enthusiasm, recklessness and ambition. Half King was not happy about his association with Washington. He later said, "The colonel was a good-natured man, but had no experience. He took upon him to command the Indians as his slaves, and would have them every day upon the scout, and to attack the enemy by themselves, but would by no means take advice from the Indians."

Washington had been promoted to full colonel during the campaign. Now Dinwiddie decided to break up the Virginia regiment into independent companies and offered Washington the captaincy of one. George indignantly refused and promptly resigned, saying, "I think the disparity between the present offer of a company and my former rank too great to expect any real satisfaction or enjoyment in a corps where I once did, or thought I had a right to, command." To add insult to injury Washington's commission would be a colonial not a royal one. "In short," he wrote, "every captain bearing the King's commission, every half-pay officer, or other, appearing with such a commission, would rank before me."

After paying a board bill in Williamsburg of £1 7s 6d and a much more formidable bar bill of £5, 9s 6d in Finnie's ordinary —where he presumably had done some entertaining—Washington took his hurt pride and thwarted ambition home. But in a letter to

Governor Sharpe of Maryland he wrote, "My inclinations are strongly bent to arms."

Soon he had a new opportunity to follow his inclinations without loss of prestige and to learn more of his chosen profession. The king sent two regiments of regulars from Ireland under the highly regarded Major General Edward Braddock. One of Braddock's aides wrote Washington in March 1755, "The general having been informed that you expressed some desire to make the campaign, but that you declined it upon the disagreeableness that you thought might arise from the regulation of command, has ordered me to acquaint you that he will be very glad of your company in his family [i.e., on his staff] by which all inconveniences of that kind will be obviated.

George replied the next day, "It's true, sir, I have, ever since I declined a command in this service, expressed an inclination to serve the ensuing campaign as a volunteer; and this, believe me sir, is not a little increased, since it's likely to be conducted by a gentleman of the general's great good character." On May 10, 1755 a general order stated, "Mr. Washington is appointed Aide-de-camp to His Excellency General Braddock." George immediately wrote to two friends to announce that he was an unpaid volunteer. To William Byrd he said, "If I can gain any credit, or if I am entitled to the least countenance and esteem, it must be from serving my country with a free, voluntary will; for I can very truly say, I have no expectation of reward but the hope of meriting the love of my country and friendly regard of my acquaintaces."

American history has rather unfairly labeled Braddock a fool and a bungler. Mistakes he did make; but his expedition was doomed from the start by the fact that he had little support from the colonies, which seemingly preferred destruction to cooperation. He was delayed for months in getting provisions and transport, which he finally received only after Benjamin Franklin pried it out of Pennsylvania farmers by combining a pledge of his own credit with a threat of reprisals from nonexistent British hussars if the wagons and horses were not forthcoming.

While they were waiting to advance, Washington had little to do.

When the general, who was of choleric temper, expressed his wrath at the colonists, George did not hesitate to argue with Braddock, and wrote to William Fairfax:

THE GENERAL, by frequent breaches of contract, has lost all patience; and for want of that temper and moderation which should be used by a man of sense upon these occasions will, I fear, represent us in a light we little deserve; for instead of blaming the individuals, as he ought, he charges all his disappointments to public supineness, and looks upon the country, I believe, as void of honor and honesty.

We have frequent disputes on this head, which are maintained with warmth on both sides, especially on his, who is incapable . . . of giving up any point he asserts, let it be ever so incompatible with reason or common sense.

Washington made a trip home to replace his mounts, and borrowed Sally Fairfax's riding horse. He went to Williamsburg to take four thousand pounds to Braddock. While he was there John Carlyle, a member of the House of Burgesses, mentioned an upcoming vacancy in that body and, perhaps jokingly, suggested that George might fill it. As a result Washington wrote his brother John Augustine—whom he called Jack—the first letter in which he touched on politics. After asking his brother to sound out the opinions of certain leading local men on his chances, he continued:

IF YOU DO ANYTHING in this, pray let me know by the first opportunity how you have succeeded in it and how those gentlemen stand affected. If they seem inclinable to promote my interest, and things should be drawing to a crisis, you then may declare my intentions and beg their assistance. If, on the contrary, you find them more inclined to favor some other, I would have the affair entirely dropped. . . . Conduct the whole till you are satisfied of the sentiments of those I have mentioned with an air of indifference and unconcern; after that you may regulate your conduct accordingly.

George's mother had objected to his going on the campaign. Then, in the midst of it, she wrote him a characteristic letter asking him to get her "some butter and a 'Dutch man'" (probably a German farmer). George answered with the cool politeness which marked most of his relations with his mother. "Honored Madam . . . am sorry it is not in my power to provide you with either a Dutch man, or the butter as you desire, for we are quite out of that part of the country where either are to be had. . . ." Although he signed this "Your Affectionate and Dutiful Son," there was little evidence of deep affection on George's part for his unreasonable and demanding mother.

There were two letters to Sally Fairfax. First, he asked her to write him: "In order to engage your correspondence, I think it expedient just to deserve it; which I shall endeavor to do by embracing the earliest and every opportunity of writing to you." Then, when she did not write, he penned a rather pathetic appeal:

WHEN I HAD THE PLEASURE to see you last, you expressed an inclination to be informed of my safe arrival at camp with the charge that was entrusted to my care [her horse] but at the same time desired it might be communicated in a letter to somebody of your acquaintance. This I took as a gentle rebuke and polite manner of forbidding me corresponding with you. . . . If I am right in this I hope you will excuse my present presumption. . . . If on the contrary these are fearful apprehensions only, how easy is it to remove my suspicion, enliven my [spirits?] and make me happier than the day is long, by honoring me with a correspondence which you did once partly promise."

Washington was distressed and somewhat fearful at the slow progress of hacking a road through the wilderness. The army had made but twenty-two miles in ten days. Then Washington was stricken with the "bloody flux." He wrote his brother, Jack. "I was seized with violent fevers and pains in my head which continued without the least intermission. . . . My illness was too violent to suffer me to ride, therefore I was indebted to a covered wagon for some part of my transportation."

But Washington was not too ill to advise his commander. In the same letter to Jack, he wrote:

THE GENERAL, before they met in council, asked my private opinion concerning the expedition. I urged it, in the warmest terms I was master of, to push on; if we even did it with a chosen detachment for that purpose, with the artillery and such other things as were absolutely necessary; leaving the baggage and other convoys with the remainder of the army, to follow by slow and regular marches, which they might do safely, while we were advanced in front. As one reason to support this opinion, I informed the [general] if we could credit our intelligence, the French were weak at the Forks but hourly expected reinforcements which to my certain knowledge could not arrive with provisions or any supplies during the continuance of the drought, as the Buffalo River down which is their only communication to Venango must be . . . dry. . . . This was a scheme that took, and it was determined that the general with 1200 chosen men and . . . with such a certain number of wagons as the train would absolutely require, should march as soon as things could be got in readiness for them. . . .

We set out with less than thirty carriages (including those that transported the ammunition for the howitzers, twelve-pounders, and six-pounders, etc.) and all of them strongly horsed; which was a prospect that conveyed infinite delight to my mind, though I was excessively ill at the time. But this prospect was soon clouded, and my hopes brought very low indeed, when I found that instead of pushing on with vigor, without regarding a little rough road, they were halting to level every molehill, and to erect bridges over every brook, by which means we were four days getting twelve miles.

At this camp I was left by the doctor's advice, and the general's absolute orders . . . without which I should not have been prevailed upon to remain behind. As I then imagined, and now believe, I shall find it no easy matter to join my own corps again, which is twenty-five miles advanced before us. Notwithstanding, I had the general's word of honor, pledged in the most solemn manner, that I should be brought up before he arrived at Fort Duquesne.

Washington's most complete description of Braddock's debacle on the bank of the Monongahela was written fifty years later when David Humphreys started to write his biography. The writer submitted twelve pages to Washington for criticism. In a memorandum to Humphreys Washington, writing in the third person, described his part in the battle:

THE FIRST DIVISION approached the Monongahela ten miles short of Fort Duquesne the 8th of July; and [at?] which time and place, having so far recovered from a severe fever and delirium . . . he [Washington] joined him [Braddock] and the next day though much reduced and very weak mounted his horse on cushions, and attended as one of his aides.

About ten o'clock on the 9th, after the van had crossed the Monongahela . . . and the rear yet in the river, the front was attacked and by the unusual hallooing and whooping of the enemy, whom they could not see, were so disconcerted and confused as soon to fall into irretrievable disorder. The rear was forced forward to support them but, seeing no enemy, and themselves falling every moment from the fire, a general panic took place among the troops from which no exertions of the officers could recover them. In the early part of the action some of the irregulars (as they were called) without directions advanced to the right, in loose order, to attack. But this, unhappily from the unusual appearance of the movement, being mistaken for cowardice and a running away, was discountenanced.

Before it was too late, and the confusion became general, an offer was made by G. W. to head the provincials and engage the enemy in their own way; but the propriety of it was not seen into until it was too late for execution. After this many attempts were made to dislodge the enemy from an eminence on the right but they all proved ineffectual and fatal to the officers who by great exertions and good examples endeavored to accomplish it. In one of these the general received the wound of which he died; but previous to it had several horses killed and disabled under him. Captains Orme and Morris, his two aides-de-camp, having received wounds which rendered them unable to attend, G. W. remained the sole aide through the day to the general. He also had one horse killed and two wounded under him; a ball through his hat, and several through his clothes, but escaped unhurt.

No person knowing, in the disordered state things were, who the surviving senior officer was, and the troops by degrees going off in confusion without a ray of hope left of further opposition from those that remained, G. W. placed the general in a small covered cart, which carried some of his most essential equipage and in the best order he could . . . brought him over the first ford of the Monongahela. . . .

After crossing the Monongahela the second time and ascending the heights he found Lieutenant Colonel Gage . . . to whom he delivered the general's order and then returned to report the situation he found them in. When he was again requested by the general . . . to proceed (it then being after sundown) to the second division under the command of Colonel Dunbar, to make arrangements for covering the retreat and forwarding on provisions and refreshments to the retreating and wounded soldiery.

To accomplish this (for the second division was forty-odd miles in the rear) it took up the whole night and part of the next morning; which from the weak state in which he was and the fatigues and anxiety of the last twenty-four hours, rendered him in a manner wholly unfit for the execution of the duty he was sent upon when he arrived at the Dunbar's camp. To the best of his power, however, he discharged it, and remained with the second division till the other joined it.

The shocking scenes which presented themselves in this night's march are not to be described. The dead, the dying, the groans, lamentation, and crys along the road of the wounded for help . . . were enough to pierce a heart of adamant. The gloom and horror . . . was not a little increased by the impervious darkness occasioned by the close shade of thick woods which in places rendered it impossible for the two guides which attended to know when they were in or out of the track but by groping on the ground with their hands.

Happy was it for . . . the remains of the first division that they left such a quantity of valuable and enticing baggage on the field as to occasion a scramble and contention in the seizure and distribution of it among the enemy; for had a pursuit taken place . . . and they had got into our rear, the whole, except for a few woodsmen, would have fallen victims to the merciless savages.

Of about twelve or thirteen hundred which were in this action eight or nine hundred were either killed or wounded; among whom a large proportion of brave, valuable officers were included. The folly and consequence of opposing compact bodies to the sparse manner of Indian fighting in woods, which had in a manner been predicted, was now so clearly verified that from hence forward another mode obtained in all future operations.

As soon as the two divisions united, the whole retreated toward Fort Cumberland; and at an encampment near the Great Meadows the brave but unfortunate General Braddock breathed his last. He was interred with the honors of war. . . . It was left to G. W. to see this performed, and to mark out the spot for the reception of his remains. To guard against a savage triumph, if the place should be discovered, they were deposited in the road over which the army, wagons, etc. passed to hide every trace by which the entombment could be discovered. Thus died a man whose good and bad qualities were intimately blended. He was brave even to a fault and in regular service would have done honor to his profession. His attachments were warm, his enmities were strong, and having no disguise about him both appeared in full force. He was generous and disinterested, but plain and blunt in his manner even to rudeness.

When Washington wrote the foregoing in October 1783, modesty and humility still were not among his prominent characteristics. Earlier in the memorandum he wrote that, in the initial stages of the campaign, he "used every proper occasion . . . to impress the general and the principal officers around him with the necessity of opposing the nature of his defense to the mode of the attack which, more than probably, he would experience from the Canadian French and their Indians on his march through the mountains and covered country; but so prepossessed were they in favor of regularity and discipline and in such absolute contempt were these people held that the admonition was suggested in vain." Later in the memorandum he wrote "As G. W. foresaw, so it happened."

Immediately after the battle he wrote several letters dealing with the Braddock campaign. In none of these did he report that he had specifically warned Braddock or that he had foreseen the outcome. He did suggest to Braddock that better speed could be made with pack horses than with wagons; advice which the general ignored. And it was Washington who suggested the fatal step of dividing the army. He obviously did not expect an attack from the French outside of the fort; in fact in one letter he wrote, "As to any danger from the enemy, I look upon it as trifling."

After the battle Colonel Thomas Dunbar, senior surviving British officer, took the regulars into "winter quarters" in Philadelphia —in August. This meant, George wrote, "there will be no men left here unless it is the poor remains of the Virginia troops who survive and will be too small to guard our frontiers." Washington, as Braddock's aide, had no connection with these Virginia troops. He rode slowly home to Mount Vernon and poured out his woes in a letter to his half-brother Augustine:

I WAS EMPLOYED to go a journey in the winter [to Fort Le-Boeuf] . . . and what did I get by it? My expenses borne! I then was appointed, with trifling pay, to conduct a handful of men to the Ohio. What did I get by this? Why, after putting myself to a considerable expense in equipping and providing necessaries for the campaign, I went out, was soundly beaten, lost them all—came in, and had my commission taken from me or, in other words, my command reduced, under pretense of an order from home. I then went out a volunteer with General Braddock and lost all my horses and many other things, but this being a voluntary act, I should not have mentioned it, was it not to show that I have been upon the losing order ever since I entered the service, which is now near two years. So that I think I can't be blamed, should I, if I leave my family again, endeavor to do it upon such terms as to prevent my suffering. (To gain by it, is the least of my expectation.)

Less than two weeks later Washington wrote to his brother-in-law, Warner Lewis, hinting that he would like to be back in harness—but only on his own terms. He said:

THE CHIEF REASON (next to indisposition) that prevented me from coming down to this Assembly was a determination not to offer myself, and that determination proceeded from the following reasons. First, A belief that I could not get a command upon such terms as I should care to accept; as I must confess I never will quit my family, injure my fortune, and (above all) impair my health to run the risk of such changes and vicissitudes as I have done; but shall now expect, if I am employed again, to have something certain. . . . Was I to have the command, I should insist upon some things which ignorance and inexperience made me overlook before. . . .

I believe our circumstances are now [in] that unhappy dilemma that no man can gain any honor by conducting our forces at this time, but rather lose in his reputation. . . .

It is possible you may infer from what I have said that my

intention is to decline at all events, but my meaning is entirely different. I was determined not to offer, because to solicit the command and at the same time to make my proposals I thought would look a little incongruous, and to carry a face of too much self-sufficiency—as if I imagined there were none others equally (if not more) capable of conducting the affair than myself. But if the command should be offered the case is then altered as I am at liberty to make such objections as my reason and my small experience have pointed out.

The Burgesses promptly voted George three hundred pounds to cover his losses in the previous campaign and Dinwiddie sent him a commission as "Colonel of the Virginia regiment and Commander-in-Chief of all the forces now raised and to be raised for the defense of this His Majesty's Colony. . . . And you are hereby charged with full power and authority to act defensively or offensively, as you shall think for the good and welfare of the service." The pay was thirty shillings a day, plus a hundred pounds for his table, allowance for a batman and 2 per cent commission of all funds which he handled. Washington's health promptly improved and he galloped to Williamsburg to become Commander-in-Chief at the age of twenty-three.

CHAPTER III

THE YOUNG COMMANDER-IN-CHIEF

❦

First the new Commander-in-Chief needed an army. It did not exist. He had to recruit it, clothe it, arm it, feed it, train it and then employ it to guard 350 miles of frontier in forts which he must also construct. He had to try to induce the Indians to cooperate. Most of his writing late in 1755 had to do with the need for, "shoes, stockings, shirts, hats . . . blankets, kettles, tomahawks, cartridge paper, stationery and a proper assortment of Indian goods."

Alarms of Indian burnings, butcherings and torturings came from all points on the frontier—some real, some panicky. Washington reported one case in which he personally led a hastily gathered detachment to the point "where these horrid murders were said to be committed. . . . Who should we find . . . but three drunken soldiers of the light horse, carousing. . . . The party of Indians discovered by Isaac Julian proved to be a mulatto and Negro seen hunting cattle."

Two months after his appointment Washington described the general situation to Dinwiddie by writing:

I WAS DESIROUS of proceeding immediately, at the head of some militia, to put a stop to the ravages of the enemy, believing their numbers to be few, but was told by Colonel Martin, who had attempted to raise the militia for the same purpose, that it was impossible to get above twenty or twenty-five men; they having absolutely refused to stir—choosing, as they say, to die with their wives and families. . . . They are more encompassed by fear than by the enemy. . . .

In all things I meet with the greatest opposition. No orders are obeyed, but what a party of soldiers, or my own drawn sword, enforces. Without this, a single horse, for the most urgent occasion, cannot be had; to such a pitch has the insolence of these people arrived. . . . However, I have given up none, where His Majesty's service requires the contrary, and where my proceedings are justified by my instructions. Nor will I, unless they execute what they threaten, i.e., "to blow out my brains."

After recruiting, discipline was the greatest problem. For the enlisted man, frequent flogging was Washington's prescription, then and during the Revolution. He ordered his officers, "If they hear any man swear, or make use of an oath or execration, to order the offender twenty-five lashes immediately, without a court-martial." If any man feigned illness, the officer of the day "is expressly ordered to give him in the face of all the men, fifty lashes with a cat-and-nine-tails; and set him to work again." He put most of the "tippling houses and gin shops" of Winchester off limits, and any man "found ever going into or sitting down" in these places "shall immediately receive fifty lashes." However, if the men behaved themselves, "the colonel promises to give them, so long as they deserve it, four gallons of rum, made into punch, each day."

To cope with the steady stream of deserters Washington threatened that "any soldier who shall desert, though he return again, shall be hanged without mercy." At first this was an idle threat. Not until the summer of 1757 did the Assembly enact a military code which permitted capital punishment. Washington then wrote, "I have a gallows near forty-foot high erected (which has terrified the rest exceedingly) and I am determined, if I can be justified in the proceeding, to hang two or three on it, as an example to others." He promptly carried out his threat and hanged two deserters, of whom he wrote Dinwiddie, "Your Honor will, I hope, excuse my hanging instead of shooting them. It conveyed much more terror to others; and it was for example sake we did it." Then, and later, he maintained, "Discipline is the soul of the army."

Problems of discipline were not confined to the men. To one captain Washington wrote, "I am very much surprised to hear the great irregularities which were allowed of in your camp. The rum, although sold by Joseph Coombs, I am credibly informed is your property. There are continual complaints to me of the misbehavior of your wife, who I am told sows sedition among the men and is chief of every mutiny. If she is not immediately sent from the camp, or I hear any more complaints of such irregularities in behavior upon my arrival there, I shall take care to drive her out myself, and suspend you." When he cashiered an ensign for cheating at cards he made the act an occasion for warning the others:

REMEMBER, THAT IT IS the actions, and not the commission, that makes the officer and that there is more expected from him than the title. . . . I think it my duty, gentlemen, as I have the honor to preside over you, to give this friendly admonition; especially as I am determined, as far as my small experience in service, my abilities and interest of the service dictate, to observe the strictest discipline through the whole economy of my behavior. On the other hand, you may as certainly depend upon having the strictest justice administered to all. And . . . I shall make it the most agreeable part of my duty to study merit, and reward the brave and deserving. I assure you, gentlemen, that partiality shall never bias my conduct; nor shall prejudice injure any. . . . Throughout the whole tenor of my proceedings, I shall endeavor, as far as I am able, to reward and punish without the least dimunition.

Washington was always very remote from the enlisted man, always courteous but reserved with his officers. He did promote on merit, but it is surprising that, during the entire tenure of his early command, he did not write a single line of praise or commendation for any of his subordinates.

The question of rank again threatened Washington's pride late in 1755. A John Dagworthy marched into Fort Cumberland with thirty men from Maryland and announced that he commanded there by virtue of his royal commission as captain. Governor Sharpe of Maryland ranked Dinwiddie in the colonial military establishment. He refused to intervene. Governor Shirley of Massachusetts was superior to both his southern colleagues. In February 1756, George set out for Boston, with two aides and two servants, to have his superiority to Dagworthy confirmed. It was an expensive trip, but to the sensitive commander position was more important than money.

It was also a leisurely trip. He paused to replenish his wardrobe in Philadelphia and lose eight shillings at cards. In New York he escorted Miss Mary Philipse, who owned 51,000 acres of Hudson Valley land, to "Mr. Baron's rout, six shillings," and to the News Exchange to see "The Microcosm of the World in Miniature," which cost £1 8s. He lost another eight shillings at cards. In Rhode Island he gave "By cash to Mr. Malbone's servants four pounds; to a bowl broke, four pounds." In Boston he found the exchange between Massachusetts and Virginia currency so favorable that he spent £200 on clothes and silver lace. He also lost £5 6s at cards—but all this came to only £26 Virginia currency. Shirley, whose son had been an aide to Braddock with Washington, confirmed that Dagworthy was under Washington's command and gave him an order to that effect.

Back in the Shenandoah Valley conditions were deteriorating steadily. Settlers were streaming out of the valley. In April 1756 George advised the governor:

DESOLATION and murder still increase, and no prospects of relief. The Blue Ridge is now our frontier, no men being left in this county except a few that keep close with a number of women and children in forts, which they have erected for the purpose. There are now no militia in this county. When there were, they could not be brought to action.

Another disappointment for the young Commander-in-Chief was the attitude of the Indians. He considered the assistance of friendly Indians essential to cope with the tawny allies of the French. White men could not do it, he said, "the cunning and vigilance of Indians in the woods are no more to be conceived, than they are to be equaled by our people. Indians are the only match for Indians; and without these, we shall ever fight upon unequal terms."

When Washington was told that war parties of Cherokee and Catawbas were to join him he expressed his pleasure:

THEY WILL BE of particular service—more than twice their number of white men. When they arrive, which I pray may be soon, we may deal with the French in their own way; and, by visiting their country, will keep their Indians at home. . . . Those Indians who are now coming should be showed all possible respect, and the greatest care taken of them, as upon them much depends. 'Tis a critical time, they are very humoursome, and their assistance very necessary! One false step might not only lose us that, but even turn them against us. All kinds of necessary goods, etc., should be got from [for] them.

But the promised support resulted in only seven braves from one tribe and eleven from the other. Washington's difficulty with the Indians may have been partly his own fault, for the reasons given by Half King, who was now dead. Washington blamed it on the lack of a unified chain of command in dealing with them. "We receive fresh proofs every day of the bad direction of our Indian affairs," he wrote. "It is . . . easy to tell . . . how dissatisfied they are, and how gloomy the prospect of pleasing them appears, while we pursue our present system of management." He described the French system of single control, "whereas, with us it is everybody's business, and no one's, to supply. Every person attempts to please, and few succeed in it, because one promises this, and another that; and few can perform anything, but are obliged to shuffle and put them off, to get rid of their importunities. Hence they accuse us of perfidy and deceit!"

Washington organized scalping parties of the few friendly Indians and cheerfully reported, "a party of our Indians, under command of Lieutenant Baker, with some Cherokee Indians met with ten Frenchmen at Turtle Creek, near Fort Duquesne, and killed and scalped five; two of which were officers." On another occasion, when the Indians came in with the scalp of a French officer he wrote to Williamsburg, "I hope, although it is not an Indian's, they will meet with an adequate reward at least, as the monsieur's is of much more consequence. The whole party jointly claim the reward, no person pretending solely to assume the merit." He later reported, "I must confess that I think these scalping parties of Indians we send out will more effectually harass the enemy . . . than any parties of white people can do." It is interesting in connection with the legendary Washington that in the earliest collection of his writings and in Washington Irving's biography this letter is quoted—but the word "scalping" is omitted. To the Father of his Country, scalping was part of the day's work.

Reports of misconduct of the military on the frontier were rife in Williamsburg. The *Virginia Gazette* published an editorial calling the officers "drunken debauchees." Governor Dinwiddie wrote, "I hope the affairs of the regiment are not in so bad a condition as represented here. The Assembly were greatly inflamed, being told that the greatest immoralities and drunkenness have been much countenanced, and proper discipline neglected." To this Washington replied with one of the longest sentences he ever penned.

HOW FAR ANY of the individuals may have deserved such invidious reflections, I will not take upon me to determine, but this I am certain of, and can call my conscience, and what, I suppose will still be a more demonstrable proof in the eyes of the world, my orders, to witness how much I have, by both threats and persuasive means, endeavored to discountenance gaming, drinking, swearing, and irregularities of every other kind; while I have, on the other hand, practiced every artifice to inspire a laudable emulation in the officers for the service of their country, and to encourage the soldiers in the unerring exercise of their duty.

Apparently Washington brooded about this criticism. Four days later he addressed another, impassioned, letter to Dinwiddie:

I AM TOO LITTLE ACQUAINTED, sir, with pathetic language to attempt a description of the people's distresses, though I have a generous soul, sensible of wrongs, and swelling for redress. But what can I do? If bleeding, dying, would glut their insatiate revenge, I would be a willing offering to savage fury, and die by inches to save a people! I see their situation, know their danger and participate their sufferings, without having it in my power to give them further relief than uncertain promises. In short, I see inevitable destruction in so clear a light that, unless vigorous measures are taken by the Assembly and speedy assistance sent from below, the poor inhabitants that are now in forts must unavoidably fall, while the remainder of the country are flying before the barbarous foe.

In fine, the melancholy situation of the people, the little prospect of assistance, the gross and scandalous abuses cast upon the officers in general, which is reflecting upon me in particular for suffering misconducts of such extraordinary kinds, and the distant prospects, if any, that I can see of gaining honor and reputation in the service, are motives which cause me to lament the hour that gave me a commission, and would induce me, at any other time than this of imminent danger, to resign without one hesitating moment a command which I never expect to reap either honor or benefit from; but, on the contrary, have almost an absolute certainty of incurring displeasure below, while the murder of poor innocent babes and helpless families may be laid to my account here!

The supplicating tears of the women and moving petitions

from the men melt me into such deadly sorrow that I solemnly declare, if I know my own mind, I could offer myself a willing sacrifice to the butchering enemy, provided that would contribute to the people's ease.

By the end of 1756 things had improved slightly. A string of twenty-four forts and stockades were built or abuilding down the western side of the Shenandoah from Fort Cumberland in Maryland to the North Carolina line. Some were rude stockades; few were properly manned—but a system of defense was taking shape.

In January 1757, Lord Loudoun, the new commander-in-chief of all His Majesty's forces in the colonies, arrived in America. Without going through channels or consulting Dinwiddie, Washington wrote him a long report of conditions in Virginia, repeating all the complaints he had been dinning at Dinwiddie of the militia, the pay, the lack of provisions and equipment, and much else. He emphasized the folly of trying to defend the frontier with the men he had. He told Loudoun, "how strongly I have urged the Governor and Assembly to pursue different measures, and to convince them, by all the reasons I was capable of offering, of the impossibility of covering so extensive a frontier from Indian incursions without more force than Virginia can maintain. I have endeavored to demonstrate that it would require fewer men to remove the cause than to prevent the effects while the cause subsists." The solution, thought Washington, was an attack on Fort Duquesne; and the not yet twenty-five-year-old colonel did not hesitate to advise His Lordship that this was the way the war should be fought.

George's letter ended on a personal note and an appeal for Loudoun's favor:

I HAVE LONG BEEN SATISFIED of the impossibility of continuing in this service without loss of honor. Indeed, I was fully convinced of it before I accepted the command the second time . . . and did for this reason reject the offer (until I was ashamed any longer to refuse), not caring to expose my character to public censure. But the solicitations of the country overcame my objections and induced me to accept it.

Another reason of late had continued me in it until now, and that is the dawn of hope that arose when I heard Your Lordship was destined by His Majesty for the important command of his armies in America. . . . Hence it was that I drew my hopes, and fondly pronounced Your Lordship our patron. Although I had not the honor to be known to Your Lordship, Your Lordship's name was familiar to my ear, on account of the important services performed to His Majesty in other parts of the world. Do not think, my Lord, that I am going to flatter. Notwithstanding I have exalted sentiments of Your Lordship's character and respect your rank, it is not my intention to adulate. My nature is open and honest and free from guile. . . .

With regard to myself, I cannot forbear adding that, had His Excellency General Braddock survived his unfortunate defeat, I should have met with preferment agreeable to my wishes. . . . I do not know, my Lord, in what light this short and disinterested relation may be received by Your Lordship; but with the utmost candor and submission it is offered.

Some of Washington's concerns in the summer of 1757 came to light as recently as 1920, when a notebook titled *A Role of Artificers* was discovered among some manuscripts in the New York Public Library. Much of it was filled with memorandum made by Washington:

8 June 1757. Get the prices of all the soldiers clothing from Colonel Carlyle . . . and give it to each captain with orders to examine his company's necessary roll once a week. . . . Write the governor that Captain Paris has got a commission in the Maryland force—that Governor Denny [of Pennsylvania] has sent invitations to the Cherokees to treat with him at Fort Loudoun. . . . That I am apprehensive the different colonies striving against each other must be bad.

Also know how far and in what points I am to pay obedience to the orders of Colonel Stanwix and if it should happen that I receive orders from himself and Colonel Stanwix differing (which is not unlikely) whose orders I am to obey. . . . Take care also to acquaint the governor about the bad provisions at Fort Cumberland. . . . There has been foul play used with it.

June 13th—Drafts. Not to receive any but what is fit for the service. Reject all that are old—subject to fits—and otherwise infirm. . . .

Memorandum of sundry things to be done in Williamsburg if I go down in November: Get my accounts with the governor and committee settled. . . . Get some tea—Hysoon. . . . Is all the parties of Indians to be furnished with ammunition from the public stores here? . . . Unless troops march out in the spring there won't be one inhabitant left in this county—the people have been persuaded to wait the event of the spring. If this county breaks the others will go (being much thinner settled) infinitely faster and then an army can never be supported."

In the same book was an item in Washington's hand that had nothing to do with colonial defense—a recipe for making beer;

To make small Beer

Take a large sifter full of bran hops to your taste—boil these three hours then strain out thirty gallons into a cooler. Put in three gallons molasses while the beer is scalding hot—or rather draw the molasses into the cooler and strain the beer on it while boiling hot. Let this stand till it is little more than blood warm then put in a quart of yeast. If the weather is very cold cover it over with a blanket and let it work in the cooler twenty-four hours then put it into the cask. Leave the bung open till it is almost done working. Bottle it that day week it was brewed.

The year 1758 was important in Washington's life for two non-military happenings. Early in the year he returned to Mount Vernon in ill health. He thought that he had tuberculosis and wrote, "At certain periods I have been reduced to great extremity, and I have now too much reason to apprehend an approaching decay, being visited with several symptoms of such a disease." In a fit of despondency he added, "My constitution is certainly greatly impaired, and . . . nothing can retrieve it but the greatest care and the most circumspect conduct. I now have no prospect left of preferment in the military way, and as I despair of rendering that immediate service which my country may require from the person commanding their troops, I have some thought of quitting my command and retiring from all public business."

This melancholy mood was soon improved by a meeting with a plump little widow, Martha Custis. There is some mystery surrounding the meeting. Seventy-five years later Martha's grandson, George Washington Parkes Custis, wrote a romantic tale, presumably told to him when he was a child by his grandmother, that Martha first met George when he stopped, by chance, at the home of a Mr. Chamberlayne where she was visiting. Washington expected to stay only for dinner; his servant did not even unsaddle. But he was so captivated by the young widow that they talked all night, and when he left in the morning, they were engaged.

There may have been some such meeting, but there is little likelihood that it was their first, or that it resulted in their engagement. Before her first husband's death Martha and George, two months apart in age, had moved in the same small circle of hospitable Williamsburg society. It is unbelievable that they did not meet. In the spring of 1758 Martha was the wealthiest widow in Virginia. George called on her on March 16 and again a week later. He then hastened home and ordered from London "by the first ship bound to any part of Virginia . . . as much of the best superfine blue cotton velvet as will make a coat, waistcoat and breeches for a tall man, with a fine gilt button to suit it . . . six pairs of the very neatest shoes . . . [and] six pair gloves." At the same time Martha wrote to England for "one genteel suite of clothes for myself to be grave but not to be extravagant and not to be mourning." This is the best evidence of the date of the engagement to the woman who would provide George with a mistress for Mount Vernon, a sizable fortune in land and cash, 150 slaves and a ready-made family of two small children.

George's courtship of Martha shall remain forever a secret because after his death she burned all his premarital letters to her. The following, which appears in collections of his writings, is almost certainly a forgery:

JULY 20, 1758

WE HAVE BEGUN our march for the Ohio. A courier is starting for Williamsburg, and I embrace the opportunity to send a few words to one whose life is now inseparable from mine. Since that happy hour when we made our pledges to each other, my thoughts have been continually going to you as another self. That an all-powerful Providence may keep us both in safety is the prayer of your ever faithful and affectionate friend.

The original of this letter has never been found and Washington's most recent and reliable biographer, Douglas Southall Freeman, condemns the copy on several counts. It is in every way foreign to Washington's style. On July 20 the march to the Ohio had not begun, and Washington did not know when and if it would begin. Washington always started his letters to women with a salutation such as "Dear Madam" or "Honored Madam" and always ended with a flowery peroration. Less than two months later he ended the letter to Sally Fairfax, quoted below, with "Be assured that I am, dear Madame, with the most unfeigned regard, your most obedient and most obliged humble servant." Washington never used the word "courier" at this period; he always wrote "express." Finally, if Washington wrote this letter it is the only time in his life that he spelled "opportunity" properly. He usually spelled it "oppertunity."

The letter of this period that intrigues students of Washington is one to Sally Fairfax. Early biographers maintained that this was written to Martha—it was addressed merely "Dear Madam"—on the grounds that the "plaster saint" Washington of their creation would not write a love letter to one woman while engaged to another. The words "prospect of possessing Mrs. Custis" certainly rule out this contention. Also, Sally's husband wrote George under the date of September 1 acknowledging receipt of two letters and saying that his wife would answer one, by the same messenger that carried his. Washington's letter, dated September 12, follows:

YESTERDAY I WAS HONORED with your short but very agreeable favor of the first instant. How joyfully I catch at the happy occasion of renewing a correspondence which I feared was disrelished on your part I leave to time, the never failing expositor of all things, and to a monitor equally faithful in my own breast, to testify. In silence I now express my joy; silence which, in some cases . . . speaks more intelligently than the sweetest eloquence.

If you allow that any honor can be derived from my opposition to our present system of management, you destroy the merit of it entirely in me by attributing my anxiety to the animating prospect of possessing Mrs. Custis. . . . 'Tis true I profess myself a votary of love. I acknowledge that a lady is in the case, and further I confess that this lady is known to you. Yes, Madame, as well as she is to one who is too sensible of her charms to deny the power whose influence he feels and must ever submit to. I feel the force of her amiable beauties in the recollection of a thousand tender passages that I could wish to obliterate till I am bid to revive them. But experience, alas, sadly reminds me how impossible this is and evinces an opinion which I have long entertained; that there is a destiny which has the control of our actions, not to be resisted by the strongest efforts of human nature.

You have drawn me, dear Madame, or rather I have drawn myself, into an honest confession of a simple fact. Misconstrue not my meaning; doubt it not, nor expose it. The world has no [business] to know the object of my love, declared in this manner to you, when I want to conceal it. One thing above all things in this world I wish to know, and only one person of your acquaintance can solve me that, or guess my meaning. But adieu to this till happier times, if I ever shall see them.

No other interpretation of this letter is possible than that, before marrying Martha, he felt compelled to profess his love for Sally. He stated his love as a simple fact, excepting the inevitable conclusion that nothing could be done about it; "there is a destiny that has control of our actions, not to be resisted by the strongest efforts of human nature." He wanted to know whether Sally returned his love. Apparently in her reply, which has never come to light, she did not tell him, for his next letter to her started: "Do we still misunderstand each other's letters? I think it must appear so, although I would feign hope the contrary as I cannot speak plainer without. But I'll say no more, and leave you to guess the rest." He then continued with a gossipy letter to the wife of his neighbor.

The other nonmilitary happening of 1758 was Washington's election, in absentia, to the Burgesses of Virginia. Although he had permission to go to Williamsburg to campaign he decided "to leave the management of that matter to the care of my friends [rather] than to be absent from my regiment when there is a probability of its being called upon." His friends did their work well and Washington was elected by a handsome majority. But the campaign was not cheap. His account book shows election expenses for:

	£	s	d
To 40 gallons of rum Punch @ 3/6 pr. galn.	7	0	0
12 gallons of Wine @ 10/ pr. galn.	7	10	0
13½ gallons of Wine @ 10s	6	15	0
3½ pints of Brandy @ 1/3		4	4½
13 gallons Beer @ 1/3		16	3
8 qts. Cider Royal @ 1/6		12	0
Punch		3	9
30 gallons of strong Beer @ 8d pr. gall.	1	0	0

	£	s	d
1 hhd. & 1 barrel of punch, consisting of			
26 gallons best Barbadoes rum 5/	6	10	0
12½ lbs. refined sugar 1/6		18	9
6 gallons best Madeira Wine 10/	3	0	0
3 gallons and 3 qts. of Beer @ 1/ pr. gallon		3	9
10 bowls of Punch @ 2/6 each	1	5	0
9 half pints of rum @ 7½ each		5	7½
1 pint of Wine		1	6

This 160 gallons of liquor was presumably consumed by the 391 eligible voters of Frederick County—almost a half gallon a man. Washington was not dismayed at the expense or its purpose. Rather, he wrote, "I hope no exceptions were taken to any that voted against me but that all were alike treated and all had enough; it is what I much desired. My only fear is that you spent with too sparing a hand."

In thanking his campaign manager, Colonel James Wood, for his efforts Washington started to sound like a politician:

IF THANKS FLOWING from a heart replete with joy and gratitude can in any measure compensate for the fatigue, anxiety and pain you had at my election, be assured you have them. . . .

How shall I acknowledge my sense of obligation to the people in general for their choice of me, I am at a loss to resolve on. But why? Can I do it more effectually than by making their interest (as it really is) my own, and doing everything that lies in my little power for the honor and welfare of the country? I think not; and my best endeavors they may always command.

He had no program to propose to the legislature. He said, "I don't like to touch upon our public affairs; the prospect is overspread by too many ills to give a favorable account. I will therefore say little but yet say this, that backwardness appears in all things but the approach of winter; that jogs on apace."

Early in 1758 Lord Pitt relieved Lord Loudoun of command in America and announced a three-pronged offensive for the year with expeditions toward Louisburg, Ticonderoga and Fort Duquesne. The last was to be commanded by Colonel John Forbes. Counting the three governors, this was Washington's eighth commander in four years. In all this time he had received no recognition of any kind from the home country. He promptly wrote to Brigadier General John Stanwix, a British officer, "I must . . . beg that you will add one more kindness to the many I have experienced, and that is to mention me in favorable terms to General Forbes . . . as a person who would gladly be distinguished in some measure from the common run of provincial officers, as I understand there will be a motley herd of us."

As always, preparations for the advance took far longer than Washington thought they should, but in some respect the military prospect was brightening. Forbes, with lavish gifts, weaned a substantial number of Indians from the French. Recruiting in Virginia picked up. There were now two regiments of almost a thousand men each, of which Washington was senior colonel. His immediate superior was British Colonel Henry Bouquet.

But Washington was not happy. Forbes was up in Pennsylvania. With an eye to the profit possibilities of supplying the expedition, the Pennsylvanians were trying to convince him that the best way to reach Fort Duquesne was to cut a new road through their colony, rather than use the old Braddock route. Washington was a colonial Englishman; but first and last he was a Virginian: as yet there were no united Americans. Washington had little love for the neighboring colonies—particularly Pennsylvania. He wrote to Speaker Robinson that the English officers were "dupes, or something else, to Pennsylvanian artifice, to whose selfish views I attribute the miscarriage of this expedition. . . . It has long been the luckless fate of poor Virginia to fall victim to the views of her crafty neighbors, and yield her honest efforts to promote their common interest at the expense of much blood and treasure."

Washington advanced his reasons for using Braddock's road in a letter to Bouquet. He wrote:

INDIANS AFTER HAVING TAKEN the greatest pains to gain the rewards then offered for this discovery, declared the path leading from Wills Creek was infinitely preferable to any that could be made at any other place. Time and experience so clearly demonstrated this truth . . . [that] the Ohio Company in 1753, at a considerable expense, opened a road thither. In 1754 the troops I had the honor to command greatly repaired it . . . and in 1755 it was widened and completed by General Braddock within six miles of Fort Duquesne. Consequently a road that has been so long opened, so well repaired and so often, must be much firmer and better than a new one, allowing the ground to be originally equally as good.

This letter continued for several pages to give a complete exposition of Washington's thesis that the Braddock route was the only reasonable one to the Forks. He gave relative distances, streams and swamps to be crossed, and much else.

Not content with pushing his views on Bouquet, George did the unforgivable thing, in the military, of going over his superior's head. He wrote to Major Francis Halkett, who had been with Braddock and was now an aide to Forbes:

I AM JUST RETURNED from a conference held with Colonel Bouquet. I find him fixed, I think I may say fixed, upon leading you a new way to the Ohio; through a road, every inch of it to cut, at this advanced season, when we have scarce time left to tread the beaten track; universally confessed to be the best passage through the mountains.

If Colonel Bouquet succeeds in this point with the general, all is lost! All is lost by Heavens! Our enterprise ruined; and we stopped at the Laurel Hill this winter; not to gather laurels, by the by, desirable in their effects.

Forbes' opinion of this action was reflected in a later letter to Bouquet in which he said, "Consult Colonel Washington, although perhaps not follow his advice, as his behavior about the roads was no ways like a soldier."

The decision was made for a new road. Washington served well in helping to build it and, for a time, was a brigadier in charge of two regiments. But he never stopped arguing. When the new route had reached the last ridge before Duquesne he wrote Forbes apropos of garrisoning and supplying the fort after it was captured: "I do not know so effectual a way of doing it as by the communication of Fort Cumberland and General Braddock road, which is in the first place good, and in the next, fresh; affording good food if the weather keeps open, which is more than a road can do as much used as this one has been." George Washington was a very stubborn man.

The English did not have to attack Fort Duquesne. French losses in the North had made it impossible to supply the garrison at the Forks, and at the approach of the British their remaining Indians had melted into the forest. When the English arrived the stronghold was a deserted, smoking ruin. But Washington did see some action in this campaign. In his memorandum to Humphreys, almost fifty years later, he wrote that

> . . . a circumstance occurred which involved the life of G. W. in as much jeopardy as it had ever been before or since. The enemy sent out a large detachment to reconnoiter our camp, and to ascertain our strength. In consequence of intelligence that they were within two miles of the camp a party commanded by Lieutenant Colonel Mercer of the Virginia line . . . was sent to dislodge them; between whom a severe conflict and hot firing ensued . . . lasting some time and appearing to approach the camp.

Washington led a party of reinforcements to relieve Mercer, and sent a scout ahead to announce their coming.

. . . But it being near dusk and the intelligence not having been fully disseminated among Colonel Mercer's corps, and they taking us for the enemy . . . approaching in another direction, commenced a heavy fire upon the relieving party which drew fire in return in spite of all the exertions of the officers; one of whom and several privates were killed and many wounded before a stop could be put to it—to accomplish which G. W. never was in more imminent danger, by being between two forces, knocking up with his sword the presented pieces.

Thus ended Washington's early military career. He resigned at the end of 1758 after slightly less than five years service—and in age two months short of twenty-seven. He had accomplished more and gained more recognition than any of the other Founding Fathers in their early years. At the same age John Adams was trying to build up a new law practice. His cousin Samuel was running a brewery. Benjamin Franklin had paid off the debts of his print shop and published the first edition of *Poor Richard's Almanac*. Thomas Jefferson was, unhappily and rather unsuccessfully, riding the backcountry circuit courts of Virginia.

The accomplishments of Washington's first military career are a study in contrasts. He had demonstrated his capacity for assuming responsibility. He had proved a stern disciplinarian, but with a reputation for inflexible justice. He was a first-rate administrator. He had learned a lesson that would later be invaluable—the necessity for endless patience. He was admired and respected by his junior officers.

On the debit side he was not so highly regarded by his equals in rank nor by his superiors. He was a failure at recruiting; principally because his background, training and inclination made it impossible for him to have contact with the private soldier. He had, and always maintained, a lack of appreciation for and understanding of militia. He never did learn how to handle the citizen soldier.

His motivations were somewhat paradoxical. In many of his letters he sounded like a mercenary—"I must now beg leave to know . . . upon what terms your honor proposes to continue me, and what may be my certain dependence?" He made enough from his military service to buy more land and slaves. Only once, early in his service did he mention a patriotic impulse—"a glowing zeal," as he termed it—when he referred to "The heroic spirit of every free-born Englishman to attest the rights and privileges of our king (if we don't consult the benefit of ourselves) and rescue from the invasions of a usurping enemy our Majesty's property, his dignity and land." Later he wrote, "We are defending the king's dominions." And he felt that the wealthy king should pay for this service.

He was almost pushingly ambitious. The close of his letter to Lord Loudoun, seeking advancement, sounds like a fawning courtier rather than the dignified Washington. When his position was not, in his opinion, properly respected he threatened to resign—seven times in all before his final resignation.

But more important than ambition or money was honor. Throughout his letters are expressions of his concern for this: "I believe our circumstances are now to that happy dilemma that no man can gain any honor by conducting our forces at this time, but rather lose in his reputation." Again, he reported, "the chief part of my happiness, i.e., the esteem and notice the country has been pleased to honor me with." And, "If I can gain credit," he told William Byrd just before joining Braddock, "or if I am entitled to the least countenance or esteem, it must be from serving my country with a free, voluntary will."

Washington's code of conduct, his ideals, also seems at variance with his ambition and acquisitiveness. What he called "the principles by which I govern myself" were rigid and inflexible. He took the "Rules of Civility and Decent Behavior," which he had copied as a boy, very much to heart. Honesty, justice and courtesy were, with Washington, stern taskmasters, as was truth. "I may be blamed possibly for expressing my opinions so freely," he wrote, "but never can be ashamed of the truth."

Perhaps the best summary of the young Commander-in-Chief, although not necessarily an objective one, is contained in a memorial signed by twenty-seven of his junior officers when he resigned:

WE, YOUR MOST OBEDIENT and affectionate officers, beg leave to express our great concern at the disagreeable news we have received of your determination to resign the command of that corps in which we have under you long served. The happiness we have enjoyed, and the honor we have acquired, together with the mutual regard that has always subsisted between you and your officers, have implanted so sensible an affection in the minds of us all, that we cannot be silent on this critical occasion.

In our earliest infancy you took us under your tuition, trained us up in the practice of that discipline which alone can constitute good troops; from the punctual observance of which you never suffered the least deviation. Your steady adherence to impartial justice, your quick discernment and invariable regard to merit, wisely intended to inculcate those genuine sentiments of true honor and passion for glory from which the great military achievements have been derived, first heightened our natural emulation, and our desire to excel.

The memorial continued, in even more florid language, to laud Washington's service to his country and the loss which his leaving entailed for king, country and the officers themselves. Then the young men concluded:

. . . Frankness, sincerity, and a certain openness of soul, are the true characteristics of an officer, and we flatter ourselves that you do not think us capable of saying anything contrary to the purest dictates of our minds. Fully persuaded of this, we beg leave to assure you that, as you have hitherto been the actuating soul of the whole corps, we shall at all times pay the most invariable regard to your will and pleasure, and will always be happy to demonstrate, by our actions, with how much respect and esteem we are, sir, your most affectionate and most obedient humble servants.

CHAPTER IV

THE PEACEFUL SQUIRE

❦

"I am now, I believe, fixed at this seat with an agreeable consort for life and hope to find more happiness in retirement than I ever experienced amidst a wide and bustling world." So wrote Washington in the fall of 1759. On January 6 of that year he had married Martha in the White House, the handsome residence which she had inherited from her first husband. With Martha's wealth and George's fame it was a wedding long remembered in eastern Virginia. After a brief honeymoon at the bride's home, Washington journeyed to Williamsburg to take his seat in the House of Burgesses, for the first time, on his twenty-seventh birthday. George Mercer, a friend and fellow member of the House, described him as follows:

HE MAY BE DESCRIBED as being straight as an Indian, measuring six feet two inches in his stockings and weighing 175 lbs when he took his seat in the House of Burgesses in 1759. His frame is padded with well-developed muscles, indicating great strength. His bones and joints are large; as are his hands and feet. He is wide-shouldered but has not a deep or round chest; is neat waisted, but is broad across the hips, and has rather long legs and arms. His head is well shaped, though not large, but is gracefully poised on a superb neck. A large and straight rather than a prominent nose; blue-gray penetrating eyes which are widely separated and overhung by a heavy brow. His face is long rather than broad, with high round cheek bones, and terminates in a good firm chin. He has a clear though rather colorless pale skin which burns with the sun. A pleasing and benevolent though a commanding countenance, dark brown hair which he wears in a queue. His mouth is large and generally firmly closed, but which from time to time discloses some defective teeth. His features are regular and placid with all the muscles of his face under perfect control, though flexible and expressive of deep feeling when moved by emotions. In conversation he looks you full in the face, is deliberate, deferential and engaging. His demeanor at all times [is] composed and dignified. His movements and gestures are graceful, his walk majestic, and he is a splendid horseman.

Other descriptions of Washington are generally in accord with this except for his weight. G. W. P. Custis says that he tipped the scales at 210 to 225 in his prime; a more likely weight for a man of his height and build.

There are few records of Washington's activities as a member of the House of Burgesses. He seldom spoke. Thomas Jefferson, a fellow member in later years, remembered, "I served with General Washington in the legislature of Virginia before the Revolution and, during it, with Dr. Franklin in Congress. I never heard either of them speak for ten minutes at a time, nor to any but the main point which was to decide the question. They laid their shoulders to the great points, knowing that the little ones would follow of themselves." Washington was initially made a member of the important Committee of Propositions and Grievances, a most appropriate appointment because this committee dealt with commercial affairs and, for the next fifteen years, Washington would be a man of business. One of the few bills which he proposed was to "preserve the water for the use of the inhabitants of the town of Winchester and the limits thereof by preventing hogs from running at large therein." Most of his early interests had to do with legislation for the relief of soldiers who had served with him.

After seven pleasant weeks in the capital the newlyweds started for home, accompanied by "Jacky" Custis, aged four, Patsy Custis, aged two, and a small retinue of servants. Apparently it did not occur to George until they were halfway to Mount Vernon that his domain of bachelor days might not be presentable in the eyes of his wife. In any event, he sent a servant galloping forward to get the key from the neighbors and to carry a note to his plantation manager, John Alton:

JNO: I have sent Miles on today, to let you know that I expect to be up tomorrow, and to get the key from Colonel Fairfax's, which I desire you will take care of. You must have the house very well cleaned, and were you to make fires in the rooms below it would air them. You must get two of the best bedsteads put up, one in the hall room, and the other in the little dining room that used to be, and have beds made on them against we come. You must also get out the chairs and tables, and have them very well rubbed and cleaned; the staircase ought also to be polished in order to make it look well.

Inquire about in the neighborhood, and get some eggs and chickens, and prepare in the best manner you can for our coming; you need not, however, take out any more of the furniture than the beds and tables and chairs in order that they may be well rubbed and cleaned.

In truth, Mount Vernon had run down during his years at the wars. Brother Jack had been there at times, but his casual supervision had not served to prevent buildings from collapsing and stock from running off or to provide provender even to feed the family during the first year. Since his teens, Washington had been first a surveyor and then a soldier. Now he had to learn to be a farmer, a bookkeeper, a financier and a businessman. He started, in those days when wives were not supposed to have minds of their own, by writing a firm letter to Carey and Company, the London merchants who handled the bulk of the Custis business:

THE ENCLOSED IS the minister's certificate of my marriage with Mrs. Martha Custis, properly, as I am told, authenticated. You will, therefore, for the future please to address all your letters which relate to the affairs of the late Daniel Parke Custis, Esq., to me, as by marriage I am entitled to a third part of that estate, and invested likewise with the care of the other two thirds [held in trust for the Custis children]. . . .

On the other side is an invoice of some goods which I beg of you to send me by the first ship, bound either to Potomac or Rappahannock, as I am in immediate want of them.

The list of goods on the back of the letter was a long one, starting with furniture for the bridal chamber:

One tester bedstead 7½ feet pitch with fashionable blue or blue and white curtains to suit a room laid with yellow Ireland paper.

Window curtains of the same for two windows; with either papier mache cornish [valances] . . . or cornish covered with the cloth.

One fine bed coverlid to match the curtains. Four chair bottoms of the same; that is, as much covering suited to the above furniture as will go over the seats of four chairs (which I have by me) in order to make the whole furniture of this room uniformly handsome and genteel.

The list continued through carpeting and candlestands for Mount Vernon to hose, gloves, shoes and a suit for George. It reflected a new interest by including, "The newest and most approved treatise of agriculture—besides this, send me a small piece in octavo—called a *New System of Agriculture,* or a *Speedy Way to Grow Rich.*" And an old interest by ending with, "Order from the best house in Madeira a pipe of the best old wine, and let it be secured from pilferers."

Washington's "daily grind" during the first half of the 1760s, when he was trying to build up Mount Vernon to put it on a paying basis and manage the plantations of his wife and stepchildren, is indicated by excerpts from his diary in January 1760. His daily record of the weather—which he kept throughout his life when at home—has been omitted on most days:

Tuesday, 1st: Visited my plantations and received an instance of Mr. French's great love of money in disappointing me of some pork, because the price had risen to 22/6 after he had engaged to let me have it at 20/.

Called at Mr. Possey's on my way home and desired him to engage me 100 barrels of corn upon the best terms he could in Maryland.

And found Mrs. Washington upon my arrival broke out with the measles.

Wednesday, 2d: . . . the weather being too bad . . . together with Mrs. Washington indisposition, confined me to the house and gave me an opportunity of posting my books and putting them in good order.

Fearing a disappointment elsewhere in pork I was fein to take Mr. French's upon his own terms and engaged them to be delivered at my house on Monday next.

Thursday 3d: . . . Hauled the sein and got some fish, but was near being disappointed of my boat by means of any oyster man, who had lain at my landing and plagued me a good deal by his disorderly behavior. . . .

Sunday 6th: . . . Mrs. Washington was a good deal better today; but the oyster man still continuing his disorderly behavior at my landing I was obliged in the most peremptory manner to order him and his company away, which he did not incline to obey till next morning. . . .

Tuesday, 8th: Directed an indictment to be formed by Mr.

Johnston against Jno. Ballendine for a fraud in some iron he sold me.

Got a little butter from Mr. Dalton, and wrote to Colonel West for pork.

In the evening, eight of Mr. French's hogs from his Ravensworth quarter came down, one being lost on the way—as the others might as well have been for their goodness.

Carpenter Sam was taken with the Measles. . . .

Saturday, 12th: Set out with Mrs. Bassett on her journey to Port Royal. . . . We passed Occoquan without any great difficulty . . . and lodged at Mr. McCraes in Dumfries. . . .

Here I was informed that Colonel Cocke was disgusted at my house and left because he saw an old Negro there resembling his own image. . . .

Monday, 14th: . . . Mr. Bassett brought me a letter from Captain Langbourn enclosing a bill of lading for twenty Hhds. [shipped on] the *Deliverance,* Captain William Whyte. One other was sent by the ship, neither of which signifying to whom the tobacco was consigned; which is not less strange than that only two bills should be given when four, and never less than three, is customary in wartime. . . .

Tuesday, 15th: . . . Several gentlemen dined with us at Colonel Carter's [neighbors], but we spent a very lonesome evening at Colonel Champe's, not anybody favoring us with their company but himself. . . .

Wednesday, 16th: I parted with Mr. Gibourne, leaving Colonel Champe's before the family was stirring, and at ten reached my mother's, where I breakfasted and then went to Fredericksburg with my brother Sam, who I found there.

About noon it began snowing, the wind at southwest, but not cold; was disappointed of seeing my sister Lewis and getting a few things which I wanted out of the stores. Returned in the evening to mother's—all alone with her. . . .

Saturday, 19th: . . . Received a letter from my overseer Hardwick, informing me that the smallpox was surrounding the plantations he overlooked, and requiring sundry working tools.

Bought four hogs . . . and delivered them to Richard Stephens, which fully completes his own and son's allowance of provisions.

Sunday, 20th: My wagon, after leaving two hogsheads of tobacco at Alexandria, arrived here with three sides of butter, one of which for Colonel Fairfax and fifteen bushels of salt which she took in at Alexandria.

Visited at Belvoir today, carrying Doctor Craik with us, who spent the evening there. . . .

Friday, 25th: . . . Went to Alexandria and saw my tobacco as it came from the mountains lying in an open shed, with the ends of the hogsheads out and in very bad order. Engaged the inspection of it on Monday.

Wrote to Doctor Ross to purchase me a joiner, bricklayer and gardener, if any ship of servants was in.

Also wrote to my old servant Bishop to return to me again, if he was not otherwise engaged. Directed for him at Philadelphia but no certainty of his being there. . . .

Saturday, 26th: . . . Visited my plantation. Severely reprimanded young Stephens for his indolence, and his father for suffering of it.

Found the new Negro Cupid ill of a pleurisy at Dogue Run quarter and had him brought home in a cart for better care of him.

Tuesday, 29th: . . . Darcus, daughter of Phyllis, died, which makes four Negroes lost this winter; viz, three dower Negroes namely, Beck, appraised to £50, Doll's child born since, and Darcus . . . and Belinda, a wench of mine, in Frederick. . . .

Wednesday, 30th: . . . Cupid was extremely ill all this day, and at night when I went to bed I thought him within a few hours of breathing his last.

Thursday, 31st: He was somewhat better, the wind continued at northwest all day, very cold and clear.

When smallpox spread among the slaves on his plantation in Frederick, Washington mounted and rode to supervise their care himself. Fortunately, he was immune to the disease since his trip to Barbados. His diary records:

> . . . Reached Mr. Stephenson's in Frederick about four o'clock, just time enough to see Richard Mounts interred. Here I was informed that Harry and Kit, the two first of my Negroes that took the smallpox, were dead, and Roger and Phyllis the only two down with it were recovering from it. . . .
>
> After taking the doctor's directions in regard to my people, I set out for my quarters and got there about twelve o'clock—time enough to go over them and find everything in the utmost confusion, disorder and backwardness; my overseer (Hardwick) lying upon his back of a broken leg, and not half a crop, especially of corn ground, prepared. . . .
>
> Got blankets and every other requisite from Winchester and settled things upon the best footing I could to prevent the smallpox from spreading, and in case of its spreading, for the care of the Negroes.
>
> Mr. Vall Crawford agreeing, in case any more of the people at the lower quarter getting it, to take them home in his house, and if any more at the upper quarter get it, to have them removed into my room and the nurse sent for.

The number of slaves on Washington's several plantations increased through the years, finally reaching more than three hundred. His records show continuing purchases of black slaves, the indentures of white servants, and transported felons. As with his troops, Washington was fair to his slaves and indentured servants, but a strict disciplinarian and stern taskmaster. His stepgrandson said of him, "As a master of slaves, General Washington was consistent, as in every other relation of his meritorious life. They were comfortably lodged, fed and clothed, required to do a full and fair share of duty, well cared for in sickness and old age, and kept in strict and proper discipline. These, we humbly conceive, comprise all the charities of slavery."

He seldom sold his Negroes. He considered them, with his land, the basis of his wealth. But when he had to sell an unruly one he did not hesitate to consign him the region most dreaded by the Virginia slaves; the West Indies. A letter to a ship's captain records one such transaction:

SIR: With this letter comes a Negro (Tom) which I beg the favor of you to sell, in any of the islands you may go to, for whatever he will fetch, and bring me in return from him

One hogshead of best molasses
One ditto of best rum
One barrel of limes, if good and cheap
One pot of tamarinds, containing about ten pounds
Two small ditto of mixed sweetmeats, about five pounds each
And the residue, much or little, in good old spirits.

That this fellow is both a rogue and a runaway . . . I shall not pretend to deny. But that he is exceeding healthy, strong and good at the hoe the whole neighborhood can testify . . . which gives me reason to hope he may, with your good management, sell well, if kept clean and trimmed up a little when offered for sale.

I shall very cheerfully allow you the customary commissions on this affair, and must beg the favor of you (lest he should attempt his escape) to keep him handcuffed till you get to sea, or in the bay, after which I doubt not but you may make him very useful to you.

Despite Washington's best efforts his plantations did not make money during the early 1760s. There were three reasons. He was too generous, he was too extravagant and the land was not suitable for raising tobacco. On this latter head he at first refused to admit that his tobacco was inferior. When a Liverpool merchant sold a hogshead of his leaf for £8 4s he wrote them, " 'Tis unreasonable, therefore, to expect that I can continue a correspondence under such obvious disadvantages." He would do no more business with this house; but at the same time he wrote Cary and Company that they were not treating him fairly: "I am at a loss to conceive the reason why Mr. Wormeley's, and indeed some other gentlemen's tobaccos, should sell at 12s last year and mine . . . only fetch 11½. . . . Certain I am no person in Virginia takes more pains to make their tobacco fine than I do and 'tis hard then I should not be as well rewarded for it." It did not seem to be so much a matter of money as of pride. Nobody else should grow better tobacco than George Washington.

His unsatisfactory income did not restrict Washington's spending. He loved nice things. So did Martha, for herself, her home and her children. There were orders for four dozen knives "properly disposed of in neat mahogany cases for decorating a sideboard," a dozen chairs from England and eight busts "according to the enclosed directions and measure." This order continued to specify fifteen-inch busts of Alexander the Great, Caesar, Charles XII of Sweden and the King of Prussia; with smaller busts of Prince Eugene, the Duke of Marlborough and two wild animals. When he was advised that the only fifteen-inch busts available were those of poets, he turned them down.

For Martha there were egrets for her headdress, "One cap, handkerchief, tucker and ruffles to be made of Brussels lace, proper to wear with the above negligee, to cost £20. . . . Six pounds of perfumed powder," and much else. "For Master Custis" there were Irish Holland, fine cambric, "two laced hats, one pair handsome silver shoe and knee buckles, 10s worth of toys, six little books for children beginning to read." "For Miss Custis" there were fine printed linen and Irish Holland, "two fans; two masks; two bonnets; one stiffened coat of fashionable silk, made to packthread stays; one fashionable-dressed baby 10s, and other toys 10s."

For Miss Custis there was also soon ordered "one very good spinet, to be made by Mr. Plinius, harpsicord maker in South Audley Street, Grosvenor Square. Note: it is begged as a favor that Mr. Cary would bespeak this instrument as for himself or a friend, and not let it be known that it is intended for exportation. Send a good assortment of spare strings to it." For poor Master Custis there was ordered at the same time a dozen different Latin grammars, readers and dictionaries. The indulgent stepfather would have his daughter cultured, his son intellectual.

When he rode abroad Washington was given to a certain ostentation. This tendency would later cause Thomas Jefferson to speculate that he might have monarchial aspirations. Now it caused Washington to order, with meticulous care for detail, a new chariot from Cary and Company:

I WOULD WILLINGLY have the chariot you may now send me made in the newest taste, handsome, genteel and light; yet not slight and consequently unserviceable. To be made of the best seasoned wood, and by a celebrated workman. . . . green being a color little apt . . . to fade, and grateful to the eye, I would give it the preference, unless any other color more in vogue and equally lasting is entitled to precedency. In that case I would be governed by fashion.

A light gilding on the mouldings . . . and any other ornaments that may not have a heavy and tawdry look (together with my arms agreeable to the impression here sent) might be added, by way of decoration. . . . Together with a handsome set of harness for four middle-sized horses. . . . On the harness let my crest be engraved.

If such a chariot as I have here described could be got at second hand little or nothing the worse of wear, but at the same time a good deal under the first cost of a new one (and sometimes, though perhaps rarely, it happens so), it would be very desirable; but if I am obliged to go near the original cost I would even have one made; and have been thus particular, in hopes of getting a handsome chariot, through your direction, good taste, and management; not of copper, however, for these do not stand the powerful heat of our sun.

The vehicle he received was new and cost, with shipping charges, £315 13s 6d.

It is not to be wondered that Cary and Company soon wrote their valued customer reminding him that he was in their debt in the amount of £1811 and that they would like a small remittance. Washington considered this a dunning letter and replied indignantly that, no matter "in whatsoever light it may appear to you, it is not less evidently certain that mischances rather than misconduct hath been the causes of it. . . ."

Washington's financial straits did not prevent him from loaning money liberally. Neighbors, friends and even acquaintances looked to him for frequent financial aid, and seldom in vain. When one of his captains in the Virginia regiment, Robert Stewart, appealed for a loan of £411 to buy a royal commission, Washington wrote him a long letter of explanation and apology because he did not have that sum. He enclosed "a copy of Mr. Cary's last account current against me, which upon my honor and the faith of a Christian is a true one, and transmitted to me with the additional aggravation of a hint at the largeness of it." He went on to explain at great length that the restoration of his plantation "swallowed up before I well knew where I was, all the money I got by marriage; nay more, brought me in debt." He did not make this explanation, he told Stewart, "in order to lay open the distress of my affairs, but rather to evince my inability of exceeding £300; a sum I am now laboring to procure by getting money to purchase bills of that amount to remit to yourself, that Mr. Cary may have no knowledge of the transaction since he expected this himself."

Washington's shortage of cash was not peculiar to him. It was a condition of the Virginia economy in which tobacco shipped to England resulted in credits with British merchants against which planters purchased manufactured goods. There was very little hard money in the colony; and perhaps too much paper money printed in Williamsburg. A system of barter was commonplace, which vastly complicated Washington's bookkeeping. There was a good blacksmith at Mount Vernon. Washington traded his services to one neighbor for butter, to another for eggs and chickens, to a third for a cow and a fourth for old iron. He traded wagonage for leather; fifteen hundred pounds of pork for a boat; brick, salt and wheat for a quarter cask of port wine. When one planter ran up a sizable blacksmith's bill Washington accepted part payment in the services of a stallion at stud.

In 1764 Washington turned over a new leaf. Or, rather, he started to cut down on the tobacco leaf that he could not raise successfully and substituted wheat. He also sought new sources of income. He purchased a new schooner and went into the fishing business. By the end of the decade he was selling 700,000 salted herring and a lesser volume of shad. He built a second mill and went into the flour business with his own "G. Washington" brand. Here, as with tobacco, he tried to produce the best, but when the product was inferior he sought to sell it to the best advantage far from home. Of one shipment to the West Indies he wrote the factor:

IN THE DISPOSAL of this flour, I recommend its being lumped . . . rather than sold in small parcels for trial as it was ground out of indifferent wheat; and will, I fear, look better to the eye than it will prove agreeable to the taste, being a little musty.

The money arising from the sales I would have laid out in Negroes, if choice ones can be had under forty pounds sterling; if not, then in rum and sugar from Barbados, or any of the Windward Islands; and sugar and molasses if the flour should be sold in Jamaica.

If the returns are in slaves let there be two thirds of them males, the other third females. The former not exceeding (at any rate) twenty years of age, the latter sixteen. All of them to be straight-limbed and in every respect strong and likely with good teeth, and good countenances, to be sufficiently provided with clothes.

Economy also become the watchword in the mid-1760s—very temporarily. The weaving room at Mount Vernon was enlarged to supply all of the cloth for "the people." A new still was purchased to produce applejack and peach brandy from the plantation's orchards. Most of this was traded or used by tenants and servants; Washington still preferred his very expensive imported Madeira.

In 1763 Washington was elected to the Vestry in Truro Parish. This, and his several orders for worship services by troops in camp, contributed to the legend that Washington was a stanch churchman. Actually, although he was devoutly religious, his attendance at church was spotty. During these years he went about once a month, and apparently never took communion. His diaries seem to indicate that he would rather go hunting or fishing; but Martha had other ideas. The Vestry was an administrative body to which, in his position, Washington was virtually required to belong.

Unlike Franklin, Jefferson and John Adams, who speculated at length on religion and theology, Washington wrote little on these subjects although he firmly believed in God: "It is impossible to reason without arriving at a Supreme Being." During the dark times of the Revolution he repeatedly echoed the theme that success would be possible only with the aid of a Divine Providence.

He felt that religious exercises were good for the people, good for his troops and good for the country. During the Revolution he wrote:

WHILE WE ARE ZEALOUSLY performing the duties of good citizens and soldiers we certainly ought not to be inattentive to the higher duties of religion. To the distinguished character of patriot it should be our highest glory to add the more distinguished character of Christian. The signal instances of Providential goodness which we have experienced, and which have now almost crowned our labors with complete success, demand from us in a peculiar manner the warmest returns of gratitude and piety to the Supreme Author of all good.

The important aspect of Washington's religious beliefs, in a day of rabid sectarianism, was tolerance. Certainly the Catholic-hating clergy of the colonies would have frowned had they read his orders to Benedict Arnold for the invasion of Canada, in which he wrote: "as far as lays in your power you are to protect and support the free exercise of the religion of the country and the undisturbed enjoyments of the rights of conscience in religious matters with your utmost influence and authority. I also give it in charge to you to avoid all disrespect or contempt of the religion of the country and its ceremonies."

Washington seemed to attend church more frequently in times of stress—and the denomination did not matter. Although he was an Episcopalian his diary records that while he was a delegate to the first Continental Congress he on one Sunday "Went to the Presbyterian meeting in the forenoon and the Romish Church in the afternoon." On another occasion he went to the Dutch Reformed Church in Pennsylvania and remarked, with a rare touch of humor, that the service "being in that language not a word of which I understood I was in no danger of becoming a proselyte to its religion by the eloquence of the preacher."

In later years he wrote to the quakers:

THE LIBERTY ENJOYED by the people of these states, of worshipping Almighty God agreeable to their consciences, is among the choicest not only of their blessings but also of their rights. . . . Your principles and conduct are well known to me, and it is doing the people called Quakers no more than justice to say that (excepting their declining to share with others the burden of the common defense) there is no denomination among us who are more exemplary or useful citizens.

And again to a Hebrew congregation in Newport Rhode Island:

IT IS NOW NO MORE that toleration is spoken of as if it was by indulgence of one class of people that another enjoyed the exercise of their inherent natural rights. . . . May the Father of Mercies scatter light and not darkness on our paths, and make us all, in our several vocations useful here, and in his own due time and way everlastingly happy.

In his later years he was an honorary member of the Friendly Sons of St. Patrick, perhaps the only Protestant in that Hibernian association.

Washington was a practicing, rather than a prating, Christian. He wrote nothing of Jesus, but his own code of conduct, except for a certain acquisitiveness, paralleled the Sermon on the Mount. He summed up his views on religion in his Farewell Address:

MORALITY is a necessary spring of popular government. . . . let us with caution indulge the supposition that morality can be maintained without religion. Whatever may be conceded to the influence of refined education on minds of peculiar structure, reason and experience both forbid us to expect that national morality can prevail in exclusion of religious principle.

In 1765 the Virginia Burgesses first took a strong position on England's unfair treatment of the colonies by passing the resolutions against the Stamp Act proposed by Patrick Henry. Washington was probably not present when Henry dramatically proclaimed, "If this be treason, make the most of it." His accounts show that he was not paid for four days of that session; probably the last four, during which Henry made his memorable speech.

Washington was not so violently opposed to the Stamp Act as many of the hotheads. His only comment on it before its repeal was:

THE STAMP ACT IMPOSED on the colonies by the Parliament of Great Britain engrosses the conversation of the speculative part of the colonists, who look upon this unconstitutional method of taxation as a direful attack upon their liberties, and loudly exclaim against the violation. What may be the result of this and some other (I think I may add) ill-judged measures, I will not undertake to determine; but this I may venture to affirm that the advantage accruing to the mother country will fall greatly short of the expectations of the Ministry; for certain it is our whole substance does already in a manner flow to great Britain, and that whatsoever contributes to lessen our importations must be hurtful to their manufacturers. And the eyes of our people, already beginning to open, will perceive that many luxuries which we lavish our substance to Great Britain for can well be dispensed with whilst the necessaries of life are (mostly) to be had within ourselves.

The letter continued to say that the Stamp Act simply would not work because, "we have no money to pay for the stamps. . . . I fancy the merchants of Great Britain trading to the colonies will not be among the last to wish for a repeal of it."

The Stamp Act was replaced by the equally obnoxious Townshend Act, which placed a tax upon paints, glass, paper and tea. Washington was among the Virginia leaders who formed an association dedicated to nonimportation of taxed goods from Britain. He expressed his views on the subject to George Mason:

AT A TIME WHEN our lordly masters in Great Britain will be satisfied with nothing less than the depreciation of American freedom, it seems highly necessary that something should be done to avert the stroke and maintain the liberty which we have derived from our ancestors; but the manner of doing it to answer the purpose effectually is the point in question.

That no man should scruple or hesitate a moment to use arms in defense of so valuable a blessing, on which all the good and evil of life depends, is clearly my opinion; yet arms, I would beg leave to add, should be the last resource; the *dernier* resort.

This was Washington's first tentative reference to the possibility of armed resistance.

Mason drew up a list of articles on the proposed nonimportation list. Washington took these to Williamsburg for presentation to the Burgesses. When the governor dissolved this body, Washington joined his colleagues in a rump session in the Apollo Room of the Raleigh Tavern and presented his plan. It was promptly adopted, and he was appointed to a committee to carry it out.

Meanwhile, back at Mount Vernon, the financial position was much better in the late 1760s, and Washington was very much the county squire. He had become a warden of the church and a justice of the peace. In fact, before the Revolution, he held almost every position in the county except those of sheriff and coroner. He became, to a greater extent, an unofficial banker to many of his friends and a councilor to many more. Despite all these duties, with his plantations on a paying basis he had more time to play. His diaries for this period abound with records of hunting and fishing, like these from January 1768.

"Fox hunting in my own Neck." "Started a fox and run him four hours, took the hounds off at night." "Rid up to Toulston in order to fox hunt it." "Fox hunting with Jacky Custis and L(un)d Washington. Catched a fox after a three hours chase." "Never started a fox, but did a deer." "Fishing for sturgeon from breakfast to dinner but catched none." "Went a ducking and killed two mallards and five bald faces."

When the weather was inclement and during his frequent stays in Williamsburg, cards were a favorite pastime. His meticulous accounting shows losses of £24 during one session of the Burgesses, although on one night he won £9 10s. Washington was also a devotee of the theater in the colonial capital. During one seven-day period he attended five times:

16: Dined at the club at Mrs. Campbell's and went to the play in the evening.

17: Went to church in the forenoon, and from thence to Colonel Burwell's, where I dined and lodged.

18: Came into Williamsburg in the morning. Dined at the club and went to the play in the afternoon.

19: Dined at the club and went to the play.

20: Dined at the President's and went to the play afterwards.

21: Dined at the club at Mrs. Campbell's at 8 o'clock and went to bed directly after.

22: Dined at the club and went to the play, after meeting the associates at the Capitol.

And he still gave his money away with a free hand. Typical of his generosity was this letter to a friend in Alexandria:

HAVING ONCE OR TWICE of late heard you speak highly in praise of the Jersey College [later Princeton] as if you had a desire of sending your son William there . . . I should be glad, if you have no other objection to it than what may arise from the expense, if you would send him there as soon as it is convenient, and depend on me for twenty-five pounds this currency a year for his support. . . . No other return is expected, or wished, for this offer, than that you will accept it with the same freedom and good will with which it is made, and that you may not even consider it in the light of an obligation, or mention it as such; for, be assured, that from me it will never be known.

The children were growing up. Jacky, particularly, was well spoiled by a doting mother and an indulgent stepfather. He had a tutor until he was fourteen. Then Washington applied for the youth's admission to a school in Annapolis run by the Reverend Jonathan Boucher, saying:

HE IS A BOY of good genius, about fourteen years of age, untainted in his morals and of innocent manners. Two years and upward he has been reading of Virgil. . . . If he comes, he will have a boy [a servant] . . . and two horses, to furnish him with the means of getting to church and elsewhere as you may permit; for he will be put entirely and absolutely under your tuition, and direction to manage as you think proper in all respects. . . . As to his board and schooling . . . I do not think it necessary to inquire into and will cheerfully pay ten or twelve pounds a year extraordinary to engage your peculiar care of and a watchful eye to him, as he is a promising boy; the last of his family and will possess a very large fortune. Add to this my anxiety to make him fit for more useful purposes than a horse racer.

When Boucher wrote that Jacky had been inoculated against smallpox Washington was pleased, but his answer reflected the attitude of the doting Martha toward the boy. Washington wrote that she "often wished that Jack would take and go through the disorder without her knowing of it, that she might escape those tortures which suspense would throw her into." He added, "When he is returned to Annapolis, you will be so good as to write me a line by post to Williamsburg which shall be the first intimation of this affair I purpose to give if I can keep it concealed so long."

Jacky was not the industrious student that his stepfather would have him. When he came home on vacation Washington wrote Boucher, "I cannot discover that he is much farther in Latin . . . knows little arithmetic, and is quite ignorant of the Greek language. . . . Not that I think his becoming a mere scholar is a desirable education for a gentleman, but I conceive a knowledge of books is the basis upon which other knowledge is to be built." To which the aggrieved minister replied, "I must confess to you I never in my life knew a youth so exceedingly indolent, or so surprisingly voluptuous: one would suppose nature had intended him for some Asiatic Prince."

Regardless of what nature intended, his stepfather's handling of Jacky's share of the estate would make him one of the richest young men in Virginia by the time he reached his majority, and he acted the part. There was not much wrong with him that time did not cure. Washington worried about his indolence: "his mind [is] a good deal released from study and more than ever turned to dogs, horses and guns; indeed upon dress and equipage, which, till of late, he has discovered little inclination of giving into . . ." And about his morals: ". . . the warmth of his own passions, assisted by the bad example of other youth, may prompt him to actions derogatory of virtue, and that innocence of manners which one could wish to preserve him in. For which reason I would beg leave to request, that he may not be suffered to sleep from under your own roof, unless it be at such places as you are sure he can have no bad examples set him; nor allow him to be rambling about of nights." Two centuries ago the Father of his Country had exactly the same problem as the parents of today's teen-agers. This did not apply to Patsy who, already suffering from epilepsy, was kept home.

During the late 1760s and early 1770s, when the colonies' troubles with the mother country were coming to a head, Washington was looking the other way. His greatest interest was in western land. By 1772 he had already extended his Virginia holdings to almost 12,500 acres. But he had a wider horizon. Future wealth lay to the west. In 1767 he wrote: "look to Frederick, and see what fortunes were made by the . . . first takers up of those lands: Nay, how the greatest estates we have in this colony were made. Was it not by taking up and purchasing at very low rates the rich back lands which were thought nothing of in those days, but are now the most valuable lands that we possess?"

When surveyors Charles Mason and Jeremiah Dixon established the western boundary of Pennsylvania, Washington immediately wrote to William Crawford, a companion from Forbes' march to the Forks:

I . . . desire the favor of you (as I understood rights might now be had for the lands which have fallen within the Pennsylvania line) to look me out a track of about 1500, 2000 or more acres somewhere in your neighborhood. . . . It will be easy for you to conceive that ordinary or even middling land would never answer my purpose or expectation so far from navigation and under such a load of expense as those lands are encumbered with. No: a track to please me must be rich. . . .

At the end of the French and Indian War in 1763 King George had established a frontier line by a proclamation that read: ". . . for the present, and until our further pleasure be known . . ." English subjects were not to settle "beyond the heads or sources of any of the rivers which fall into the Atlantic Ocean from the West and Northwest." Washington's letter to Crawford continued:

. . . I never look upon that Proclamation in any other light (but this I say between ourselves) than as a temporary expedient to quiet the minds of the Indians and must fall of course in a few years; especially when those Indians are consenting to our occupying the lands. Any person therefore who neglects the present opportunity of hunting out good lands and in some measure marking and distinguishing them for their own (in order to keep others from settling them) will never regain it. If therefore you will be at the trouble of seeking out the lands I will take upon me the part of securing them so soon as there is a possibility of doing it and will moreover be at all the cost and charges of surveying and patenting, etc., after which you shall have such a reasonable proportion of the whole as we may fix upon at our first meeting.

But the big opportunity to acquire vast western holdings went back to 1754, when Governor Dinwiddie had promised 200,000 acres to the volunteers who erected and supported the fort at the Forks. The grant was delayed by nine years of war and then by the Proclamation Line. In 1769 Washington started a campaign with the Burgesses and Governor Botetourt to have the grant made and to limit the distribution to the few men who had enlisted in 1754—not the larger regiment which he later commanded.

He hoped to get 15,000 acres from this Dinwiddie promise in his own right. In addition, there was another speculative opportunity in western land under a royal proclamation which permitted colonial governors to grant lands to veterans under which Washington's share would be 5000 acres. This latter grant was very vague, and Washington started buying up the rights of his comrades-in-arms. He bought one officer's claim to 2000 acres for ten pounds and wrote, "Could I purchase 12,000 or 15,000 acres upon the same terms I would do it, considering of it as a lottery only." He then wrote his brother Charles:

. . . as you are situated in a good place for seeing many of the officers at different times, I should be glad if you would (in a joking way, rather than in earnest, at first) see what value they seem to set upon their lands; and if you can buy any of the rights of those who continued in the service till after the Cherokee Expedition, at the rate of about five, six, or seven pounds a thousand acres, I shall be obliged to you and will pay the money upon demand. I am of the opinion that some of those who may be in want of a little money would gladly sell. . . . In the whole of your transactions, . . . do not let it be known that I have any concern therein.

In October 1770, Washington set out for the Ohio, with Dr. Craik, his old regimental surgeon, to inspect the western land under the Dinwiddie grant and arrange for surveys. He first visited the tract that Crawford had picked up for him, "about 1600 acres; some as fine land as I ever saw," and then proceeded down the Ohio in canoes with an interpreter and two Indians.

The journey was generally uneventful. Washington's diary contains descriptions of the land and estimates of the sizes of various parcels. He visited and exchanged speeches with the chiefs of the Six Nations. At one Indian town he "received the disagreeable news of two traders being killed . . . thirty-eight miles below this; which caused us to hesitate whether we should proceed or not." However, he soon learned that "only one person was killed. . . . We resolved to pursue our passage till we could get some more distinct account of this transaction." He shot some deer, wild turkeys and five buffaloes. Some of what he did between October 6 and 16 will never be known because the right halves of these diary pages were eaten by mice. After spending twenty-six pounds entertaining the officers at Fort Pitt on the return trip, he arrived home on December 1.

Washington secured 20,147 acres, more than 10 per cent of the Dinwiddie grant and including, as a result of his trip west, some of the best acreage. He justified his extensive acquisitions by writing: "my shoulders had supported the whole weight heretofore; and . . . I might add, without much arrogance, that if it had not been for my unremitted attention to every favorable circumstance, not a single acre of land would ever have been obtained."

As D-Day of the Revolution approached, life went on pleasantly and profitably at Mount Vernon. Frequent orders for furnishings and fashionable clothes for the family crossed the ocean, including, for George:

A GENTLEMAN'S hunting cap, covered with black velvet, to fit a pretty large head, cushioned round or stuffed to make it sit easy thereon. A silk band, and handsome silver buckle to it.

One pair of silver spurs of the newest fashion. . . . One best whole hunting whip, pretty stout and strong, capped with silver and my name and the year engraved thereon.

On May 20, 1772, Washington's diary records, "I sat to have my picture drawn." This was the first portrait of Washington, painted by Charles Willson Peale.

There are many legends of Washington's prodigious strength, the most common being the tale of pitching a dollar across the Rappahannock. This one, told by Peale, seems to have the ring of authenticity:

ONE AFTERNOON several young gentlemen, visitors at Mount Vernon, and myself were engaged in pitching the bar, one of the athletic sports common in those times, when suddenly the Colonel appeared among us. He requested to be shown the pegs that marked the bounds of our effort; then, smiling, and without putting off his coat, held out his hand for the missile. No sooner did the heavy iron bar feel the grasp of his mighty hand than it lost the power of gravitation and whizzed through the air, striking the ground far, very far, beyond our utmost limits. We were indeed amazed, as we stood around all stripped to the buff, with shirt sleeves rolled up, and having thought ourselves very clever fellows, while the Colonel, on retiring, pleasantly observed, "When you beat my pitch, young gentlemen, I'll try again."

The time was approaching for Jacky to go to college. Washington had a low opinion of Virginia's William and Mary:

I CANNOT THINK [IT] a desirable place to send Jack Custis to; the inattention of the masters, added to the number of holidays, is the subject of general complaint, and affords no pleasing prospect to a youth who has a good deal to attain and but a short time to do it in.

It was decided to send the youth to King's College in New York (now Columbia University). But eighteen-year-old Jacky had another idea—marriage to Miss Nelly Calvert, of Baltimore.

Washington wrote a letter of a type that was new, for him, to the girl's father. After assuring Calvert that he had no objection to an alliance with the Maryland family he added:

. . . This acknowledgment being made you must permit me to add, sir, that at this, or in any short time, his youth, inexperience and unripened education is, and will be, insuperable obstacles in my eye to the completion of the marriage. . . . at present, I do not conceive that he is capable of bestowing that due attention to the important consequences of a marriage state which is necessary to be done by those who are inclined to enter into it; and, of course, am unwilling he should do it till he is. . . .

Delivering my sentiments thus will not, I hope, lead you into a belief that I am desirous of breaking off the match; to postpone it is all I have in view; for I shall recommend it to the young gentleman with the warmth that becomes a man of honor (notwithstanding he did not vouchsafe to consult either his mother or me on the occasion) to consider himself as much engaged to your daughter as if the indissoluble knot was tied; and as the surest means of effecting this, to stick close to his studies (in which I flatter myself you will join me), by which he will, in a great measure, avoid those little flirtations with other girls which may, by dividing the attention, contribute not a little to divide the affection.

Washington continued to outline young Mr. Custis's estate and closed by expressing his hope that Calvert "would also be willing to do something genteel by your daughter." He then took Jacky off to New York on a leisurely trip which included dinners with the governors of Maryland, Pennsylvania and New Jersey—the executive of the last-named state was Benjamin Franklin's son William. It was all to no avail. When Jack came home for the Christmas holidays he was resolved on immediate marriage. Like so many fathers before and since, Washington expressed his disapproval of early marriage in a letter to the President of Columbia:

I HAVE YIELDED, contrary to my judgment, and much against my wishes, to Jack's quitting college, in order that he may enter soon into a new scene of life, which I think he would be much fitter for some years hence than now. But having his own inclination, the desires of his mother and the acquiescence of almost all of his relatives to encounter, I did not care, as he is the last of the family, to push my opposition too far, and therefore have submitted to a kind of necessity.

Tragedy struck Mount Vernon in June 1773. For the nineteenth of that month Washington's diary reports, "At home all day. About five o'clock poor Patsy Custis died suddenly." A letter written the next day to Burwell Bassett, Martha's brother-in-law, was more explicit:

SHE ROSE FROM DINNER about four o'clock in better health and spirits than she appeared to have been in some time; soon after which she was seized with one of her usual fits, and expired in it, in less than two minutes without uttering a word, a groan, or scarce a sigh.

A few months previously Washington had consoled Burwell on the loss of the latter's daughter by writing:

THE WAYS OF PROVIDENCE being inscrutable, and the justice of it not to be scanned by the shallow eye of humanity, nor to be counteracted by the utmost efforts of human power or wisdom, resignation, and as far as the strength of our reason and religion can carry us, a cheerful acquiescence to the Divine Will is what we are to aim.

CHAPTER V

THE VIRGINIAN BECOMES AN AMERICAN

❦

About New Year's Day, 1774, word reached Mount Vernon that some Sons of Liberty in Boston, thinly disguised as Indians, had dumped chests of tea into the harbor. It was more than six months before Washington rather casually expressed his disapproval of this delinquency, but calmly voiced his support of Massachusetts in a letter to George Fairfax, who was now in England. Buried amid neighborhood gossip and business news, Washington wrote:

. . . the Ministry may rely on it that Americans will never be taxed without their own consent; that the cause of Boston . . . now is and ever will be considered as the cause of America (not that we approve their conduct in destroying the tea) and that we shall not suffer ourselves to be sacrificed by piecemeal; though God only knows what is to become of us, threatened as we are with so many hovering evils as hang over us at present.

The distant British were but one of Virginia's problems—the Indians and the weather they had always with them. Washington lumped their woes in his letter to Fairfax:

. . . of this colony the minds of people in it never were more disturbed or our situation so critical as at present; arising, as I have said before, from an invasion of our rights and privileges by the Mother Country and our lives and properties by the savages; whilst cruel frost, succeeded by as cruel a drought, contributed not a little to our unhappy situation.

Washington's letters during the winter and spring of 1774 do not reflect the hectic happenings of the times. He had more pressing and immediate personal affairs. In early February he journeyed to the bride's home for Jacky's wedding. He went to Alexandria unwillingly to buy a brig. The Captain Daniel Adams to whom he had entrusted his musty flour had not purchased the straight-limbed slaves that Washington ordered. Instead, he had pocketed the money and Washington compelled him to auction his vessel to pay it back. When there were no bidders, Washington wrote, "I was compelled to buy it in myself at the price of £175 this currency; much against my inclination, as I had no desire of being concerned in shipping. But I was obliged to make the best of a bad matter." The brig, renamed the *Farmer,* turned out out to be a profitable addition to the Mount Vernon enterprises.

He was anxious to secure settlers for his western lands. He considered importing some Germans, whom he called Pallatines, and wrote to Pennsylvania, "be so good as to ask some of the Pallatine importers what they would deliver two hundred families (not much encumbered with children) at Alexandria for, or even at Philadelphia. Also inquire whether a request of mine, to my correspondent in London, to send me a parcel of these people would be a ready method of getting them. You may perceive I am for trying all things." He also advertised for settlers, but ended by buying four convicts, four indentured servants and a man and wife.

The western land brought other problems, and Washington wrote one of his few ill-tempered letters in connection with one of them. Captain George Muse had admitted to cowardice at Fort Necessity and been cashiered; but he still demanded, and received, his share of the Dinwiddie grant. Then he decided that he had been cheated and wrote Washington a vehement letter of protest, the bearer of which told Washington that Muse was drunk when he penned it. Washington replied:

SIR, Your impertinent letter . . . was delivered to me yesterday by Mr. Smith. As I am not accustomed to receive such from any man, nor would have taken the same language from you personally . . . I would advise you to be cautious in writing me a second of the same tenor; for though I understand that you were drunk when you did it, yet give me leave to tell you that drunkenness is not excuse for rudeness; and that but for your stupidity and sottishness you might have known . . .

And with that he explained the apportionment. He added: "all my concern is that I ever engaged in behalf of so ungrateful and dirty fellow as you are." Such a letter was asking for a duel under the contemporary code of Virginia gentlemen. But Muse was still the coward. He replied with a cringing reference to his "infirmness and old age."

In addition to his personal affairs, Washington was engulfed in many time-consuming "extracurricular" activities. Their extent is indicated by this letter to a friend who asked him to be an executor for his estate:

FOR WHAT WITH my own business, my present wards', my mother's (which is wholly in my hands), Colonel Colville's, Mrs. Savage's, Colonel Fairfax's, Colonel Mercer's . . . and the little assistance I have undertaken to give in the management of my brother Augustine's affairs [Augustine had died] . . . keeps me, together with the share I take in public affairs, constantly engaged in writing letters, settling accounts and negotiating one piece of business or another in behalf of one or another of these concerns; by which means I really have been deprived of every kind of enjoyment, and had almost fully resolved to engage in no fresh matter till I had entirely wound up the old.

In May of 1774 Washington put all of this behind him—temporarily, he thought—and went to Williamsburg for what proved to be an important session of the Burgesses. The British Parliament had closed the port of Boston in retaliation for the Tea Party, and the young radicals of the Virginia Burgesses, who now formed an unofficial steering committee for the body, were bent on action. Washington was not part of this inner circle. He was as adamant for justice as Patrick Henry, Thomas Jefferson and the Lees, but calmer and more moderate. He approved of their strong resolution condemning king and Parliament and calling for a day of fasting and prayer. When Governor Dunmore dissolved the Burgesses he joined his fellows in a protest session at the Raleign Tavern and endorsed a call for a joint meeting of delegates from all colonies. But he could not fully approve a proposal for nonintercourse with England which included the repudiation of colonial debts to British merchants.

His views at this critical time were expressed in a letter to Bryan Fairfax, son of Colonel William Fairfax. Bryan wrote Washington suggesting that an appeal should be sent to the king to wipe out the offensive laws—"unaccompanied with any threats or claims." To this Washington replied:

HAVE WE NOT TRIED this already? Have we not addressed the Lords, and remonstrated to the Commons? And to what end? Did they deign to look at our petitions? Does it not appear, as clear as the sun in its meridian brightness, that there is a regular, systematic plan formed to fix the right and practice of taxation upon us? Does not the uniform conduct of Parliament for some years past confirm this? . . . Is there anything to be expected from petitioning after this? Is not the attack upon the liberty and property of the people of Boston . . . a plain and self-evident proof of what they are aiming at? . . . Ought not we, then, to put our virtue and fortitude to the severest test?

With you I think it a folly to attempt more than we can execute, as that will not only bring disgrace upon us, but weaken our cause; yet I think we may do more than is generally believed. . . . As to the withholding of our remittances, that is another point, in which I own I have my doubts on several accounts, but principally on that of justice; for I think, whilst we are accusing others of injustice, we should be just ourselves; and how this can be, whilst we owe a considerable debt, and refuse payment of it to Great Britain, is to me inconceivable. Nothing but the last extremity, I think, can justify it. Whether this is now come is the question.

Washington stood for resistance, patient, full and fair—if necessary by an appeal to that "last resort" of which he had written George Mason. Of his views on independence at this time a fellow member of the Burgesses later said, "I have heard [Washington] declare a thousand times, and he does it every day in the most public company, that independence was farthest of anything from his thoughts, and that he never entertained the idea until he plainly saw that absolute conquest was the aim and unconditional submission the terms which Britain meant to grant." That time was now approaching. In another letter to Bryan Fairfax Washington wrote, "I could wish, I own, that the dispute had been left to posterity to determine, but the crisis is arrived when we must assert our rights or submit to every imposition that can be heaped upon us, till custom and use shall make us as tame and abject slaves as the blacks we rule over with such arbitrary sway."

One of the most momentous days in Washington's life was August 5, 1774. On that date he was chosen as one of seven Virginia delegates to the first Continental Congress. He contributed little at this assembly; but he did meet and favorably impress the delegates from the northern colonies. Had it not been for the friendly dinners in 1774 at which the Adamses, Hancock and others came to know him, it is unlikely that Washington would have been selected to command the American army a year later. He might well have spent the war in a subordinate position commanding Virginia troops.

Washington sat quietly through the long-drawn sessions of the first Congress. He made no speeches, was appointed to no committees, is not mentioned in any of the letters of other delegates. He was one of the few delegates who was not, in the words of John Adams, always "nibbling and quibbling." He was not among those of whom Adams sarcastically said, "These great wits, these subtle critics, these refined geniuses, these learned lawyers, these wise statesmen, are so fond of showing their parts and powers as to make their consultations very tedious." Washington expressed his views quietly in the social evening meetings. He also won seven pounds playing cards during the session.

And he wrote a letter in which he first mentioned independence. Captain Robert MacKenzie, formerly one of Washington's company officers, was now with the British at Boston. He wrote his old commander defending the English point of view. Washington replied:

PERMIT ME with the freedom of a friend . . . to express my sorrow that fortune should place you in a service that must fix curses to the latest posterity upon the diabolical contrivers, and if success (which, by the by, is impossible) accompanies it, execrations upon all those who have been instrumental in the execution. . . .

For my own part, I confess to you candidly that I view things in a very different point of light to the one in which you seem to consider them; and though you are led to believe by venal men . . . that the people of Massachusetts are rebellious, setting up for independency and what not, give me leave, my good friend, to tell you that you are abused, grossly abused. . . . I think that I can announce it as a fact that it is not the wish or interest of that government or any other upon this continent, separately or collectively, to set up for independency. But this you may at the same time rely on: that none of them will ever submit to the loss of those valuable rights and privileges which are essential to the happiness of every free state and without which, life, liberty, and property are rendered totally insecure. . . .

Give me leave to add as my opinion that more blood will be spilt on this occasion, if the Ministry are determined to push matters to extremity, than history has ever yet furnished instances of in the annals of North America, and such a vital wound given to the peace of this great country as time itself cannot cure or eradicate the remembrance of.

After he returned from Philadelphia, Washington had but a brief time at home before the Burgesses again met in January 1775. The main question before that body was how to arm the colony without bringing reprisals from Great Britain. The tension had eased somewhat. Washington wrote that, while "things wear a disagreeable aspect," he learned, *"by private letters from London,* there is reason to believe the Ministry would willingly change their ground, from a conviction that forcible measures will be inadequate to the end designed. A little time must now unfold the mystery, as matters are drawing to a point."

Washington heard Patrick Henry electrify his audience with the words, "Is life so dear, or peace so sweet, as to be purchased at the price of chains and slavery? Forbid it, Almighty God! I know not what course others may take; but as for me, give me liberty or give me death!" But if he was inflamed by Henry's clarion call he gave no sign. His diary entry for that day reads, "Dined at Mr. Patrick Cooley's and lodged where I had done the night before." But during the session he expressed his calm resolution in a letter to brother Jack; "it is my full intention to devote my life and fortune in the cause we are engaged in, if need be."

News of Lexington and Concord must have reached Washington five or six days before he left Mount Vernon to attend the second Continental Congress on May 4, 1775, but his earliest reference to it is in a letter to George William Fairfax on the last day of that month, in which he wrote:

FROM THE BEST ACCOUNTS I have been able to collect of that affair; indeed from every one, I believe the fact, stripped of all coloring, to be plainly this: that if the retreat had not been as precipitate as it was (and God knows it could not well have been more so) the Ministerial troops must have surrendered, or been totally cut off; for they had not arrived in Charlestown (under cover of their ships) half an hour before a powerful body of men from Marblehead and Salem were at their heels, and must, if they had happened to have been up one hour sooner, have inevitably intercepted their retreat to Charlestown. Unhappy it is, though, to reflect that a brother's sword has been sheathed in a brother's breast, and that the once happy and peaceful plains of America are either to be drenched with blood or inhabited by slaves. Sad alternative! But can a virtuous man hesitate in his choice?

The "shot heard round the world" made a great difference in Washington's position in the Congress. With Massachusetts troops besieging the British in Boston the opinion of a soldier was more important than those of quibbling lawyers. Washington was the most experienced military man in the Congress and the only member who attended its sessions in uniform—almost certainly his red and blue colonel's garb from the French and Indian War, as there is no record that he had, at that time, purchased the buff and blue uniform in which he is always pictured.

He was promptly appointed to three committees: to plan the defenses of New York; "to consider ways and means to supply these colonies with ammunition and military stores"; and to estimate the funds needed to buy them. But a more important appointment was in the offing. On June 14 New England's most influential delegate, John Adams, rose on the floor to propose that the gentleman from Virginia was the best man to lead the colonial army. His cousin Samuel immediately endorsed this view. Washington left the hall while they were speaking and was not present the next day when the unanimous appointment was made official. The following day John Hancock solemnly proclaimed, "The President has the order of Congress to inform George Washington, Esq., of the unanimous vote in choosing him to be General and Commander-in-Chief of the forces raised and to be raised in defense of American liberty. The Congress hopes the gentleman would accept."

Washington bowed, took his prepared speech from his pocket, and read:

MR. PRESIDENT: Though I am truly sensible of the high honor done me in this appointment, yet I feel great distress from a consciousness that my abilities and military experience may not be equal to the extensive and important trust. However, as the Congress desires, I will enter upon the momentous duty, and exert every power I possess in their service for the support of the glorious cause. I beg they will accept my most cordial thanks for this distinguished testimony of their approbation.

But lest some unlucky event should happen unfavorable to my reputation, I beg it may be remembered by every gentleman in the room, that I this day declare with the utmost sincerity, I do not think my self equal to the command I am honored with.

As to pay, sir, I beg leave to assure the Congress that as no pecuniary consideration could have tempted me to have accepted this arduous employment (at the expense of my domestic ease and happiness) I do not wish to make any profit from it. I will keep an exact account of my expenses. Those I doubt not they will discharge and that is all I desire.

Then he conveyed his deep feelings about this turn of fate to his wife.

MY DEAREST: I am now set down to write you on a subject which fills me with inexpressible concern, and this concern is greatly aggravated and increased when I reflect upon the uneasiness I know it will cause you. It has been determined in Congress that the whole army raised for the defense of the American cause shall be put under my care, and that it is necessary for me to proceed immediately to Boston to take upon me the command of it.

You may believe me, my dear Patsy, when I assure you in the most solemn manner that, so far from seeking this appointment, I have used every endeavor in my power to avoid it; not only from unwillingness to part with you and the family but from a consciousness of its being a trust too great for my capacity, and that I should enjoy more real happiness in one month with you at home than I have the most distant prospect of finding abroad if my stay were to be seven times seven years. But as it has been a kind of destiny that has thrown me upon this service, I shall hope that my undertaking it is designed to answer some good purpose. . . .

It was utterly out of my power to refuse this appointment without exposing my character to such censure as would have reflected dishonor upon myself and have given pain to my friends. This, I am sure, could not and ought not to be pleasing to you, and must have lessened me considerably in my own esteem. I shall rely, therefore, confidently on that Providence which has heretofore preserved and been bountiful to me, not doubting but that I shall return safe to you in the fall. I shall feel no pain from the toil or the danger of the campaign; my unhappiness will flow from the uneasiness I know you will feel from being left alone. I therefore beg that you will summon your whole fortitude and pass your time as agreeably as possible. Nothing will give me so much sincere satisfaction as to hear this, and to hear it from your own pen. . . .

As life is always uncertain, and common prudence dictates to every man the necessity of settling his temporal concerns while . . . the mind is calm and undisturbed, I have, since I came to this place . . . got Colonel Pendleton to draft a will for me, by the directions I gave him, which will I now enclose. . . .

A comparison between this letter to his wife and one to his mother written exactly twenty years before is interesting. To

Martha he wrote, "It was utterly out of my power to refuse this appointment without exposing my character to such censure as would have reflected dishonor upon myself and have given pain to my friends. This, I am sure, could not and ought not to be pleasing to you, and must have lessened me considerably in my own esteem." To Mary Washington he had written, "If the command is pressed upon me by the general voice of the country, and offered upon such terms as can't be objected against, it would reflect eternal dishonor upon me to refuse it; and that, I am sure must, or ought, to give you greater cause of uneasiness than my going in an honorable command." Two decades had not changed his concept of honor and duty one iota.

Washington traveled toward Cambridge—pausing, reluctantly, to meet the demands of politeness and receive flowery addresses in the cities through which he passed. Major General Phillip Schuyler, who accompanied him, was dropped in New York where he was to command. Washington's first military order as Commander-in-Chief was addressed to Schuyler. It outlined the New York general's responsibilities but indicated that he was to have considerable independence.

SIR: You are to take upon you the command of all the troops destined for the New York Department, and see that the orders of the Continental Congress are carried into execution, with as much precision and exactness as possible. . . . Delay no time in occupying the several posts recommended by the provincial Congress of this colony, and putting them in fit posture to answer the end designed. Neither delay any time in securing the stores, which are or ought to have been removed from this city by order of the Continental Congress. Keep a watchful eye upon Governor Tryon, and if you find him directly or indirectly attempting any measures inimical to the common cause, use every means in your power to frustrate his designs. . . . In like manner watch the movements of the Indian agent (Colonel Guy Johnston), and prevent, as far as you can, the effect of his influence to our prejudice with the Indians.

Obtain the best information you can of the temper and disposition of those people, and also of the Canadians, that a proper line may be marked out to conciliate their good opinion, or facilitate any future operation. . . . Your own good sense must govern in all matters not particularly pointed out, as I do not wish to circumscribe you within narrow limits.

Almost before he dismounted at Cambridge the endless problems of the poorly organized and untrained army fell upon his shoulders. He had good cause to write, "I have launched into a wide and extensive field too boundless for my abilities and far, very far, beyond my experience." General officers were unhappy with the seniority of Continental commissions which Congress had given Washington to dispense. Wisely he kept all but Major General Israel Putnam's in his trunk. The immediate need was to strengthen the feeble defenses that had been erected to contain the British in Boston. Washington put the men to work with shovels. He described conditions as he found them in a letter to brother Jack.

DEAR BROTHER: I found a mixed multitude of people here under very little discipline, order or government. I found the enemy in possession of a place called Bunker's Hill, on Charles Town Neck, strongly entrenched, and fortifying themselves, I found part of our army on two hills (called Winter and Prospect Hills) about a mile and a quarter from the enemy on Bunker's Hill, in a very insecure state. I found another part of the army at this village; and a third part at Roxbury, guarding the entrance in and out of Boston. My whole time, since I came here, had been employed in throwing up lines of defense at these three several places: to secure, in the first instance, our own troops from any attempts of the enemy, and, in the next, to cut off all communication between their troops and the country. . . . We have a semicircle of eight or nine miles to guard, to every part of which we are obliged to be equally attentive; whilst they, situated as it were in the center of the semicircle, can bend their whole force . . . against any one part of it with equal facility. . . . Our works and those of the enemy are so near and quite open between that we see everything that each other is doing.

In his first report to Congress, Washington described the situation in more detail and said that, although he was "sensible of the difficulties which attend the defense of lines of so great extent," a council of war had the "unanimous opinion to hold and defend these works as long as possible." He then continued, to create a pattern for hundreds of letters and reports which he would write during the next six years, by listing all that was lacking to fight a war:

THESE CONSIST of a want of engineers to construct proper works and direct the men. A want of tools and a sufficient number of men to man the works in case of attack. . . . We labor under great disadvantages for want of tents, for though they have been helped by a collection of sails from the seaport towns the number is yet far short of our necessities. . . . I find myself already much embarrassed for want of a military chest; these embarrassments will increase every day. I must therefore most earnestly request that money may be forwarded to me as soon as possible. . . . I find the army in general, and particularly the troops raised in Massachusetts Bay, very deficient in necessary clothing. . . . I am of the opinion that a number of hunting shirts, not less than 10,000, would in a great degree remove the difficulty in the cheapest and quickest manner. . . . Upon the article of ammunition, I must re-echo the former complaints on this subject; we are so exceedingly destitute that our artillery will be of little use without a supply both large and seasonable; what we have must be reserved for the small arms and that managed with the utmost frugality. . . .

The state of the army you will find ascertained, with tolerable precision, in the returns which accompany this letter. . . . From the number of boys, deserters and Negroes which have enlisted in this province, I entertain some doubts whether the number required can be raised here; and all the general officers agree that no dependence can be put on the militia for a continuance in camp, or regularity and discipline during the short time they may stay. . . . I would humbly submit to the Congress the propriety of making some further provision of men from the other colonies. . . . It requires no military skill to judge of the difficulty of introducing discipline and subordination into an army while we have the enemy in view and are in daily expectation of an attack, but it is of so much importance that every effort will be made to this end which time and circumstances will admit. In the meantime I have the pleasure of observing that there are materials for a good army, a great number of men, able-bodied, active, zealous in the cause and of unquestionable courage.

Washington had expected to find 20,000 men under arms around Boston. There were only 16,000 fit for duty. But more critical than the shortage of manpower was the scarcity of powder. He was told when he arrived that there were "303½ barrels. . . . But on ordering a new supply of cartridges yesterday, I was informed to my great astonishment that there was no more than thirty-six barrels of the Massachusetts store, which with the stock of Rhode Island, New Hampshire and Connecticut makes 9937 rounds; not more than nine rounds a man."

The British must not learn of this shortage. Washington's order forbidding the casual firing of guns emphasized how silly, rather than how wasteful, were the men who "fire at a distance, where there is not the least probability of hurting the enemy, and where no other end is answered but to . . . expose themselves to the ridicule of the enemy and keep their own camps harassed by frequent and continual alarms, to the hurt of every good soldier who is thereby disturbed of his natural rest and will at length never be able to distinguish between a real and a false alarm." He appealed to Congress and the governors of the northern colonies for aid, and he asked Governor Nicholas Cooke of Rhode Island to undertake a seemingly wild scheme for capturing some powder from the English:

ONE HARRIS IS LATELY COME from Bermuda, where there is a very considerable magazine of powder in a remote part of the island and the inhabitants well disposed, not only to our cause in general, but to assist in this enterprise in particular. We understand there are two armed vessels in your province commanded by men of known activity and spirit; one of which it is proposed to dispatch on this errand. . . . I am very sensible that at first view the project may appear hazardous and its success must depend on the concurrence of many circumstances, but we are in a situation which requires us to run all risks.

Washington wrote a dramatic address to the "Inhabitants of the Island of Bermuda," calling them "descendants of freemen and heirs with us of the same glorious inheritance. We flatter ourselves that, though divided by our situation, we are firmly united in sentiment. The cause of virtue and liberty is confined to no continent or climate; it comprehends within its capacious limits the wise and good, however dispersed and separated in space or distance." He continued to say that he did not want them to do anything that might get them into trouble. But, he added, "if your favor and friendship to North America and its liberties have not been misrepresented, I persuade myself you may, consistent with your own safety, promote and further this scheme so as to give it the fairest prospect of success." The secret supply of powder in Bermuda turned out to be nonexistent.

As week after week passed in the stalemate at Boston, Washington hoped that the war would, somehow, be settled shortly. He was concerned about affairs at Mount Vernon and worried about Martha. A remote cousin, Lund Washington, was managing things at home. Late in August Washington wrote him that he was not to "buy a single bushel of wheat till you can see with some certainly what market flour is to go to." "Spinning should go forward with all possible dispatch, as we shall have nothing else to depend on if these disputes continue another year." Two carpenters were to be put to work making casks, "for it is not reasonable . . . that I am to pay them £100 a year to be idle." Lund was to quicken the work on "the dining room chimney piece . . . as I could wish to have that end of the house completely finished before I return. I wish you had done the end of the new kitchen next the garden, as also the old kitchen, with rusticated boards. However, as it is not, I would have the corners done so in the manner of our new church."

At the end of August he wrote to Richard Henry Lee that his position was temporarily secure—and then loosed a tirade against the men and officers from Massachusetts:

AS WE HAVE NOW nearly completed our lines of defense, we [have] nothing more, *in my opinion,* to fear from the enemy, provided we can keep our men to their duty and make them watchful and vigilant. But it is among the most difficult tasks I ever undertook in my life to induce these people to believe that there is, or can be, danger till the bayonet is pushed at their breasts; not that it proceeds from any uncommon prowess, but rather from an unaccountable kind of stupidity in the lower class of these people which, believe me, prevails but too generally among the officers of the Massachusetts *part* of the army; who are *nearly* of the same kidney with the privates, and adds not a little to my difficulties; as there is no such thing as getting of officers of this stamp to exert themselves in carrying orders into execution. To curry favor with the men (by whom they were chosen and on whose smiles possible they may think they may again rely) seems to be one of the principal objects of their attention. . . .

I have made a pretty good slam among such kind of officers as the Massachusetts government abound in since I came to this camp, having broke one colonel and two captains for cowardly behavior in the action on Bunker's Hill. . . . In short I spare none yet fear it will not all do, as these people seem to be too inattentive to everything but their interest.

The Commander-in-Chief did not entirely agree with the accepted historical view of American valor at Bunker Hill. He wrote:

THE PARTY TO BUNKER'S HILL had some good and some bad men engaged in it. One or two courts have been held on the conduct of part of it. To be plain, these people—among friends—are not to be depended upon if exposed; and any man will fight well if he thinks himself in no danger.

In September, the Commander-in-Chief of the army decided to start a navy. He wrote to Nicholson Broughton:

YOU, BEING APPOINTED a captain in the army of the United Colonies of North America, are hereby directed to take the command of a detachment of said army and proceed on board the schooner *Hannah,* at Beverly, lately fitted out and equipped with arms, ammunition and provisions at the Continental expense.

You are to proceed, as commander of said schooner, immediately on a cruise against such vessels as may be found, on the high seas or elsewhere, bound inward and outward to or from Boston, in the service of the Ministerial army, and to take and seize all such vessels, laden with soldiers, arms, ammunition or provisions for or from said army, or which you shall have good reason to suspect are in such service.

Other vessels were later added to "Washington's Navy," and the *Hannah* brought in a British supply ship whose cargo somewhat eased the shortage of powder.

To carry the war to the enemy Washington proposed an invasion of Canada which would deprive the English of the St. Lawrence as an invasion route and might lead the Canadians to join the other colonies in revolt. Schuyler was to send one column, under General Robert Montgomery, via Lake Champlain to attack Montreal. Washington dispatched another up the Kennebec River to attack Quebec. This was commanded by his most energetic and capable young officer, Colonel Benedict Arnold. The Commander-in-Chief gave Arnold explicit orders as to purpose, but not method.

You are immediately, on their march from Cambridge, to take the command of the detachment from the Continental army against Quebec and use all possible expedition, as the winter season is now advancing and the success of this enterprise (under God) depends wholly upon the spirit with which it is pushed, and the favorable disposition of the Canadians and Indians. . . .

You are by every means in your power to endeavor to discover the real sentiments of the Canadians toward our cause, and particularly as to this expedition, ever bearing in mind, that if they are averse to it and will not cooperate, or at least willingly acquiesce, it must fail of success. . . .

In order to cherish those favorable sentiments to the American cause that they have manifested you are, as soon as you arrive in their country, to disperse a number of the addresses you will have with you, particularly in those parts where your route shall lay, and observe the strictest discipline and good order, by no means suffering any inhabitant to be abused. . . .

You are to endeavor, on the other hand, to conciliate the affections of those people and such Indians as you may meet with by every means in your power, convincing them that we come, at the request of many of their principal people, not as robbers or to make war upon them but as the friends and supporters of their liberties, as well as ours. . . .

Check every idea, and crush in its earliest stage every attempt to plunder even those who are known to be enemies to our cause. It will create dreadful apprehensions in our friends and, when it is once begun, none can tell where it will stop.

Arnold was further ordered to capture King's stores, gather intelligence, be kind to prisoners, pay for what he took from civilians and respect the Catholic religion. Washington then gave him one of his most dramatic addresses to spread among the Canadian French, exhorting them to

> come, then, my brethren, unite with us in an indissoluble union. Let us run together to the same goal. We have taken up arms in defense of our liberty, our property, our wives and our children: we are determined to preserve them or die. We look forward with pleasure to that day not far remote (we hope) when the inhabitants of America will have one sentiment and the full enjoyment of the blessings of a free government. . . . To frustrate those cruel and perfidious schemes which would deluge our frontier with the blood of women and children, I have detached Colonel Arnold into your country with a part of the army under my command. . . . The cause of America and of liberty is the cause of every virtuous American citizen. Whatever may be his religion or his descent, the United Colonies know no distinction but such as slavery, corruption and arbitrary domination may create. Come, then, ye generous citizens, range yourselves under the standard of general liberty, against which all the force and artifice of tyranny will never be able to prevail.

Meanwhile at Cambridge the leaves were turning. Winter would soon be upon the ragged army, shivering under their threadbare blankets, if they had such. "So far as regards the preservation of the army from cold," Washington had to tell Congress, "they may be deemed in a state of nakedness. . . . Many of the men have been without blankets the whole campaign, and those which have been in use during the summer are so much worn as to be of little service."

A start was made on constructing barracks, and plans made to send the men to Harvard when the snow flew, to quarter them in the college buildings—if, that is, there were any men to quarter. Enlistments would expire with the year's end, those of Connecticut somewhat sooner. Washington queried Congress, "how then shall we be able to keep soldiers to their duty, already impatient to get home, when they come to feel the severity of winter without proper covering?"

Washington wanted to attack. So did a committee from Congress which came to Cambridge, headed by Benjamin Franklin. All of the other generals opposed this rashness. If he had powder he might bombard the British. But, he asked, would Congress approve? "The General wishes to know how far it may be deemed proper and advisable to avail himself of the season to destroy the troops who propose to winter at Boston by a bombardment when the harbor is blocked up; or, in other words, whether the loss of the town and the property therein are to be so considered as that an attack upon the troops there should be avoided, when it evidently appears that the town must of consequence be destroyed." Congress told him to bombard if necessary.

He had another question. He believed that New York should be put in a better position of defense. Did he have the authority to order this? He wrote John Adams, "In giving me your opinion of this matter I have no doubt of your taking a comprehensive view of it. . . . Whether such a step, though right in itself, may not be looked upon as beyond my line etc., etc."

Adams told him to take whatever action he thought necessary regarding New York, but this question of Washington's authority to act independently of Congress was one that would plague him throughout the war.

As the year end neared and much of the army prepared to go home, Washington wrote a bitter letter:

SUCH A DEARTH of public spirit and want of virtue . . . I never saw before, and pray God I may never be witness to again. What will be the ultimate end of these maneuvers is beyond my scan. I tremble at the prospect. We have been till this time enlisting about 3500 men. . . . The Connecticut troops will not be prevailed upon to stay longer than their term . . . and such a dirty, mercenary spirit pervades the whole that I should not be at all surprised at any disaster that may happen. In short, after the last of this month our lines will be so weakened that the minutemen and militia must be called in for their defense. . . . These [men], being under no kind of government themselves, will destroy the little subordination I have been laboring to establish and run me into one evil whilst I am endeavoring to avoid another; but the lesser evil must be chosen. Could I have foreseen what I have, and am likely to, experience no consideration upon earth should have induced me to accept this command. A regiment or any subordinate department would be accompanied with ten times the satisfaction, and perhaps the honor.

Some militia were called out, but by mid-January 1776 there were but 5582 men fit for duty in the lines at Boston, and 2000 of these had no muskets. At this low point Washington wrote:

THE REFLECTION ON MY SITUATION and that of this army produces many an unhappy hour when all around me are wrapped in sleep. Few people know the predicament we are in on a thousand accounts; still fewer will believe, if any disaster happens to these lines, from what cause it flows. I have often thought how much happier I should have been if, instead of accepting a command under such circumstances, I had taken my musket on my shoulder and entered the ranks. Or, if I could have justified the measure to posterity and my own conscience, had retired to the backcountry and lived in a wigwam. . . . Could I have foreseen the difficulties which have come upon us; could I have known that such a backwardness would have been discovered in the old soldiers to the service, all the generals upon earth should not have convinced me of the propriety of delaying an attack upon Boston till this time. When it can now be attempted I will not undertake to say; but this much I will answer for, that no opportunity can present itself earlier than my wishes.

By this time he had learned that Benedict Arnold had been wounded in an abortive attack on Quebec, but he still had hopes that the future traitor would yet bring Canada into the fold. He wrote Arnold:

THE GLORIOUS WORK must be accomplished in the course of this winter, otherwise it will become difficult, most probably impracticable; for [the] Administration, knowing that it will be impossible ever to reduce us to a state of slavery and arbitrary rule without it [i.e., Canada] will certainly send a large reinforcement there in the spring. I am fully convinced that your exertions will be invariably directed to this grand object, and I already view the approaching day when you and your brave followers will enter this important fortress with every honor and triumph attendant on victory and conquest. Then will you have added the only link wanting in the great chain of continental union, and render the freedom of your country secure.

In February Washington conceived a desperate scheme for an attack, which he reported to Congress:

THE LATE FREEZING WEATHER having formed some pretty strong ice from Dorchester Point to Boston Neck . . . thereby affording a more expanded and consequently a less dangerous approach to the town, I could not help thinking, notwithstanding . . . we had little or no powder to begin our operation by a regular cannonade and bombardment, that a bold and resolute assault upon the troops in Boston with such men as we had . . . might be crowned with success; and therefore, seeing no certain prospect of a supply of powder, on the one hand, and a certain dissolution of the ice, on the other, I called the general officers together for their opinion. . . .

All of his generals advised against the attack. Washington did not persist. He told Congress, again with his constant concern for the esteem with which he was regarded:

PERHAPS THE IRKSOMENESS of my situation may have given different ideas to me than those which influenced the gentlemen I consulted and might have inclined me to put more to the hazard than was consistent with prudence. If it had, I am not sensible of it, as I endeavored to give it all the consideration that a matter of such importance required. True it is, and I cannot help acknowledging, that I have many disagreeable sensations on account of my situation; for to have the eyes of the whole continent fixed with anxious expectation of hearing of some great event, and to be restrained in every military operation for want of the necessary means of carrying it on is not very pleasing; especially as the means used to conceal my weakness from the enemy conceals it also from our friends and adds to their wonder.

The council of war had suggested that the occupation of some of the hills on Dorchester Neck might bring the British out to attack, as had the occupation of Breed's Hill the previous year. Washington told Schuyler, "If anything will induce General Howe to risk an engagement, it will be this. I am determined to do everything in my power to bring on one, and that as soon as possible. How far my views may be answered, time must determine."

The result of this final phase of the siege of Boston he described in a letter to brother Jack:

HAVING RECEIVED a small supply of powder, very inadequate to our wants, I resolved to take possession of Dorchester Point. . . . To do this . . . it was necessary, in the first instance, to possess two heights . . . which had the entire command of the point. The ground at this point being frozen upward of two feet deep, and as impenetrable as a rock, nothing could be attempted with earth. We were obliged, therefore, to provide an amazing quantity of chandeliers and fascines for the work and, on the night of the 4th, after a previous severe cannonade and bombardment for three nights together to divert the enemy's attention from our real design, we removed every material to the spot under cover of darkness and took full possession of those heights without the loss of a single man.

Upon their discovery of the works next morning great preparations were made for attacking them; but not being ready before the afternoon, and the weather getting very tempestuous, much blood was saved and a very important blow, to one side or the other, was prevented. That this most remarkable interposition of Providence is for some wise purpose, I have not a doubt. But, as the principal design of the maneuver was to draw the enemy to an engagement under disadvantages to them; as a premeditated plan was laid for this purpose, and seemed to be succeeding to my utmost wish . . . I can scarcely forbear lamenting the disappointment; unless the dispute is drawing to an accommodation and the sword going to be sheathed.

But, to return, the enemy thinking, as we have since learned, that we had got too securely posted before the second morning to be much hurt by them; and apprehending great annoyance from our new works, resolved upon a retreat, and accordingly on the 17th embarked in as much hurry, precipitation, and confusion as ever troops did, not taking time to fit their transports but leaving the King's property in Boston to the amount, as is supposed, of thirty or forty thousand pounds in provisions and stores. . . . The enemy left all their works standing in Boston and on Bunker's Hill; and formidable they were. The town has shared a much better fate than was expected, the damage done to the houses being nothing equal to report.

Privately, to his brother, Washington ended with some justifiable self-praise.

I BELIEVE I MAY with great truth affirm that no man, perhaps since the first institution of armies, ever commanded one under more difficult circumstances than I have done. To enumerate the particulars would fill a volume. . . . I am happy, however, to find and to hear from different quarters that my reputation stands fair, that my conduct hitherto has given universal satisfaction. . . . It is a great stake we are playing for, and sure we are of winning, if the cards are well managed.

CHAPTER VI

THE DARKEST YEARS

❦

"Georgio Washington supreme duci exercituum adsertori libertatis Cimitia Americana."

Washington probably knew a little Latin. Some knowledge of the classic languages was almost a "must" for gentlemen of his day. But, unlike all of the other Founding Fathers, he certainly was not fluent in it, and one of his more erudite aides probably translated for him the above inscription from the gold medal which Congress awarded him for the victory at Boston—"The American Congress, to George Washington, the supreme commander of the armies and the defender of freedom." The same aide may have translated the avalanche of Latin on the honorary degree from Harvard making "Georgium Washington" a "Doctorem utrius Juris." Benjamin Franklin was always called "Doctor" after he received his honorary degrees, but somehow the title Doctor Washington never caught on.

There were other honors for the success at Boston, and Washington needed no translator to appreciate these lines from a poem.

> Thee first in place and honours,—we demand
> The grace and glory of thy martial land.
> Fam'd for thy valour, for thy virtues more,

Hear every tongue thy guardian aid implore! . . .
Anon Britannia droops the pensive head,
While round increase the rising hills of dead. . . .
Proceed, great chief, with virtue on thy side,
Thy ev'ry action let the goddess guide.
A crown, a mansion, and a throne that shine,
With gold unfading, WASHINGTON! be thine.

The poem is of interest because it was written by America's first Negro poet, Phyllis Wheatley, who was brought as a slave from Africa. Washington's acknowledgement, too, is an interesting indication of a paradox in his character:

I THANK YOU most sincerely for your polite notice of me in the elegant lines you enclosed; and however undeserving I may be of such encomium and panegyric, the style and manner exhibit a striking proof of your poetical talents; in honor of which, and as a tribute justly due to you, I would have published the poem had I not been apprehensive that, while I only meant to give the world this new instance of your genius, I might have incurred the imputation of vanity. This, and nothing else, determined me not to give it place in the public prints.

Repeatedly Washington wrote of his concern for public esteem. What people thought of him was vitally important to his ego and his honor. Yet, basically, he was a very modest man. This was also evident in his willing subordination to the will of Congress, to whom he wrote from New York City on May 5, 1776.

THE DESIGNS OF THE ENEMY are too much behind the curtain, for me to form any accurate opinion of their plan of operations for the summer's campaign. . . . As no place . . . seemed of more importance in the execution of their grand plan than possessing themselves of Hudson's River I thought it advisable to remove, with the Continental Army, to this city. . . . But if the Congress, from their knowledge, information, or belief, think it best for the general good of the service that I should go to the northward or elsewhere, they are convinced, I hope, that they have nothing more to do than signify their commands.

The enemy did not leave him long in the dark. At the end of June, General Howe arrived in New York Bay with the army from Boston. Here he was soon joined by another fleet under his brother, Admiral Sir William Howe, carrying the hated Hessians, and by a third contingent of British which had failed in an attack on Charlestown. In all, the British had some 20,000 trained, well-equipped troops. Washington had about 8300, plus what militia might come in from New York. Calmly and piously the Commander-in-Chief wrote his brother:

WE EXPECT a very bloody summer of it at New York . . . and I am sorry to say that we are not, in either men or arms, prepared for it. However, it is to be hoped that if our cause is just, as I do most religiously believe it to be, the same Providence which has in many instances appeared for us will still go on to afford its aid.

While he awaited the British, Washington saw to New York's defenses and expressed himself on some matters political. He was many months ahead of Congress in the conviction that independence was inevitable. When a rumor spread that British peace commissioners were on the way he wrote:

I WOULD NOT BE DECEIVED by artful declarations nor specious pretenses; nor would I be amused by unmeaning propositions; but [would] in open, undisguised and manly terms proclaim our wrongs and our resolution to be redressed. I would tell them that . . . we had done everything which could be expected from the best subjects; that the spirit of freedom beats too high in us to submit to slavery; and that, if nothing else could satisfy a tyrant and his diabolical Ministry, we are determined to shake off all connections with a state so unjust and unnatural. This

I would tell them, not under cover, but in words as clear as the sun in its meridian brightness.

When he learned that Congress was divided on the question of independence he wrote:

I AM EXCEEDINGLY CONCERNED to hear of the divisions and parties . . . on the score of independence. These are the shelves we have to avoid or our bark will split and tumble to pieces. Here lies our great danger, and I almost tremble when I think of this rock. Nothing but disunion can hurt our cause.

When he learned that Virginia had called a convention to form a new state constitution he wrote his brother:

TO FORM A NEW GOVERNMENT requires infinite care and unbounded attention, for if the foundation is badly laid the superstructure must be bad. Too much time, therefore, cannot be bestowed in weighing and digesting matters well. We have, no doubt, some good parts in our present constitution. Many bad ones we know we have. Wherefore no time can be misspent that is employed in separating the wheat from the tares. My fear is that you will all get tired and homesick; the consequence of which will be that you will patch up some kind of constitution as defective as the present. This should be avoided. Every man should consider that he is lending his aid to frame a constitution which is to render millions happy, or miserable, and that a matter of such moment cannot be the work of a day.

Little did he know then that he would apply these ideas seventeen years later when he presided at a convention to create a more far-reaching charter of government.

In June a plot to assassinate Washington was uncovered which involved, among others, members of his personal bodyguard, one of whom, Thomas Hickey, was hung. After the army watched the execution Washington lectured them in this general order.

THE UNHAPPY FATE of Thomas Hickey, executed this day for mutiny, sedition and treachery, the General hopes will be a warning to every soldier in the army to avoid those crimes, and all others, so disgraceful to the character of a soldier and pernicious to his country, whose pay he receives and bread he eats —and in order to avoid those crimes the most certain method is to keep out of the temptation of them and particularly to avoid lewd women, who, by the dying confession of this poor criminal, first led him into practices which ended in an untimely and ignominious death.

On the evening of July 4, 1776, the rumor ran through New York taverns that Congress had declared for independence two days previously, but it was not until July 9 that Washington received a copy of the document advertising that fact. In the general orders for that day he confirmed the sentence of twenty-nine lashes for an attempted desertion, appointed a committee to issue passes to leave the city, moved the location of the North River guard, announced that each regiment would thereafter have a chaplain and enjoined regimental commanders "to see that all inferior officers and soldiers pay them a suitable respect and attend carefully upon religious exercises." After these items he added:

THE HONORABLE, the Continental Congress, impelled by the dictates of duty, policy and necessity, having been pleased to dissolve the connection which subsisted between this country and Great Britain, and to declare the United Colonies of North America, free and independent STATES:—The several brigades are to be drawn up this evening on their respective parades at six o'clock, when the declaration of Congress, showing the grounds and reasons of this measure, is to be read with an audible voice.

The General hopes this important event will serve as a fresh incentive to every officer and soldier to act with fidelity and courage, as knowing that now the peace and safety of his country depends (under God) solely on the success of our arms; and that he is now in the service of a state, possessed of sufficient power to reward his merit, and advance him to the highest honors of a free country.

After the ceremony many of the troops went to cheer the mob which celebrated the event by pulling down a statue of George III. Washington could not approve such vandalism. In the general order for the next day he wrote:

THOUGH THE GENERAL doubts not the persons who pulled down and mutilated the statue in the Broadway last night were actuated by zeal in the public cause; yet it has so much the appearance of riot and want of order in the army that he disapproves the manner, and directs that in future these things shall be avoided by the soldiery, and left to be executed by proper authority.

Washington waited throughout most of the summer for the British to make a move. To Lund at Mount Vernon he wrote in mid-August:

THERE IS something exceedingly mysterious in the conduct of the enemy. Lord Howe takes pains to throw out, upon every occasion, that he is the messenger of peace, that he wants to accommodate matters.

This was, in fact, true; but Washington distrusted Howe's motives and believed that his peace overtures might be explained by "some disagreeable advices from Europe, or by having some maneuver in view which is to be effected by procrastination."

As with most of his letters to Lund this one contained with advice on things to be done at Mount Vernon; a subject never entirely out of his mind. At the moment he was concerned with landscaping and told his cousin:

. . . There is no doubt but that the honey locust if you could procure seed enough . . . will make . . . a very good hedge;

so will the haw or thorn, and if you cannot do better I wish you to try these, but cedar or any kind of evergreen would look better.

Lund was to plant groves at both ends of the house:

. . . Trees to be planted without any order or regularity . . . and to consist . . . of all the clever kind of trees (especially flowering ones) that can be got.

New York City, which then occupied only the lower end of Manhattan Island, was really indefensible against a determined opponent, which Howe did not seem to be. With control of the water the British might go up either the East or the North River and isolate the Continental Army on the tip of the island. Or they might bombard the city from Brooklyn Heights, across the East River on the western end of Long Island. To guard against this Washington divided his forces, which had now increased to over 20,000, and dug in on Brooklyn Heights. When the British landed on Long Island he transferred more troops and went across the river himself to direct, and lose, his first large-scale battle.

Before the engagement he exhorted his troops with an order that read:

THE ENEMY have now landed on Long Island, and the hour is fast approaching on which the honor and success of this army and the safety of our bleeding country depend. Remember, officers and soldiers, that you are freemen, fighting for the blessings of liberty, that slavery will be your portion and that of your posterity if you do not acquit yourselves like men. . . . Be cool but determined. Do not fire at a distance, but wait for orders from your officers.

It is the General's express orders that if any man attempts to skulk, lay down or retreat without orders, he be instantly shot down as an example. He hopes no such scoundrel be found in this army, but on the contrary every one . . . trusting to the smiles of Heaven upon so just a cause, will behave with bravery and resolution.

There were four roads approaching the American advance positions on Long Island. One of them was left unguarded. The British used this to outflank the Americans, cut off a portion of them and force the rest back into their works on the heights. Howe then prepared to take the works by regular approaches. Under cover of a fog Washington abandoned the fortifications and drew his troops back to New York. Washington's letters and reports minimize this decisive and costly defeat. In writing to Congress during the action he called it an "engagement between a detachment of our men and the enemy." Two days later he reported:

INCLINATION AS WELL AS DUTY, would have induced me to give Congress the earliest information of my removal of the troops from Long Island and its dependencies to this city the night before last; but the extreme fatigue which myself and family [i.e., staff] have undergone . . . since the encampment of the 27th rendered me entirely unfit to take a pen in hand. Since Monday, we have scarce any of us been out of the lines till our passage across the East River was effected yesterday morning, and for the forty-eight hours preceeding that I had hardly been off my horse and had never closed my eyes, so that I was quite unfit to write or dictate till this morning.

In a more complete account of the battle he later said:

THIS MISFORTUNE happened in great measure by two detachments of our people, who were posted in two roads leading through a wood in order to intercept the enemy in their march, suffering a surprise and making a precipitate retreat: which enabled the enemy to lead a great part of their force against the troops commanded by Lord Stirling . . . who behaved with great bravery and resolution; charging the enemy and maintaining their posts from about seven or eight o'clock in the morning 'till two in the afternoon; when they were obliged to attempt a retreat, being surrounded and overpowered by numbers on all sides, and in which many of them were taken. . . .

As to the retreat from the Island, it was effected without loss of men and with but very little baggage; a few heavy cannon were left, not being movable on account of the grounds being soft and miry. . . . The enemy's loss, in killed we could never ascertain, but have many reasons to believe that it was pretty considerable, and exceeded ours a good deal. The retreat from thence was absolutely necessary, the enemy having landed the main body of their army there to attack us in front, while their ships of war were to cut off the communication with the city, from whence resources of men, provisions, etc., were to be drawn.

Actually, Washington's losses were over 1000 men, mostly captured. Howe's were under 300.

The battle was a serious setback. Early in September Washington wrote:

OUR SITUATION is truly distressing. The check our detachment sustained on the 27th . . . has dispirited too great a proportion of our troops and filled their minds with apprehension and despair. The militia, instead of calling forth their utmost efforts to a brave and manly opposition in order to repair our losses, are dismayed, intractable and impatient to return. Great numbers of them have gone off, in some instances almost whole regiments, by half ones and by companies at a time. This circumstance of itself, independent of others, when fronted by a well-appointed enemy superior in number to our whole collected force, would be sufficiently disagreeable, but . . . with the deepest concern I am obliged to confess my want of confidence, in the generality of the troops. . . . 'Till of late I had no doubt in my own mind of defending this place, nor should I have yet if the men would do their duty, but this I despair of. . . .

If we should be obliged to abandon the town, ought it to stand as winter quarters for the enemy? They would derive great conveniences from it, on the one hand, and much property would be destroyed, on the other. It is an important question, but will admit of but little time for deliberation. At present I dare say the enemy mean to preserve it if they can. If Congress therefore should resolve upon the destruction of it the resolution should be a profound secret, as the knowledge of it will make a capital change in their plans.

Washington himself wanted to burn the city, but Congress thought otherwise. He wrote to Lund:

HAD I BEEN LEFT to the dictates of my own judgment New York should have been laid in ashes before I quitted it; to this end I applied to Congress, but was absolutely forbid. That they will have cause to repent the order I have not a moment's doubt. . . . This, in my judgment, may be set down among one of the capitol errors of Congress.

Although he could not burn New York, Washington decided to abandon it and take a position at Fort Washington on the upper end of Manhattan Island. He hoped to hold the Hudson River with this work and Fort Lee directly across the river. In advising Congress of his plans, he outlined what would become his basic strategy for the future:

IT WAS IMPOSSIBLE to forget that history, our own experience, the advice of our ablest friends in Europe . . . demonstrate that on our side the war should be defensive, . . . that we should on all occasions avoid a general action, or put anything to the risk, unless compelled by a necessity, into which we ought never to be drawn. . . . With these views, and being fully persuaded that it would be presumption to draw out our young troops into open ground against their superiors both in number and discipline, I have never spared the spade and pick ax.

Before Washington could complete his withdrawal, Howe, for once, moved with sufficient swiftness to prevent him from departing in peace. A few British troops landed at Kip's Bay, partway up the western shore of the island, and brought on an engagement which ended in a disgraceful rout of the Americans which Washington described by writing:

I RODE with all possible dispatch toward the place of landing, when to my great surprise and mortification I found the troops that had been posted in the lines retreating with the utmost precipitation, and those ordered to support them . . . flying in every direction and in the greatest confusion, notwithstanding the exertions of their generals to form them. I used every means in my power to rally and get them into some order, but my attempts were fruitless and ineffectual; and on the appearance of a small party of the enemy, not more than sixty or seventy in number, their disorder increased and they ran away in the greatest confusion without firing a single shot.

There are stories of Washington throwing his hat on the ground in his rage and beating the men with his sword at this action. At the end of it he was in grave danger as he sat his horse, alone with his aides, facing the Hessians.

After a spirited fight at Harlem Heights in which the American troops behaved well enough to hold the British, Washington dropped slowly back to White Plains during the fall of 1776. Again the army was melting away. The General records:

A REGIMENT . . . that had in it fourteen rank and file fit for duty only, and several that had less than fifty. In short, such is my situation that if I were to wish the bitterest curse to an enemy on this side of the grave I should put him in my stead with my feelings.

Looting was second only to desertion.

SUCH A SPIRIT has gone forth in our army that neither public or private property is secure—every hour brings the most distressing complaints of the ravages of our own troops who are become infinitely more formidable to the poor farmers and inhabitants than the common enemy. . . . No man is secure in his effects, and scarcely in his person; for in order to get at them we have several instances of people being frightened out of their houses under pretense of those houses being ordered to be burned, and this is done with a view of seizing the goods. Nay, in order that the villainy may be more effectually concealed, some houses have actually been burned to cover the theft. I have with some others used my utmost endeavors to stop this horrid practice, but under the present lust after plunder and want of laws to punish offenders I might almost as well attempt to remove Mount Atlas.

Conventional punishment was no longer effective, said Washington:

FOR THE MOST ATROCIOUS OFFENSES, one or two instances only excepted, a man receives no more than thirty-nine lashes; and these, perhaps through the collusion of the officer who is to see it inflicted, are given in such a manner as to become rather a matter of sport than punishment. . . . When inflicted as they ought, many hardened fellows who have been the subjects have declared that for a bottle of rum they would undergo a second operation.

He wrote a long and desperate appeal to Congress pleading for better treatment for the army. He told them:

YOUR ARMY . . . is upon the eve of . . . dissolution. True it is, you have voted a larger one in lieu of it, but the season is late, and there is a material difference between voting of battalions and raising of men. In the latter there are more difficulties than Congress are aware of, which makes it my duty . . . to inform them that unless the pay of the officers . . . is raised, the chief part of those that are worth retaining will leave the service at the expiration of the present term.

As to enlisted men:

NOTHING LESS, in my opinion, than a suit of clothes annually, given to each noncommissioned officer and soldier, in addition to the pay and bounty, will avail.

What was essential, Washington wrote, was a standing army with long-term enlistments. Many members of Congress feared the potential political power of such an army. Washington thought this fear groundless. He said:

THE EVILS to be apprehended from one are remote and, in my judgment, situated and circumstanced as we are, not at all to be dreaded. But the consequence of wanting one, according to my ideas formed from the present view of things, is certain and inevitable ruin. For if I was called upon to declare upon oath whether the militia have been most serviceable or hurtful, upon the whole, I should subscribe to the latter.

He poured out the list of his woes to Lund and added:

I SEE THE IMPOSSIBILITY of serving with reputation, or doing any essential service to the cause by continuing in command, and yet I am told that if I quit the command inevitable ruin will follow from the distraction that will ensue. In confidence I tell you that I never was in such an unhappy, divided state since I was born. . . . But I will be done with the subject, with the precaution to you that it is not a fit one to be publicly known or discussed. If I fall it may not be amiss that these circumstances be known and declaration made in credit to the justice of my character. And if the men will stand by me (which, by the by, I despair of) I am resolved not to be forced from this ground while I have life.

But apparently, despite his dramatic concept of his duty, he expected to live. His letter to Lund continued without pause:

With respect to the chimney, I would not have you, for the sake of a little work, spoil the look of the fireplaces, though that in the parlor must, I should think, stand as it does.

In November, fearing that Howe might march on Philadelphia, Washington divided his little army and crossed into New Jersey with part of it. This strategy was questionable, but he could not hope to protect properly against every eventuality. The British quickly gobbled up Fort Washington. With this work gone Fort Lee on the opposite bank was worthless, and Washington started a steady withdrawal across New Jersey, with Howe slowly following.

As he retreated toward the Delaware River he kept calling for his senior major general, Charles Lee, to join him with part of the army that had been left in New York. Lee, a strange egotist whom Washington had called fickle, craved independent command and, secretly, supreme command. He moved slowly and sent excuses. Washington, always loath to give peremptory orders to his senior subordinates, pleaded with Lee to hasten on:

THE UTMOST EXERTIONS that can be made will not be more than sufficient to save Philadelphia. Without the aid of your force I think there is but little, if any, prospect of doing so. . . . Do come on. Your arrival may be . . . the means of preserving a city whose loss must prove of the most fatal consequences to the cause of America.

As he was finally about to join his chief, Lee was captured, alone, in a tavern several miles away from his troops. His solitary presence in the tavern was never explained.

Washington had expected the militia of New Jersey and eastern Pennsylvania to swell his forces. When none replied to his call he complained:

A LARGE PART of the Jerseys have given every proof of disaffection that they can do, and . . . part of Pennsylvania are equally inimical. In short, your imagination can scarce extend to a situation more distressing than mine.

Thomas Paine was with Washington on this retreat, marching in the ranks with a musket. It was here that he crouched over a fire and, with a drum for support, wrote:

THESE ARE THE TIMES that try men's souls. The summer soldier and the sunshine patriot will, in this crisis, shrink from the service of their country; but he that stands it *now,* deserves the love and thanks of man and woman. Tyranny, like hell, is not easily conquered; yet we have this consolation with us, that the harder the conflict, the more glorious the triumph. . . . Heaven knows how to put a proper price upon its goods; and it would be strange indeed if so celestial an article as FREEDOM should not be highly rated.

Paine also wrote of Washington:

VOLTAIRE has remarked that King William never appeared to full advantage but in difficulties and in action. The same remark may be made on General Washington, for the character fits him. There is a natural firmness in some minds which cannot be unlocked by trifles but which, when unlocked, discovers a cabinet of fortitude; and I reckon it among those kind of public blessings which we do not immediately see, that God hath blessed him with . . . a mind that can even flourish with care.

There were, as ever, many cares for Washington to surmount, other than immediate tactical problems. The panicky Congress had moved from threatened Philadelphia to Baltimore after giving Washington dictatorial powers "To order and direct all things relative to the department and the operations of war." Of this enlarged authority Washington wrote:

THEY HAVE DONE ME the honor to entrust me with powers, in my military capacity, of the highest nature and almost unlimited in extent. Instead of thinking myself freed from all civil obligations by this mark of their confidence I shall constantly bear in mind that, as the sword was the last resort for the preservation of our liberties, so it ought to be the first thing laid aside when those liberties are firmly established.

But though Congress had given Washington authority, they had not given him an army, nor means of clothing the few men that he had against the December cold. When a committee of women in Philadelphia sent bundles to the troops, Washington wrote:

YOUR COLLECTION of old clothes for the use of our army deserves my warmest thanks. They are of the greatest use, and shall be distributed where they are most wanted."

By mid-December Howe and British General Charles Cornwallis had established their forces in New Jersey at Brunswick and Princeton with an advance unit of Hessians in Trenton. After giving orders that "The boats and craft all along the Delaware side should be secured; particularly the Durham boats used for the transportation of produce down the river," Washington crossed into Pennsylvania. With the year's end the army would again dissolve. On the day before Christmas Washington advised Congress:

I SHALL BE LEFT with . . . from fourteen to fifteen hundred effective men. This handfull, and such militia as may choose to join me, will then compose our army.

He ended his Christmas Eve missive, "To guard against his [Howe's] designs . . . shall employ my every exertion. But how is this to be done?" The next day he decided how it might be done.

Before his army disintegrated he would attack. On Christmas Day 1776 he made the river crossing which has become one of the most famous incidents of the Revolution. What followed was a small battle, but a crucial one. Washington described it to the President of Congress as follows:

SIR: I have the pleasure of congratulating you upon the success of an enterprise which I had formed against a detachment of the enemy lying in Trenton, and which was executed yesterday morning. The evening of the 25th I ordered the troops intended for this service (which were about 2400) to parade back of McKinkey's Ferry that they might begin to pass as soon as it grew dark; imagining we should be able to throw them all over, with the necessary artillery, by twelve o'clock, and that we might easily arrive at Trenton by five in the morning—the distance being about nine miles. But the quantity of ice, made that night, impeded the passage of the boats so much that it was three o'clock before the artillery could all get over, and near four before the troops took up their line of march.

This made me despair of surprising the town, as I well knew we could not reach it before the day was fairly broke; but as I was certain there was no making a retreat without being discovered and harassed on repassing the river, I determined to push on at all events. I formed my detachments into two divisions, one to march by the lower or river road, the other by the upper or Pennington road. As the divisions had nearly the same distance to march, I ordered each of them, immediately upon forcing the out guards, to push directly into the town that they might charge the enemy before they had time to form.

The upper division arrived at the enemy's advance post exactly at eight o'clock. Three minutes after I found, from the fire on the lower road, that that division had also got up. The out guards made but small opposition, though for their numbers they behaved very well, keeping up a constant retreating fire from behind houses. We presently saw their main body formed, but from their motions they seemed undetermined how to act. Being hard pressed by our troops, who had already got possession of part of their artillery, they attempted to file off by a road on their right leading to Princeton but, perceiving their intention, I threw a body of troops in their way which immediately checked them. Finding from our disposition that they were surrounded and that they must inevitably be cut to pieces if they made any further resistance, they agreed to lay down their arms. The number that submitted in this manner was 23 officers and 886 men. . . . Our loss is very trifling indeed, only two officers and one or two privates wounded. . . . The numbers I had with me being inferior to theirs below me, and a strong battalion of light infantry at Princeton above me, I thought it most prudent to return the same evening with my prisoners and the artillery we had taken.

On the same day the Commander-in-Chief penned this congratulatory message to his troops:

THE GENERAL, with the utmost sincerity and affection, thanks the officers and soldiers for their gallant and spirited behavior at Trenton yesterday. It is with inexpressible pleasure that he can declare that he did not see a single instance of bad behavior in either officers or privates; and that if any fault could be found, it proceeded from a too great eagerness to push forward upon the enemy. Much, very much indeed, is it to be lamented that when men are brought to play the part of soldiers thus well that any of them, for the sake of a little temporary ease, should think of abandoning the cause of liberty and their country at so important a crisis. As a reward to the officers and soldiers for their spirited behavior in such inclement weather, the General will . . . have all the fieldpieces, the arms and accoutrements, horses and everything else which was taken yesterday valued and a proportionate distribution of the amount made among . . . the men who crossed the river.

The commissary is strictly ordered to provide rum for the troops that it may be served out as occasion shall require.

Perhaps inspired by success Washington sought new conquests. He had four more days before the army broke up. What else could he do? He commented, "If we could happily beat up the rest of the [enemy's] quarters bordering on and near the river, it would be attended with the most valuable consequence." On December 30 he again crossed the Delaware to Trenton. Here he paraded the regiments whose enlistments expired the next day and offered a bonus of ten dollars a man to those who would stay for six weeks. Washington left no record of the speech he made to the men. One sergeant recorded that "in a most affectionate manner he entreated us to stay."

On January 2 Cornwallis moved against Trenton from Princeton, with superior force. This was the occasion when Washington left a small force to keep campfires burning while he slipped around the British to attack their weakly held base at Princeton. On January 5 he again wrote Congress:

ON THE SECOND, according to my expectation, the enemy began to advance upon us and, after some skirmishing . . . they attempted to pass Sanpinck Creek which runs through Trenton at different places but, finding the fords guarded, halted and kindled their fires. We were drawn up on the other side of the creek. In this situation we remained till dark cannonading the enemy and receiving the fire of their fieldpieces, which did us but little damage.

Having by this time discovered that the enemy were greatly superior in numbers, and that their drift [design] was to surround us, I ordered all our baggage to be removed silently to Burlington soon after dark and at twelve o'clock, after renewing our fires and leaving guards at the bridge in Trenton . . . marched by a roundabout road to Princeton where I knew they could not have much force left, and might have stores. One thing I was sure of, that it would avoid the appearance of a retreat . . . whilst we might, by a fortunate stroke, withdraw General Howe from Trenton [and] give some reputation to our arms. Happily we succeeded.

We found Princeton about sunrise with only three regiments of infantry and three troops of light horse in it. . . . These three regiments . . . made a gallant resistance and in killed, wounded and prisoners must have lost near 500 men. . . . Our whole loss cannot be ascertained, as many who were in pursuit of the enemy (who were chased three or four miles) are not yet come in. Our slain in the field was about thirty. . . .

My original plan when I set out from Trenton was to have pushed on to Brunswick, but the harassed state of our own troops (many of them having had no rest for two nights and a day) and the danger of losing the advantage we had gained by aiming at too much, induced me . . . to relinquish the attempt. But in my judgment six or eight hundred fresh troops upon a forced march would have destroyed all their stores, and magazines; taken (as we have since learned) their military chest containing £70,000 and put an end to the war.

So ended the campaign of which the great German strategist Von Moltke later said, "No finer movement was ever executed than the retreat across the Jerseys, the return across the Delaware a first time, and then a second, so as to draw out the enemy in a long, thin line." At the time General Howe reported:

THE UNFORTUNATE and untimely defeat at Trenton has thrown us further back than was at first apprehended, from the great encouragement it has given to the rebels. I do not now see a prospect of terminating the war but by a general action, and I am aware of the difficulties in our way to obtain it, as the enemy moves with so much more celerity than we possibly can.

The British dropped back to Brunswick to protect their base there and went into winter quarters. Washington led his small army north to Morristown, New Jersey, from whence he wrote Congress, "The fluctuating state of an army composed chiefly of militia bids fair to reduce us to the situation in which we were some little time ago, that is, of scarce having any army at all." Weary men wandered off to their homes, and their commander commented, "We shall be obliged to detach one half the army to bring back the other." The militia, he said, "are here today and gone tomorrow—whose way, like the ways of Providence are almost inscrutable. . . . Desertion is a growing evil. It is become a kind of business, under the present bounty, to desert one corps to enlist in another." Men took the twenty-dollar bonus to join the Continentals, then deserted to re-enlist in state regiments for a second bonus.

Although Washington constantly expected to be attacked by Howe's superior force, the dilatory Britisher sat tight in Brunswick and Amboy on the coast through the winter and spring of 1777. It angered Washington that he could not bring his own officers and men out of a state of langour that seemed to pervade the huts at Morristown. He wrote, "It is next to impossible, I find, to get either officers or men out of comfortable winter quarters, issue what orders you will."

During Howe's advance across the state many Jerseyites had accepted offers of amnesty and protection from the British. Washington now issued a proclamation to those who were "so lost to the interest and welfare of their country, as to repair to the enemy." His order proclaimed, "I do, therefore, in behalf of the United States, by virtue of the powers committed to me by Congress, hereby strictly command and require every person having subscribed such declaration . . . to repair to headquarters . . . and there deliver up such protection, certificate and passports, and take the oath of allegiance to the United States of America." Congress promptly appointed a committee to investigate the propriety of this, and one New Jersey congressman advised his state's legislature to repudiate the proclamation and "not tamely submit their authority to the control of a power unknown in our constitution. We are set out to oppose tyranny in all its strides, and I hope we shall persevere."

Deterioration in the Continental Congress was, if possible, worse than in the army. Only six or seven of the delegates who had unanimously voted for Washington's appointment were left in the legislature. Their replacements were generally men of lesser caliber. Washington was finally impelled to write to Robert Morris that he could not

. . . make Congress fully sensible of the real situation of our affairs. . . . When they are at a distance they think it is but to say, "Presto, begone," and everything is done—or in other words to resolve without considering, or seeming to have any conception of, the difficulties and perplexities attending those who are to carry those resolves into effect. Indeed, sir, your observations on our want of many principal characters in that respectable Senate are but too well founded in truth.

There were two welcome additions to Washington's headquarters in March 1777. One was of young Alexander Hamilton, who joined his staff as secretary. The other was his wife, whose presence improved the social aspect of army life. The wife of one of Washington's staff left an unusual vignette of the Commander-in-Chief, saying that he "throws off the hero and takes on the chatty, agreeable companion—he can be downright impudent at times—such impudence, Fanny, as you and I like."

Congress continued to compound Washington's problems. In appointing five major generals they passed over senior Brigadier Benedict Arnold, whom Washington favored—particularly after Arnold had prevented, almost singlehanded, a British invasion from Canada in the fall of 1776 by building a fleet to delay their movement through Lake Champlain. Washington wrote to Richard Henry Lee:

I AM ANXIOUS to know whether General Arnold's nonpromotion was owing to accident or design, and the cause of it. Surely a more active, a more spirited and sensible officer fills no department in your army. Not seeing him then in the list of major generals, and no mention made of him, has given me uneasiness, as it is not to be presumed (being the oldest brigadier) that he will continue in service under such a slight.

He then wrote Arnold asking him not to resign:

WE HAVE LATELY had several promotions to the rank of major general, and I am at a loss whether you have had a preceding appointment, as the newspapers announce, or whether you have been omitted through some mistake. Should the latter be the case, I beg you will not take any hasty steps in consequence of it; but allow proper time for recollection, which, I flatter myself, will remedy any error that may have been made. My endeavors to that end shall not be wanting.

In light of future events Arnold's answer was ironic, "I shall cautiously avoid any hasty step (in consequence of the appointments which have taken place) that may tend to injure my country." Arnold received a belated appointment which left him junior to the earlier five. It is believed that his brooding about this was the basis of his later treachery.

Of more immediate concern was the flood of foreign officers, mostly French, who were arriving at headquarters with commissions from Congress which made them superior to many American officers. It required all of Washington's patience and tact to induce Major Generals Greene, Sullivan and Knox to rescind their resignations when Congress appointed a French officer to command all the army artillery. He appealed plaintively to Richard Henry Lee:

UNDER THE PRIVILEGE of friendship I take the liberty to ask you what Congress expects I am to do with the many foreigners they have at different times promoted to the rank of field officers? . . . These men have no attachment or ties to the country further than interest binds them; they have no influence and are ignorant of the language they are to receive and give orders in. Consequently great trouble or much confusion must follow.

Most of these "military fortune hunters" from Europe, said Washington, "in the first instance, tell you they wish for nothing more than the honor of serving so glorious a cause as volunteers, the next day they solicit rank without pay, the day following want money advanced to them, and in the course of a week want further promotion and are not satisfied with anything you can do for them."

The summer of 1777 was spent in endless marching. The strategic problem could be stated, but not solved, simply. Howe might move up the Hudson to a junction with a force coming down from Canada to cut the colonies in half. He might move on Philadelphia by land or sea. Or he might attack anywhere on the coast. Washington had to keep a nice balance between the Hudson and the Delaware to thwart either of the first two moves—there was nothing he could do to prevent the third. "Our situation," he wrote, "is truly delicate and perplexing and makes us sensibly feel now, as we have often done before, the great advantage they derive from their Navy."

July 10 brought word that Fort Ticonderoga had fallen to British General John Burgoyne. Washington believed that Howe would certainly move up the Hudson for a juncture with Burgoyne. He moved his army toward West Point. Then came word that Howe had embarked his troops and the fleet was standing off Sandy Hook. This might mean a water-borne attack on Philadelphia. Back toward the Delaware marched the Americans, although Washington was by no means sure of Howe's intention. "Howe in a manner abandoning General Burgoyne is so unaccountable a matter that till I am fully assured it is so I cannot help casting my eyes continually behind me."

As usual Howe moved slowly. While waiting, Washington went into Philadelphia to confer with Congress and to attend a dinner at which he met for the first time a nineteen-year-old Frenchman whom Congress had commissioned a major general. The Marquis de Lafayette would later, to an extent, take the place of the son that Washington never had. Congress conceived Lafayette's commission as an honorary one. The personable, ambitious, intelligent youth thought otherwise. Washington said:

CERTAIN IT IS, if I understand *him,* that he does not conceive his commission is merely honorary, but given with a view to command a division of this army. He has said that he is young and inexperienced but at the same time he has always accompanied it with a hint that so soon as I shall think him fit for the command of a division he shall be ready to enter upon the duties of it, and in the meantime has offered his service for a smaller command.

Instead of attempting to sail up the Delaware to Philadelphia past forts and obstructions in the river, Howe disembarked at the head of Chesapeake Bay, about fifty-five miles from the capital. Washington paraded his forces through the Quaker city and took a position on the east bank of Brandywine Creek between the British and their objective.

The Brandywine could be crossed only at a few fords. Washington stationed his main force at Chad's Ford, where the action started with British artillery fire on the morning of September 11. At 5:00 P.M. Washington reported to Congress:

WHEN I HAD THE HONOR of addressing you this morning I mentioned that the enemy were advancing and had begun a cannonade. I would now beg leave to inform you that they have kept up a brisk fire from their artillery ever since. Their advanced party was attacked by our light troops under General Maxwell, who crossed the Brandywine for that purpose and had posted his men on some high grounds on each side the road. The fire from our people was not of long duration . . . but was very severe. . . .

After this affair, the enemy halted upon the heights where they have remained ever since, except a detachment of them which filed off about eleven o'clock from their left, and which has since passed Brandywine at Jones' Ford, between five and six miles above Chad's. . . . At half after four o'clock, the enemy attacked General Sullivan at the ford next above this, and the action has been very violent ever since. It still continues. A very severe cannonade has begun here too and I suppose we shall have a very hot evening. I hope it will be a happy one.

It was not a happy evening. At midnight Washington forwarded this sad news to Congress:

I AM SORRY to inform you that in this day's engagement we have been obliged to leave the enemy masters of the field. Unfortunately the intelligence received of the enemy's advancing up the Brandywine, and crossing at a ford about six miles above us, was uncertain and contradictory, notwithstanding all my pains to get the best. This prevented my making a disposition adequate to the force with which the enemy attacked us on the right; in consequence of which the troops first engaged were obliged to retire before they could be reinforced. In the midst of the attack on the right, that body of the enemy which remained on the other side of Chad's Ford crossed it and attacked the division there under the command of General Wayne and the light troops under General Maxwell who, after a severe conflict, also retired. . . . But though we fought under many disadvantages, and were from the causes above mentioned obliged to retire, yet our loss of men is not, I am persuaded, very considerable. . . .

Notwithstanding the misfortune of the day I am happy to find the troops in good spirits; and I hope another time we shall compensate for the losses now sustained.

The defeat at the Brandywine was due to poor reconnaissance and confused intelligence. It is doubtful whether Washington even knew of the existence of Jeffries Ford over which the British crossed to get in Sullivan's rear. Early in the battle he received conflicting reports of the movements of the enemy. He chose to believe the wrong one, a dispatch from Sullivan saying that they had not crossed the river. His sense of justice compelled him to write Sullivan, six weeks later:

. . . although I ascribed the misfortune which happened to us on the 11th of Sept. principally to the information of Major Spear, transmitted to me by you, yet I never blamed you for conveying that intelligence. On the contrary, considering from whom and in what manner it came to you, I should have thought you culpable in concealing it.

As soon as the army caught its breath after the action at Brandywine Creek, Washington moved for a second attack. This he described by writing:

I ADVANCED with the army, as soon as it was in a situation, and was pushing to gain the grounds on their left. I believe we should have effected it . . . had not my views unfortunately been totally frustrated by a most severe rain which came on the day preceding that of the intended action. This . . . rendered our arms unfit for use and destroyed almost all the ammunition in the men's pouches, who were out and exposed during the whole time.

The danger to Philadelphia had caused the Americans to move their stores from that city to Reading. When Howe moved in that direction, Washington shifted to counter him. During the night the British countermarched and entered Philadelphia unopposed. On September 27 Washington recorded:

IT IS PROBABLE some of their parties have entered the city, and their whole army may, if they incline to do it, without our being able to prevent them. Here I must remark that our distress for want of shoes is almost beyond conception, and that from this circumstance our operations and pursuit have been impracticable.

The British main force remained in Germantown, five miles outside the city. On the evening of October 3, Washington moved to attack them again. "Having obtained information of the situation of the enemy, we determined to endeavor to do something by way of surprise. We, accordingly, marched all night and reached the town by break of day." His report of the battle reads in part:

GENERAL SULLIVAN'S ADVANCED PARTY . . . attacked their picket . . . about sunrise the next morning, which presently gave way, and his main body . . . soon engaged the light infantry and other troops encamped near the picket, which they forced from the ground, leaving their baggage. . . . They retreated a considerable distance. . . .

The morning was extremely foggy, which prevented our improving the advantages we gained so well as we should otherwise have done. This circumstance, by concealing from us the true situation of the enemy, obliged us to act with more caution and less expedition than we could have wished and gave the enemy time to recover from the effects of our first impression. And what was still more unfortunate, it served to keep our different parties in ignorance of each other's movements, hindering their acting in concert. It also occasioned them to mistake one another for the enemy, which, I believe, more than anything else, contributed to the misfortune which ensued. In the midst of the most promising appearances, when everything gave the most flattering hopes of victory, the troops began suddenly to retreat and entirely left the field in spite of every effort that could be made to rally them.

Upon the whole it may be said the day was rather unfortunate than injurious. We sustained no material loss of men and brought off all our artillery. . . . The enemy are nothing the better by the event; and our troops, who are not in the least dispirited by it, have gained what all young troops gain by being in actions.

Others of Washington's letters indicate that he believed that the Americans had the Battle of Germantown won until the frightening fog caused the troops to panic. This sanguine view was not justified. British reserves had not been committed when the Americans ran. The fog may well have prevented a severe defeat.

During November the British forced the forts below the city, opened the river as a supply line and built defenses around the city which Washington was too weak to attack. There was no alternative to retiring into winter quarters—but where? Towns near Philadelphia inhospitably protested that they were too crowded with refugees to shelter the ragged army. But the Pennsylvania Assembly cried to Congress that Washington must take a position to defend all parts of the state. There was sarcasm in his comment on this:

IT WOULD GIVE ME infinite pleasure to afford protection to every individual and to every spot of ground in the whole of the United States. Nothing is more my wish. But this is not possible with our present force. In all wars, from the nature of things, individuals and particular places must be exposed. It has ever been and ever will be the case.

Finally a site was selected about eighteen miles from Philadelphia—a wooded triangle protected by streams and hills at a place called Valley Forge. A week before Christmas, 1777, the army marched off to establish winter quarters here. They had nothing left but morale, but that the few veterans had in good part. Of the little force of Continentals who took their station at Valley Forge, Washington said:

TO SEE MEN without clothes to cover their nakedness, without blankets to lie on, without shoes, by which their marches might be traced by the blood from their feet, and almost as often without provisions as with them, marching through the frost and snow, and at Christmas taking up their winter quarters within a day's march of the enemy, without a house or hut to cover them till they could be built, and submitting to it without a murmur, is a proof of patience and obedience which, in my opinion, can scarcely be paralleled.

But, as always in adversity, the leader was unbowed. To Lafayette he wrote:

I HAVE NO DOUBT that everything happens for the best; that we shall triumph over all our misfortunes and in the end be happy—when, my dear Marquis, if you will give me your company in Virginia we will laugh at our present difficulties and the folly of others.

CHAPTER VII

VALLEY FORGE TO YORKTOWN

❦

The winter of 1777–1778 was the turning point of the Revolution. It was also, paradoxically, the low point for Washington's army and its Commander-in-Chief. The surrender of British General John Burgoyne at Saratoga led to the alliance with France which assured ultimate American success—or, at least, made it far more likely. But the victory at Saratoga in October 1777 was credited to Major General Horatio Gates, acting independently, while Washington was futilely hovering around Philadelphia after losing battles at the Brandywine and Germantown.

Gates sent the news of his victory directly to Congress, bypassing the Commander-in-Chief, although the dispatch passed through Washington's camp and he joyously announced it to his troops:

THE GENERAL HAS his happiness completed. . . . General Burgoyne and his whole army surrendered themselves prisoners of war. Let every face brighten and every heart expand with grateful joy and praise to the Supreme Disposer of all human events who has granted us this signal success. The chaplains of the army are to prepare short discourses, suited to the joyful occasion.

In all of his correspondence Washington expressed sincere appreciation for Gates's victory. There is, perhaps, but one tiny sign of jealously or self-justification. When he learned of the great turn out of militia from the northern states that had made possible the victory at Saratoga, Washington wrote:

HAD THE SAME spirit pervaded the people of this and the neighboring states we might before this have had General Howe nearly in the situation of General Burgoyne—with this difference: that the former would never have been out of the reach of his ships, whilst the latter increased his danger every step he took, having but one retreat in case of a disaster and that blocked up by a respectable force.

The contrast of Gates's success with Washington's lack of accomplishment touched off a feeling in some quarters that the New Englander would be a better Commander-in-Chief than the Virginian. Washington had little personal contact with many of the delegates who now comprised the Congress, and there was some resentment to the adulation with which he was regarded. Even John Adams, who had nominated Washington as Commander-in-Chief, told Congress:

I HAVE BEEN DISTRESSED to see some members of this house disposed to idolize an image which their own hands have molten. I speak here of the superstitious veneration that is sometimes paid to General Washington.

From this situation developed what has been called the "Conway Cabal." Thomas Conway was an Irish-born officer in the French service who secured a brigadier general's commission in the American Army and then loudly protested to Congress that he should be promoted to major general over the heads of numerous Americans who were senior to him. Washington wrote that this would be

. . . as unfortunate a measure as ever was adopted. I may add (and I think with truth) that it will give a fatal blow to the existence of the army. General Conway's merit . . . as an officer, and his importance in this army, exists more in his imagination than in reality; for it is a maxim with him to leave no service of his untold, nor to want anything that is to be had by importunity.

Conway frequently expressed his low opinion of Washington, and it was obvious that he was trying to stir up strife. This came to light when American General Lord Stirling wrote Washington that General Gates's aide, Colonel Wilkinson, had told his aide, Major McWilliams, of a letter from Conway to Gates in which the former said, "Heaven has been determined to save your country; or a weak General and bad councilors would have ruined it." When Washington politely called Conway to account for this statement the Irishman protested that he had never written it. Gates now became irate that his private letters were being "stealingly copied." Washington replied that he assumed that the disclosure had come through Wilkinson at the instigation of Gates:

WITH A friendly view to forewarn and consequently forearm me against a secret foe . . . a dangerous incendiary; in which character, sooner or later, this country will know General Conway. . . . But, in this, as in other matters of late, I have found myself mistaken.

Copies of all this correspondence, and more were sent to Congress by both parties. At the same time nine American brigadiers protested to Congress against Conway's appointment as a major general, and a group of colonels protested at Wilkinson's elevation to the rank of brigadier, at Gates request, as a reward for bringing the news of Saratoga to Congress. It was obvious that any move to replace Washington with the victor of Saratoga would meet bitter resistance in the Army.

The matter came to an end when Gates wrote to Washington, saying:

[I] EARNESTLY HOPE no more of that time, so precious to the public, may be lost upon the subject of General Conway's letter. . . . I solemnly declare that I am of no faction; and if any of my letters taken aggregately or by paragraphs convey any meaning which in any construction is offensive to Your Excellency, that was by no means the intention of the writer. After this, I cannot believe Your Excellency will either suffer your suspicions or the prejudices of others to induce you to spend another moment upon the subject.

To which Washington replied:

I AM AS AVERSE to controversy as any man, and had I not been forced into it you never would have had occasion to impute to me even the shadow of a disposition toward it. Your repeatedly and solemnly disclaiming any offensive views in those matters that have been the subject of our past correspondence makes me willing to close with the desire you express of burying them hereafter in silence and, as far as future events will permit, oblivion. My temper leads me to peace and harmony with all men, and it is peculiarly my wish to avoid any personal feuds with those who are embarked in the same great national interest with myself, as every difference of this kind must in its consequences be very injurious.

Whether there was a plot or conspiracy to remove Washington is not quite clear; but if there was it seems likely that the objectionable General Conway was the victim, rather than the instigator, of the Conway Cabal. Although he detested Conway, Washington seemed to feel that the movement stemmed from Gates. When Lafayette wrote him decrying the group in Congress who were infatuated with Gates, Washington replied:

HAPPY, THRICE HAPPY, would it have been for this army and the cause we are embarked in if the same generous spirit had pervaded all the actors in it. But one gentleman, whose name you have mentioned [Gates], had, I am confident, far different views. His ambition and great desire of being puffed off as one of the first officers of the age could only be equaled by the means which he used to obtain them; but finding that I was determined not to go beyond the line of my duty to indulge him . . . he became my inveterate enemy and has, I am persuaded, practiced every art to do me an injury, even at the expense of reprobating a measure which did not succeed. . . . It is much to be lamented that things are not now as they formerly were; but we must not, in so great a contest, expect to meet with nothing but sunshine.

In the surrender terms which Gates had granted Burgoyne was a provision that the captured British army was to be permitted to return to England on parole, with the provision that they would not again bear arms against the colonies. The surrender convention also provided that the prisoners were to embark from Boston. Washington wanted to keep the prisoners or, at least, delay their departure as long as possible. He wrote to Congress:

BY A LETTER from General Howe to General Burgoyne which passed through my hands, he hinted that liberty might probably be granted for the prisoners to embark at Rhode Island or some part of the Sound. This indulgence appearing to me inadmissible, I immediately wrote to General Heath to prevent him giving the least countenance to the measure in case it should be requested. . . . The reasons I am persuaded will at once occur to Congress for my conduct in this instance, as well as General Howe's. . . . If the embarkation is confined to Boston it is likely that it will not take place before sometime in the spring, . . . a circumstance of great importance to us, as the moment they get there [to England] the most scrupulous and virtuous observance of the Convention will justify the Ministry in placing them in garrison and sending others out to reinforce General Howe, or upon any other expedition they may think proper to undertake against us.

The prisoners were later sent to Virginia, in violation of the Convention, and treated shamefully. Washington did not approve this, but it may have stemmed, at least partially, from his advice to correct Gates's mistake by holding them as long as possible without violating the Convention.

As the army wearily dragged its bleeding feet into Valley Forge, Washington sought to cheer the men with some rather bombastic rhetoric in general orders:

THE COMMANDER-IN-CHIEF, with the highest satisfaction, expresses his thanks to the officers and soldiers for the fortitude and patience with which they have sustained the fatigues of the campaign. Although in some instances we unfortunately failed, yet upon the whole Heaven hath smiled on our arms and crowned them with signal success; and we may upon the best grounds conclude that by a spirited continuance of the measures necessary for our defense we shall finally obtain the end of our warfare—Independence, Liberty and Peace. These are blessings worth contending for at every hazard. . . . The General ardently wishes it were now in his power to conduct the troops into the best winter quarters. But where are these to be found?

The orders explained why the army could not take shelter in a town or leave the vicinity of Philadelphia. Then he continued to paint a bright picture of how snug the men would be in their shelterless valley:

. . . with activity and diligence huts may be erected that will be warm and dry. In these the troops will be compact, more secure against surprises than if in a divided state, and at hand to protect the country. These cogent reasons have determined the General to take post in the neighborhood of this camp; and influenced by them, he persuades himself that the officers and soldiers, with one heart and one mind, will resolve to surmount every difficulty with a fortitude and patience becoming their profession and the sacred cause in which they are engaged. He himself will share in the hardship, and partake of every inconvenience.

Washington painted a somewhat different picture to Congress in the first of many appeals from Valley Forge, written only six days after his optimistic general order:

I AM NOW CONVINCED, beyond a doubt, that unless some great and capital change suddenly takes place . . . this army must inevitably be reduced to one or other of these three things—starve, dissolve or disperse in order to obtain subsistence in the best manner they can. Rest assured, sir, this is not an exaggerated picture but that I have abundant reason to support what I say.

Yesterday afternoon, receiving information that the enemy, in force, had left the city . . . to forage . . . I ordered the troops to be in readiness that I might give every opposition in my power; when, behold! to my great mortification, I was not only informed, but convinced, that the men were unable to stir on account of provision[s]. . . . This brought forth the only commissary in this camp and, with him, this melancholy and alarming truth; that he had not a single hoof of any kind to slaughter, and not more than 25 barrels of flour! . . .

Finding the inactivity of the army, whether for want of provisions, clothes or other essentials, is charged to my account, by not only the common vulgar but those in power, it is time to speak plain in exculpation of myself. With truth then I can declare that no man, in my opinion, ever had his measures more impeded than I have by every department of the army. Since the month of July we have had no assistance from the Quarter Master General. . . . Soap, vinegar and other articles allowed by Congress we see none of . . . since the battle of Brandywine. The first indeed we have now little occasion of [for] few men having more than one shirt, many only the moiety of one, and some none at all. . . . We have by a field return, this day made no less than 2898 men now in camp unfit for duty because they are barefoot and otherwise naked. . . . Our numbers fit for duty from the hardships and exposures they have undergone, particularly on account of blankets (numbers being obliged to sit up all night by fires, instead of taking comfortable rest in a natural way) have decreased near 2000 men.

The Pennsylvania Legislature had addressed a "remonstrance" to Washington against putting the army into winter quarters. Of this Washington wrote Congress:

I CAN ASSURE those gentlemen that it is a much easier and less distressing thing to draw remonstrances in a comfortable room by a good fireside than to occupy a cold bleak hill and sleep under frost and snow without clothes or blankets. However, although *they* seem to have little feeling for the naked and distressed soldier, I feel superabundantly for the men and from my soul pity those miseries which it is neither in my power to relieve or prevent.

It is for these reasons therefore I have dwelt upon the subject, and it adds not a little to my other difficulties and distress to find that much more is expected of me than is possible to be performed and that upon the ground of safety and policy I am obliged to conceal the true state of the army from public view and thereby expose myself to detraction and calumny.

For the first two months of 1778 almost all of the writings of Washington were pleas for food and clothing for his naked and starving men. On February 6, he wrote to General Israel Putnam:

"The army under my command is in consequence literally reduced to a starving condition." On the same day, to Governor Jonathan Trumbull of Connecticut: "We have been once on the brink of dissolution in the course of the present year . . . and our condition now is but little better." The next day he wrote the Deputy Commissary General: "A prospect now opens of absolute want, such as will make it impossible to keep the army much longer from dissolution." And again, on that day, to the Commissary General: "The spirit of desertion among the soldiery never before rose to such a threatening height as at the present time. . . . What may ensue, if a better prospect does not speedily open, I dread to conjecture."

So the letters went out, day after day, pleading for food—in a country where food was the only plentiful war material. Somehow, the army lived from day to day through the winter. By March 20, Washington could write:

BY DEATH AND DESERTION we have lost a good many men since we came to this ground, and have encountered every species of hardship that cold, wet and hunger and want of clothes were capable of producing. Notwithstanding, and contrary to my expectations, we have been able to keep the soldiers from mutiny or dispersion; although in the single article of provisions they have encountered enough to have occasioned one or the other of these in most other armies, as they have been (two or three times) days together without provisions; and once six days without any of the meat kind. Could the poor horses tell their tale it would be in a strain still more lamentable, as numbers have actually died from pure want. But, as our prospects begin to brighten, my complaint shall cease.

The army was still alive, and still in being, but the need for officers was acute. As the Continental currency depreciated and no provision was made to adjust the compensation of officers, they resigned by the score. Washington pleaded with Congress for relief; specifically a bill which would assure them a half-pay pension—pointing out that he would not benefit from such an act. He wrote:

TO . . . SUPPOSE that public virtue alone will enable men to forego the ease and comforts of life, to encounter the hardships and dangers of war for a bare subsistence, when their companions and friends are amassing large fortunes, is viewing human nature rather as it should be than as it really is.

With calm philosophy he lectured Congress on the facts of economic life:

MEN MAY SPECULATE as they will; they may talk of patriotism; they may draw a few examples from ancient story of great achievements performed by its influence; but whoever builds upon them, as a sufficient basis for conducting a long and bloody war, will find themselves deceived in the end. We must take the passions of men as nature has given them, and those principles as a guide which are generally the rule of action. I do not mean to exclude altogether the idea of patriotism. I know it exists, and I know it has done much in the present contest. But I will venture to assert that a great and lasting war can never be supported on this principle alone. It must be aided by a prospect of interest, or some reward. For a time it may, of itself, push men to action, to bear much, to encounter difficulties; but it will not endure unassisted by interest.

So long as he was lecturing Congress on one need, he continued in another area. Great Britain had passed two acts of reconciliation and appointed commissioners to treat with the colonies. Washington did not believe that their purpose was sincere. His letter to Congress continued:

. . . The enemy are beginning to play a game more dangerous than their efforts by arms. . . . They are endeavoring to ensnare the people by specious allurements of peace. It is not improbable they have had such abundant cause to be tired of the war that they may be sincere in the terms they offer which, though far short of our pretensions, will be extremely flattering to minds that do not penetrate far into political consequences. But, whether they are sincere or not, they may be equally destructive; for to discering men nothing can be more evident than that a peace on the principles of dependence, however limited, after what has happened, would be to the last degree dishonorable and ruinous. It is, however, much to be apprehended that the idea of such an event will have a very powerful effect upon the country and if not combated with the greatest address will serve, at least, to produce supineness and disunion. . . . Nothing short of independence, it appears to me, can possibly do. A peace on other terms would, if I may be allowed the expression, be a peace of war. . . .

Before I conclude there are one or two points more upon which I will add an observation or two. The first is the indecision of Congress and the delay used in coming to determinations on matters referred to them. . . . The other point is the *jealousy* which Congress unhappily entertains of the army. . . . You may be assured there is nothing more injurious, or more unjustly founded. This jealousy stands upon the commonly received opinion, which under proper limitations is certainly true, that standing armies are dangerous to a state. . . . The prejudices in other countries have only gone to them in time of *peace*. . . . It is our policy to be prejudiced against them in time of *war*. . . .

If we would pursue a right system of policy, in my opinion, there should be none of these distinctions. We should all be considered, Congress and army, as one people, embarked in one cause, in one interest; acting on the same principle and to the same end. The distinction, the jealousies set up . . . can answer not a single purpose.

During the first two years of the war Washington was pessimistic about active aid from France. As recently as August 1777 he had written:

I HAVE FROM THE FIRST been among those few who never built much upon a French war. I ever did, and still do think, they never meant more than to give us a kind of underhand assistance; that is, to supply us with arms, etc., for our money and trade. This may, indeed, if Great Britain has spirit and strength to resent it, bring on a war; but the declaration . . . must, I am convinced, come from the last-mentioned power.

It was with pleased surprise, therefore, that he wrote Congress on May 1, 1778: "I believe no event was ever received with more heartfelt joy." The event was the news that France had recognized the independence of the United States and was sending military aid. Four days later, at the end of the general orders Washington told the army:

IT HAVING PLEASED the Almighty ruler of the Universe propitiously to defend the cause of the United American States . . . by raising us up a powerful friend among the princes of the earth to establish our liberty and independence up [on] lasting foundations, it becomes us to set apart a day for gratefully acknowledging the Divine goodness and celebrating the important event which we owe to His benign interposition. The several brigades are to be assembled for this purpose at nine o'clock tomorrow morning.

The chaplains were to "offer up a thanksgiving and deliver a discourse suitable to the occasion." This was to be followed by

. . . a discharge of thirteen cannon; when the thirteen has fired a running fire of the infantry will begin on the right of Woodford's and continue throughout the whole front line; it will then be taken on the left of the second line and continue to the right. Upon a signal given, the whole army will Huzza! "Long live the King of France." The artillery then begins again and fires thirteen rounds. This will be succeeded by a second general discharge of the musketry in a running fire. Huzza! "And long live the friendly European Powers." Then the last discharge of thirteen pieces of artillery will be given, followed by a general running fire and Huzza! "To the American States."

The orders ended: "Each man is to have a gill of rum."

But Washington feared that too much dependence might be placed on the French. While his troops were celebrating he wrote:

I VERY MUCH FEAR that we, taking it for granted that we have nothing more to do because France has acknowledged our independency and formed an alliance with us, shall relapse into a state of supineness and perfect security.

The approach of summer in 1778 brought a return of the annual problem—what would the British do and how could Washington best use his limited forces to thwart their designs? General Howe had been replaced by General Sir Henry Clinton, and Washington felt that his best course was to wait at Valley Forge to see what the newcomer would do. He had not long to wait. Before the end of May intelligence indicated that Clinton was about to evacuate Philadelphia. By the middle of June, Washington wrote Gates that "appearances seem to decide that [the British] intend to traverse the Jerseys, though they do not appear to be in any hurry."

Washington moved out of Valley Forge on a route parallel to Clinton's long column. After detaching small bodies of troops to harry the British on the march he decided on a general attack. On July 1, 1778, he reported to Congress on the Battle of Monmouth:

THE ENEMY, in marching from Allen Town, had changed their disposition and placed their best troops in the rear, consisting of all the Grenadiers, Light Infantry, and Chasseurs of the line.

This alteration made it necessary to increase the number of our advanced corps; in consequence of which I detached Major General Lee with two brigades to join the Marquis [Lafayette] at English Town, on whom of course the command of the whole devolved, amounting to about five thousand men. The main body marched the same day and encamped within three miles of that place. Morgan's corps was left hovering on the enemy's right flank and the Jersey militia, amounting at this time to about seven or eight hundred men under General Dickinson, on their left. . . .

Matters being thus situated, and having had the best information that if the enemy were once arrived at the Heights of Middletown, ten or twelve miles from where they were, it would be impossible to attempt anything against them with a prospect of success, I determined to attack their rear the moment they should get in motion from their present ground. I communicated my intention to General Lee, and ordered him to make his disposition for the attack and to keep his troops constantly lying upon their arms to be in readiness at the shortest notice. This was done with respect to the troops under my immediate command.

About five in the morning General Dickinson sent an express informing that the front of the enemy had begun their march. I instantly put the army in motion and sent orders by one of my aides to General Lee to move on and attack them, unless there should be very powerful reasons to the contrary, acquainting him at the same time that I was marching to support him. . . .

After marching about five miles, to my great surprise and mortification, I met the whole advanced corps retreating and, as I was told, by General Lee's orders, without having made any opposition. . . . I proceeded immediately to the rear of the corps, which I found closely pressed by the enemy, and gave directions for forming part of the retreating troops, who by the brave and spirited conduct of the officers, and aided by some pieces of well-served artillery, checked the enemy's advance and gave time to make a disposition of the left wing and second line of the army upon an eminence and in a wood a little in the rear covered by a morass in front. On this were placed some batteries of cannon by Lord Stirling, who commanded the left wing, which played upon the enemy with great effect and, seconded by parties of infantry detached to oppose them, effectually put a stop to their advance. . . .

The enemy by this time, finding themselves warmly opposed in front, made an attempt to turn our left flank, but they were bravely repulsed and driven back by detached parties of infantry. They also made a movement to our right, with as little success, General Greene having advanced a body of troops with artillery to a commanding piece of ground which not only disappointed their design of turning our right but severely enfiladed those in front of the left wing. In addition to this, General Wayne advanced with a body of troops and kept up so severe and well directed a fire that the enemy were soon compelled to retire behind the defile where the first stand in the beginning of the action had been made.

In this situation, the enemy had both their flanks secured by thick woods and morasses, while their front could only be approached through a narrow pass. I resolved nevertheless to attack them and for that purpose ordered General Poor with his own and the Carolina Brigade to move round upon their right, and General Woodford upon their left, and the artillery to gall them in front. The troops advanced with great spirit to execute their orders, but the impediments in their way prevented their getting within reach before it was dark. They remained upon the ground they had been directed to occupy during the night, with intention to begin the attack early the next morning, and the army continued lying upon their arms in the field of action to be in readiness to support them. In the meantime the enemy were employed in removing their wounded, and about 12 o'clock at night marched away in such silence that, though General Poor lay extremely near them, they effected their retreat without his knowledge. . . .

The extreme heat of the weather, the fatigue of the men from their march through a deep, sandy country almost entirely destitute of water, and the distance the enemy had gained by marching in the night, made a pursuit impracticable and fruitless. It would have answered no valuable purpose, and would have been fatal to numbers of our men, several of whom died the preceding day with heat. . . .

The peculiar situation of General Lee at this time requires that I should say nothing of his conduct. He is now in arrest. The charges against him, with such sentence as the court-martial may decree in his case, shall be transmitted for the approbation or disapprobation of Congress as soon as it shall have passed.

Being fully convinced by the gentlemen of this country that the enemy cannot be hurt or injured in their embarkation at Sandy Hook, the place to which they are going, and being unwilling to get too far removed from the North River [the Hudson], I put the troops in motion early this morning and shall proceed that way.

Washington never functioned better, as a field commander, than at Monmouth. A few days after the battle Alexander Hamilton wrote:

I NEVER SAW the General to so much advantage. His coolness and firmness were admirable. He instantly took measures for checking the enemy's advance, and giving time to the army, which was very near, to form and make a proper disposition. He then rode back and had the troops formed on a very advantageous piece of ground. . . . America owes a great deal to General Washington for this day's work. A general rout, dismay and disgrace would have attended the whole army in any other hands but his.

Major General Charles Lee (who had been exchanged after his earlier capture) saw it differently. When Washington met Lee retreating he spoke to his second in command rather sharply. Some say that he swore mighty oaths. After the battle Lee wrote him a singular letter saying:

... I must conclude that nothing but misinformation of some very stupid, or misrepresentation of some very wicked, person could have occasioned your making use of such very singular expressions as you did on my coming up to the ground where you had taken post: they implied that I was guilty either of disobedience of orders, of want of conduct, or want of courage.

To this Washington replied:

I RECEIVED YOUR LETTER ... expressed, as I conceive, in terms highly improper. I am not conscious of having made use of any very singular expression at the time of my meeting you, as you intimate. What I recollect to have said was dictated by duty and warranted by the occasion. As soon as circumstances will permit, you shall have an opportunity either of justifying yourself to the Army, to Congress, to America and to the world in general, or of convincing them that you were guilty of a breach of orders and of misbehavior before the enemy on the 28th instant in not attacking them as you had been directed and in making an unnecessary, disorderly and shameful retreat.

This brought an even more amazing letter from Lee in which he said, "I trust the temporary power of office, and the tinsel dignity attending it, will not be able, by all the mists they can raise, to obfuscate the bright rays of truth." To this Washington replied briefly, "Sir: Your letter by Colonel Fitzgerald and also one of this date have been duly received. I have sent Colonel Scammell, the Adjutant General, to put you in arrest, who will deliver you a copy of the charges on which you will be tried." The court-martial dismissed Lee from the Army for a year. After Congress confirmed this, Lee retired to Virginia. It is generally believed that he was insane.

For almost three years after the Battle of Monmouth the writings of Washington were voluminous—and monotonous. They fill ten thick volumes of the complete collection of his correspondence; but for the most part his hundreds of letters represent variations on a few basic themes. The army is hungry; the army is naked; the army cannot be held together unless something is done. He never gave up hope nor suggested compromise; but into his writing crept a note of bitterness toward the ineffectual Congress, the negligent people, and state governments which put their minor concerns ahead of the major objective. A few excerpts are typical of many letters which he wrote between the fall of 1778 and the spring of 1781. Of the Congress and the states he wrote:

IT APPEARS AS CLEAR to me as ever the sun did in its meridian brightness that America never stood in more eminent need of the wise, patriotic and spirited exertions of her sons than at this period; and . . . it is . . . a sufficient cause for general lamentation . . . that the states, separately, are too much engaged in their local concerns, and have too many of their ablest men withdrawn from the general council, for the good of the common weal. In a word, I think our political system may be compared to the mechanism of a clock, and that our conduct should derive a lesson from it; for it answers no good purpose to keep the smaller wheels in order if the greater one, which is the support and prime mover of the whole, is neglected.

Of the attitude of the people—or some of them—toward the war, he said:

SPECULATION, peculation, engrossing, forestalling, with all their concomitants, afford too many melancholy proofs of the decay of public virtue. . . . Nothing, I am convinced, but the depreciation of our currency, proceeding in a great measure from the foregoing causes, aided by stockjobbing and party dissensions, had fed the hopes of the enemy and kept the British arms in America to this day. They do not scruple to declare this themselves, and add that we shall be our own conquerors.

Cannot our common country, America, possess virtue enough to disappoint them? Is the paltry consideration of a little dirty pelf to individuals to be placed in competition with the essential rights and liberties of the present generation and of millions yet unborn? Shall a few designing men, for their own aggrandizement and to gratify their own avarice, overset the goodly fabric we have been rearing at the expense of so much time, blood and treasure? And shall we at last become the victims of our own abominable lust of gain? Forbid it Heaven! Forbid it all and every state in the Union by enacting and enforcing efficacious laws for checking the growth of these monstrous evils, and restoring matters in some degree to the pristine state they were in at the commencement of the war!

Of the need for money and better treatment for the army he complained to Gouverneur Morris:

CAN WE CARRY ON the war much longer? Certainly NO, unless some measures can be devised and speedily executed to restore the credit of our currency, restrain extortion and punish forestallers. Without these can be effected, what funds can stand the present expenses of the Army? And what officer can bear the weight of prices that every necessary article is now got to? A rat in the shape of a horse is not to be bought at this time for less than £200; a saddle under thirty or forty;—boots twenty;—and shoes and other articles in the like proportion. How is it possible, therefore, for officers to stand this without an increase of pay?

In one letter to the President of Congress he made a suggestion which, if it did not correct the officer's troubles, would help them to forget them:

I HAVE FREQUENT APPLICATIONS from the officers for allowances of spirits. . . . I think it highly reasonable and necessary that they should be supplied at a moderate rate proportioned to their pay.

A French fleet commanded by Comte d'Estaing arrived in July 1778. Washington shifted his army to the banks of the Hudson and prepared to attack New York in cooperation with the French. Then the French sailed to Newport, Rhode Island, which was held by the British, and Washington instructed Major General John Sullivan to call out militia to expand his forces for a joint attack at that point. When all was in readiness the British fleet appeared off Newport, and d'Estaing sailed away to Boston to refit, and then to the West Indies. When Sullivan wrote a letter critical of the admiral, Washington hastened to mollify the French officers, starting with Lafayette:

LET ME ENTREAT YOU . . . my dear Marquis, to take no exception at unmeaning expressions, uttered perhaps without consideration and in the first transport of disappointed hope. Everybody . . . who reasons will acknowledge the advantages which we have derived from the French fleet and the zeal of the commander of it; but in a free and republican government you cannot restrain the voice of the multitude; every man will speak as he thinks or, more properly, without thinking. . . . The censure which have been leveled at the officers of the French fleet would more than probable have fallen in a much higher degree upon a fleet of our own (if we had one) in the same situation. . . . Let me beseech you therefore, my good sir, to afford a healing hand to the wound that, unintentionally, has been made.

The army spent the winter of 1778–1779 in New Jersey, with Washington's headquarters at Middlebrook. Clinton seemed to be shilly-shallying in New York. Washington said that his adversary was "indecisive and foolish," and that "the conduct of the enemy at New York and Rhode Island is too mysterious to be accounted for by any rule of common sense." There was some evidence that Clinton was sending troops to Charleston, South Carolina, and Washington dispatched his meager cavalry to the south. He also ordered Sullivan to head an expedition against the Six Nations.

THE IMMEDIATE OBJECTS are the total destruction and devastation of their settlements and and the capure of as many prisoners of every age and sex as possible. It will be essential to ruin their crops now in the ground and prevent their planting more.

In July 1779 he reported to Congress the success of "Mad" Anthony Wayne's attack on Stony Point, on the bank of the Hudson: "The event will have a good effect upon the minds of the people, give our troops greater confidence in themselves and depress the spirits of the enemy proportionably." In September he reported the success of Sullivan's expedition against the Indians and advised his subordinate to make "the destruction of their settlements so final and complete, as to put it out of their power to derive the smallest succor from them in case they should even attempt to return this season."

The winter of 1779–1780 was again spent at Morristown with the usual hardships. Washington wrote that the soldiers ate "every kind of horse food but hay." In January, Washington wrote one of his many letters to Congress reprising the old theme:

THE TROOPS, both officers and men, have borne their distress with a patience scarcely to be conceived. Many of the latter have been four or five days without meat entirely and short of bread, and none but on very scanty supplies. Some for their preservation have been compelled to maraud and rob from the inhabitants, and I have not in my power to punish or to repress the practice. If our condition should not undergo a very speedy and considerable change for the better, it will be difficult to point out all the consequences that may ensue.

To Lund Washington he wrote, in May: "The country exhausted; the people dispirited; the consequence and reputation of these states in Europe sunk; our enemies deriving new credit, new confidence, new resources."

In that same month two regiments of Connecticut troops mutinied. They had not been paid in five months. Washington wrote, "We have no means at this time that I know of for paying the troops but in Continental money, and as it is evidently impracticable from the immense quantity it would require to pay them in this as much as would make up the depreciation." And, he added, "If you could see what difficulties surround us on every side, how unable we are to administer to the most ordinary calls of the service, you would be convinced that . . . we have everything to dread. Indeed, I have almost ceased to hope." To complete the month of May 1780, Charleston was surrendered to the British.

As he prepared for another summer of campaigning Washington expressed his pessimisitic philosophy:

WE ARE, during the winter, dreaming of independence and peace. . . . In the spring, when our recruits should be with the army in training, we have just discovered the necessity of calling for them and, by the fall, after a distressed and inglorious campaign for want of them, we begin to get a few men—which come in just time enough to eat our provisions and consume our stores without rendering any service. Thus it is one year rolls over another and, without some change, we are hastening to our ruin.

Washington spent the summer of 1780 planning and hoping for an attack on New York City. The French fleet was finally back at Newport, but the English fleet had been reinforced. While he awaited a second division of French ships which would swing the balance of power, the Commander-in-Chief moved his army back and forth in New Jersey and New York trying to find food and forage. And he assigned Major General Benedict Arnold, at the latter's request, to command the works at West Point, the only bastion which prevented Clinton from moving up the Hudson.

On September 25, 1780, Washington rode fifteen miles before breakfast to inspect the defenses at West Point. Usually his young companions, Alexander Hamilton and the Marquis de Lafayette, detested these early morning gallops. But this morning they were eager. The party was to breakfast with Major General Benedict Arnold, and the younger men anticipated with pleasure a meal with Arnold's beautiful Tory bride.

When they arrived at Arnold's headquarters across the river from West Point an aide told them that the general had received an urgent message summoning him to the fortifications. Washington's party breakfasted, crossed the river and inspected the works, and returned to headquarters late in the afternoon. Still no Arnold —nobody had seen him all day. Washington was preparing for dinner when Hamilton handed him a bulky packet which had been sent back from the advance lines by a dragoon officer. The packet contained several papers in Arnold's handwriting which had been taken from a man captured by some militia as he was making his way to the British lines.

Washington's best description of Arnold's treachery was in a letter to Thomas Jefferson, then governor of Virginia:

YOUR EXCELLENCY will have heard . . . of the perfidy of Major General Arnold. On the 25th of September he went to the enemy. He had entered very deeply into a combination with them, as far as we can judge, for putting them in possession of the important post of West Point, where he commanded and the command of which he had solicited, For this purpose he had contrived an interview with Major André, Adjutant General to their army, on the night of the 21st and delivered to him a copy of a state of matters I had laid before a council of general officers the 6th of September; an estimate of the force at West Point and its dependencies; of men to man the works at West Point; remarks on those works; a return of ordnance at West Point and its dependencies; artillery orders for the disposition of the corps in case of an alarm at West Point; a permit to Major André, under the assumed name of John Anderson, to pass our guards.

This officer, with all those papers in Arnold's handwriting, was taken by a most extraordinary and providential intervention of circumstances . . . by a small militia patrol . . . as he was returning to New York. . . . Arnold got information of the event on the morning of the 25th before it was known to any of the officers under his command or any in authority and pushed down the river in a barge to the *Vulture* sloop-of-war [a British ship] which lay a few miles below Stony Point. Major André was tried by a board of general officers, and on his free and voluntary confession and letters was sentenced to suffer death—agreeable to the practice and usage of nations in like cases—which he has accordingly suffered. He acted with great candor after he avowed himself until he was executed.

Washington avoided meeting with the popular and mannerly Major André. After he was sentenced to death the Englishman wrote the Commander-in-Chief requesting that he be shot instead of hung. Washington did not answer the request, but in presenting the matter to Congress he wrote that André's many acknowledgments of the good treatment accorded him "must evince that the proceedings against him were not guided by passion or resentment. The practice and usage of war were against his request and made the indulgence he solicited, circumstanced as he was, inadmissible."

There was a general feeling that Arnold's plot envisioned the capture of Washington while he was at West Point, Washington did not agree and said, "How far he meant to involve me in the catastrophe of this place does not appear by any indubitable evidence, and I am rather inclined to think he did not wish to hazard the more important object of his treachery by attempting to combine two events, the lesser of which might have marred the greater." In this same letter he wrote an epilogue to the Arnold-André affair.

ANDRÉ HAS MET his fate, and with that fortitude which was to be expected from an accomplished man and gallant officer. But I am mistaken if, at *this time,* Arnold is [not] undergoing the torments of a mental Hell. He wants feeling! From some traits of his character which have lately come to my knowledge, he seems to have been so hackneyed in villainy, and so lost to all sense of honor and shame that while his faculties will enable him to continue his sordid pursuits there will be no time for remorse.

This whole incident was most distressing to Washington because he had always thought very highly of Arnold.

During the winter of 1780–1781 the army was distributed in camps between Morristown and West Point. Washington's writings tell the same dreary story—no money, little food and clothing. The men were garbed, in Washington's words, in "all our remnants, and those of a thousand colors and kinds." As to money, Washingtion wrote Lafayette, "The Chevalier De la Luzerne's dispatches came in time for the post, which is the only means left me for conveyance of letters, there not being as much money in . . . the whole army as would bear the expense of an express to Rhode Island. I could not get one the other day to ride as far as Pompton!" At this period most of Washington's orders to distant subordinates and communications with his allies were sent by regular mail—the government could not afford to pay express riders.

Congress had, at long last, overcome their distrust of a standing army and agreed to reorganization based on long-term enlistments. Washington indicated his feeling that this might not now be easy to accomplish. In a private letter he wrote:

THE MILITARY harvest which the early part of this campaign promised to yield us has vanished as the morning dew, leaving not a trace behind it but disappointment and sorrow and the recollection of past distresses. Congress, at length, have resolved to do that which an adoption of four years ago would ere this have put an end to the war and left us in peace under our own vines and fig trees. I mean the raising of an army for the war; but *now* there are wanting many concomitants to bring about this event; among which, placing our finance upon a proper footing is not the least difficult.

The evil of enlistments short of "the duration" was made evident in January 1781 by the mutiny of the Pennsylvania Line. Most of these troops, largely Germans from Pennsylvania, had enlisted for three years. Now the three years were up, and they wanted to go home. Washington described the mutiny in a circular letter to each of the New England governors:

IT IS WITH EXTREME ANXIETY and pain of mind I find myself constrained to inform Your Excellency that the event I have long apprehended would be the consequence of the complicated distresses of the army has at length taken place. On the night of the 1st instant a mutiny was excited by the non-commissioned officers and privates of the Pennsylvania Line, which soon became so universal as to defy all opposition. In attempting to quell this tumult, in the first instance, some officers were killed, others wounded, and the lives of several common soldiers lost. Deaf to the arguments, entreaties, and utmost efforts of all their officers to stop them, the men moved off from Morristown, the place of their cantonment, with their arms and six pieces of artillery . . . on their march to Philadelphia to demand a redress of their grievances. At what point this defection will stop, or how extensive it may prove, God only knows.

The letter continued with an appeal to the governors to forward money, food and clothing to prevent the spread of the mutiny.

Washington advised General Wayne, who was with the mutineers, how to handle the situation:

OPPOSITION . . . cannot be effectual while the men remain together, but will keep alive resentment and will tempt them to turn about and go in a body to the enemy. . . . I would therefore recommend it to you to cross the Delaware with them, draw from them what they conceive to be their principal grievances and promise to represent faithfully to Congress and to the state the substance of them and to endeavor to obtain a redress. . . . If you can bring them to a negotiation, matters may afterward be accommodated, but . . . an attempt to reduce them by force will either drive them to the enemy or dissipate them in such a manner that they will never be recovered.

Fearing unrest among the troops under his immediate command, Washington did not go to the scene of the mutiny, which was settled by a committee from the Pennsylvania Legislature which met all the demands of the discontented soldiers.

A few days later Washington received a dispatch that the Jersey troops had mutinied in their camp at Pompton and were marching toward Trenton. "They have lately received a part of the depreciation of their pay," said the dispatch, "and most of them are much disguised with liquor."

Washington did not wait for civil authority to handle this mutiny. He opposed intervention by Congress, saying, "This spirit of mutiny will spread itself through the remainder of the army, if not extinguished by some decisive measure. I shall as quick as possible . . . march a detachment to compel the mutineers to submission, and I beg leave strongly to recommend that no terms may be made with them." Then he dispatched Major General Robert Howe with a detachment of "the most robust and best clothed" men from West Point and orders to "compel the mutineers to unconditional submission, and I am to desire you will grant no terms while they are with arms in their hands in a state of resistance. The manner of executing this I leave to your discretion according to circumstances. If you succeed in compelling the revolted troops to a surrender you will instantly execute a few of the most active and most incendiary leaders."

General Howe obeyed his orders with a harshness which the

Commander-in-Chief considered suitable to the occasion. He surrounded the now-sober mutineers in their snow-bound huts and then paraded them without arms. The colonels of the three regiments involved were required to point out the principal ringleader in each regiment. These were promptly condemned by a drumhead court-martial. Then a dozen men were selected who had been most active in support of the ringleaders. These were divided into two groups of six to act as firing squads. In the hollow square formed by all the mutineers the first of the ringleaders was compelled to kneel. Six men were ordered to fire at him, three at his head and three at his heart. If he still squirmed, the second six were to fire. It took two volleys to kill the first man. The second died at the first volley. The colonels interceded for the third victim, saying that he had been forced into a position of leadership. He was pardoned. When this harsh treatment was reported to Washington he issued general orders which started, "The General returns his thanks to Major General Howe for the judicious measures he pursued."

As the spring of 1781 approached, Washington's thoughts turned south. After Charleston fell, General Gates had assumed command in South Carolina. When he was decisively defeated at Camden he was replaced by Major General Nathanael Greene, who faced British General Cornwallis in that state. Also, Benedict Arnold, now leading British troops, had invaded Virginia with an expedition which came within a few minutes of capturing Thomas Jefferson.

Washington dispatched Lafayette to Virginia with part of his own army to contain Arnold, and cautioned him, "You are to do no act whatever with Arnold that directly or by implication may screen him from the punishment due to his treason and desertion, which if he should fall into your hands you will execute in the most summary way."

While the British controlled the sea Washington could not prevent the junction of Cornwallis and Arnold in the South. He wrote wistfully, "How loud are our calls from every quarter for a decisive naval superiority, and how might the enemy be crushed if we had it." Then a hurricane crippled the British squadron in Long Island Sound. Washington quickly proposed to De Rochambeau that Admiral Destouches take the French fleet from Newport to Chesapeake Bay to support Lafayette. After some delay, the French sent a small naval force—too little and too late.

This led Washington to pen one of the few imprudent missives he ever wrote. In a private letter to his cousin Lund in Mount Vernon he included a passage critical of his French allies:

THIS I MENTION in confidence, that the French fleet and detachment did not undertake the enterprise they are now upon when I first proposed it to them. The destruction of Arnold's corps would have been inevitable before the British fleet could have been in a condition to put to sea. Instead of this the small squadron . . . could not, as I foretold, do anything.

His letter, sent by ordinary post, was captured and the incriminating paragraph published by General Clinton. Fortunately the cooperative De Rochambeau did not take offense easily and gracefully accepted the apology which Washington penned:

I ASSURE YOUR EXCELLENCY that I feel extreme pain at the . . . intercepted letter of mine published by the enemy. I am unhappy that an accident should have put it in their power to give to the world anything from me which may contain an implication the least disagreeable to you or the Chevalier Destouches. . . . Whatever construction it may bear, I beg Your Excellency will consider the letter as to a private friend, a gentleman who has the direction of my concerns at home, totally unconnected with public affairs and on whose discretion I could absolutely rely. No idea of the same kind has ever gone to any public body.

Other personal embarrassments harassed Washington at about the same time. He learned that some members of the Virginia Assembly had proposed to that body a pension for his mother on the grounds that she was "in great want." Washington immediately wrote to request that this not be done, saying:

TRUE IT IS I am but little acquainted with her *present* situation or distresses, if she is under any. . . . Before I left Virginia I answered all her calls for money; and since that period have directed my steward to do the same. Whence her distresses can arise therefore I know not, never having received any complaint of his inattention or neglect on that head . . . Confident I am that she has not a child that would not divide the last sixpence to relieve her from *real* distress. This she has been repeatedly assured of by me; and all of us, I am certain, would feel much hurt at having our mother a pensioner while we had the means of supporting her; but in fact she has an ample income of her own.

A third embarrassing incident was revealed to Washington in a letter from Lafayette which told him that when a British sloop came up the Potomac several Negroes had left Mount Vernon and joined the enemy. Lund had gone aboard the vessel, carried food to the officers and offered to supply provisions to secure the return of the slaves and protection for Mount Vernon. This brought from Washington a stern letter of rebuke to Lund.

YOU OUGHT TO HAVE CONSIDERED yourself as my representative and should have reflected on the bad example of communicating with the enemy and making a voluntary offer of refreshments to them with a view to prevent a conflagration. . . . To go on board their vessels, carry them refreshments, commune with a parcel of plundering scoundrels and request a favor by asking the surrender of my Negroes, was exceedingly ill-judged and, 'tis to be feared, will be unhappy in its consequences, as it will be a precedent for others and may become a subject of animadversion.

I have no doubt of the enemy's intention to prosecute the plundering plan they have begun. And, unless a stop can be put to it by the arrival of a superior naval force, I have as little doubt of its ending in the loss of all my Negroes, and in the destruction of my houses; but I am prepared for the event.

Washington had stopped keeping his daily diary on June 19, 1775, the day on which he received his commission as Commander-in-Chief. Almost six years later, on May 1, 1781, he suddenly resumed his personal record with the entry: "I begin, at this epoch, a concise Journal of Military transactions, etc. I lament not having attempted it from the commencement of the war, in aid of my memory."

The diary entries starting with August 14, 1781, announced the beginning of the end of the war.

AUGUST 14th: Received dispatches from the Count de Barras [French Admiral at Newport] announcing the intended departure of the Count de Grasse from Cape Francois [Santo Domingo] with between twenty-five and twenty-nine sail of the line and 3200 land troops . . . for Chesapeake Bay. . . .

Matters having now come to a crisis and a decisive plan to be determined on, I was obliged . . . to give up all idea of attacking New York; and instead thereof to remove the French troops and a detachment from the American army to the Head of Elk to be transported to Virginia for the purpose of cooperating with the force from the West Indies against the troops in that state.

August 15th: Dispatched a courier to the Marquis de Lafayette with information of this matter, requesting him to be in perfect readiness to second my views and to prevent if possible the retreat of Cornwallis toward Carolina. . . .

August 16th: Letters from the Marquis de Lafayette and others inform that Lord Cornwallis with the troops from Hampton Road had proceeded up York River and landed at York and Gloucester Towns where they were throwing up works on the 6th inst.

From August 19 to September 28 Washington's diary tells the story of the concentration of forces in Virginia which, all things considered, was a masterpiece of logistics.

AUGUST 19th: The want of horses, or bad condition of them in the French army, delayed the march till this day. . . .

August 21st: In the course of this day the whole of the American troops, all their baggage, artillery and stores, crossed the [Hudson] River. . . .

August 22nd, 23rd, 24th and 25th: Employed in transporting the French army, its baggage and stores over the river. . . .

August 30th: . . . the whole army was put in motion in three columns . . . to march . . . to Trenton, . . . transports being ordered to meet them there. I set out myself for Philadelphia to arrange matters there, provide vessels and hasten the transportation of the ordnance, stores, etc. . . .

August 31st: Arrived at Philadelphia to dinner and immediately hastened up all the vessels that could be procured; but finding them inadequate to the purpose of transporting both troops and stores, Count de Rochambeau and myself concluded it would be best to let the troops march by land to the Head of Elk. . . .

September 5th: The rear of the French army having reached Philadelphia. . . . I left this city for the Head of Elk to hasten the embarkation at that place and on my way (at Chester) received the agreeable news of the safe arrival of the Count de Grasse in the Bay of Chesapeake with twenty-eight sail of the line and four frigates; with 3000 land troops which were to be immediately debarked at Jamestown and form a junction with the American army under the command of the Marquis de Lafayette. . . .

September 9th: I reached my own seat at Mount Vernon (distant 120 miles from the Head of Elk) where I stayed till the 12th, and in three days afterward, that is on the 15th, reached Williamsburg. The necessity of seeing and agreeing upon a proper plan of cooperation with the Count de Grasse induced me to make him a visit at Cape Henry where he lay with his fleet after a partial engagement with the British squadron off the Capes under the command of Admiral Graves, whom he had driven back to Sandy Hook. . . .

September 17th: In company with the Count de Rochambeau, the Chevalier Chastellux, Generals Knox and Duportail I set out for the interview with the admiral and arrived on board the *Ville de Paris* off Cape Henry the next day by noon and . . . settled most points with him to my satisfaction. . . .

September 25th: Admiral de Barras having joined the Count de Grasse with the squadron and transports from Rhode Island . . . began to land the troops from them. . . .

September 28th: Having debarked all the troops and their baggage, marched and encamped them in front of the city; and having with some difficulty obtained horses and wagons sufficient to move our field artillery, entrenching tools and such other articles as were indispensibly necessary, we commenced our march for the investiture of the enemy at York.

On September 28 Washington described Cornwallis's situation in a letter to General Greene:

LORD CORNWALLIS has collected his troops on York River and taken two posts. One in York, the other in Gloucester; where he is fortifying with great assiduity and seems resolved to de fend himself against our siege with great obstinancy. By accounts, through deserters and other ways, I fear we shall have little hope to starve him into a surrender. My greater hope is that he is not well provided with artillery and military stores for such defense, not having had in contemplation the situation to which he is now reduced. . . .

Washington planned to reduce Cornwallis's works with a classic siege operation, involving trenches and artillery emplacements which were constructed progressively nearer to the enemy. He reported the progress of the siege to the President of Congress from time to time.

[On October 1:] I HAVE NOW to acquaint Your Excellency that I marched from Williamsburg with the whole army on the 28th and approached within about two miles of the enemy at York. . . . On the 29th, the American troops moved forward and took their ground in front of the enemy's works on their left; no opposition, except a few scattered shots from a small work. . . . a small fire all day from our riflemen and the enemy's Jagers. [On the] 30th, in the morning, we discovered that the enemy had evacuated all their exterior line of works and withdrawn themselves to those near the body of the town. By this means we are in possession of very advantageous grounds which command, in a very near advance, almost the whole remaining line of their defense. . . . The investment of the enemy is now fully completed and drawn very near to their lines except on the river above the town, where their communication is still open.

[On October 6:] Since mine to Your Excellency of the 1st inst. we have been employed in repairing the enemy's works upon Pidgeon Hill and in constructing a new intermediate redoubt. These will serve to give security to our troops in making their approaches. We have been assiduously employed in making fascines and gabions and in transporting our heavy cannon, mortars and stores from Trebell's landing upon James River. . . . We now have a sufficient stock to commence operations. We shall this night open trenches.

[On October 12:] My last dispatch to Your Excellency was of the 6th. I then informed you that we should open trenches on that night. We did so, and established our first parallel within 600 yards of the enemy's works. . . . The 7th and 8th we were employed in completing the first parallel and in erecting batteries somewhat advanced of it. The 9th, at 3 o'clock in the afternoon the French battery on the left . . . opened, and at 5 o'clock the American battery on the right . . . opened also. We were informed that our shells did considerable execution in the town, and we could perceive that our shot, which were directed against the enemy's embrasures, injured them much. The 10th, two French batteries . . . opened as did two more American batteries. . . . The fire now became so excessively heavy that the enemy withdrew their cannon from their embrasures . . . and scarcely fired a shot during the whole day. . . . We last night advanced our second parallel with 300 yards of the enemy's works with little or no annoyance from them.

[On October 16:] I had the honor to inform Your Excellency in my last, of the 12th instant, that we had the evening before opened our second parallel. The 13th and 14th we were employed in completing it. The engineers having deemed the two redoubts on the left of the enemy's line sufficiently injured by our shot and shells to make them practicable, it was determined to carry them by assault on the evening of the 14th. . . . I have the pleasure to inform Your Excellency that we succeeded in both. Nothing could exceed the firmness and bravery of the troops. They advanced under the fire of the enemy without returning a shot and effected the business with the bayonet only. . . .

The works which we have carried are of vast importance to us. From them we shall enfilade the enemy's whole line and I am in hopes we shall be able to command the communication from York to Gloucester. I think the batteries of the second parallel will be in sufficient forwardness to begin to play in the course of this day.

The enemy last night made a sortie for the first time. They entered one of the French and one of the American batteries on the second parallel which were unfinished. They had only time to thrust the points of their bayonets into four pieces of the French and two of the American artillery and break them off, but the spikes were easily extracted. They were repulsed the moment the supporting troops came up, leaving behind them seven or eight dead and six prisoners. . . .

The day after that report was written a red-coated drummer mounted the wall of the British works and beat a parley. An officer came out carrying a white flag. He was blindfolded and led to headquarters, where he delivered a letter to Washington, which said:

SIR, I propose a cessation of hostilities for twenty-four hours and that two officers may be appointed by each side, to meet at Mr. Moore's house, to settle terms for the surrender of the posts at York and Gloucester. I have the honor to be, etc. Cornwallis.

Washington immediately replied:

MY LORD: I have had the honor of receiving Your Lordship's letter of this date. An ardent desire to spare the further effusion of blood will readily incline me to listen to such terms for the surrender of your posts and garrisons of York and Gloucester as are admissible.

I wish, previously to the meeting of Commissioners, that Your Lordship's proposals in writing may be sent to the American lines; for which purpose a suspension of hostilities during two hours from the delivery of this letter will be granted.

In his final report to the President of Congress, on October 19, Washington said:

I HAVE THE HONOR to inform Congress that a reduction of the British army under the command of Lord Cornwallis is most happily effected. The unremitting ardor which actuated every officer and soldier in the combined army on this occasion has principally led to this important event, at an earlier period than my most sanguine hopes had induced me to expect . . .

On the 17th instant, a letter was received from Lord Cornwallis, proposing a meeting of Commissioners to consult on terms for the surrender of the posts of York and Gloucester. This letter (the first which had passed between us) opened a correspondence, a copy of which I do myself the honor to enclose. That correspondence was followed by the definitive capitulation, which was agreed to, and signed on the 19th. . . . And which I hope will meet the approbation of Congress. . . . Your Excellency and Congress will be pleased to accept my congratulations on this happy event.

CHAPTER VIII

THE BRIEF RETIREMENT

❦

AT LENGTH, MY DEAR MARQUIS, I am become a private citizen on the banks of the Potomac. . . . I am solacing myself with those tranquil enjoyments of which the soldier who is ever in pursuit of fame; the statesman whose watchful days and sleepless nights are spent in devising schemes to promote the welfare of his own [and] perhaps the ruin of other countries; . . . and the courtier who is always watching the countenance of his Prince in hopes of catching a gracious smile, can have very little conception. I am not only retired from all public employments, but I am retiring within myself, and shall be able to view the solitary walk and tread the paths of private life with heartfelt satisfaction. Envious of none, I am determined to be pleased with all. And this, my dear friend, being the order for my march, I will move gently down the stream of life until I sleep with my fathers.

Washington wrote this poor prophecy to Lafayette early in 1784, more than two years after the siege of Yorktown. They had been the two most idle and boring years of his life; spent waiting for the release which formal peace would bring.

Courtesy of The Art Museum, Princeton University

"The Princeton University Portrait" painted from life by C. W. Peale in Philadelphia in 1783, showing Washington as Commander-in-Chief at the battle of Princeton. It now hangs in Nassau Hall at Princeton University.

He had been by no means sure that Yorktown would end the fighting, and repeated the warning he had issued after the French alliance: "My greatest fear is that Congress, viewing this stroke [at Yorktown] in too favorable a light, may think our work too nearly closed and will fall into a state of langour and relaxation."

Even when the peace treaty was drawn, he was still suspicious. "The articles . . . ," he said, "are so very inconclusive . . . that we should hold ourselves in a hostile position, prepared for either alternative, war or peace." To the President of Congress he wrote, "I must confess I have my fears that we shall be obliged to worry through another campaign before we arrive at that happy period which is to crown all our toils."

If he had any thoughts for the future, other than retirement, he did not commit them to paper—although he did indignantly rebuke a colonel who reported that the army wished him to be king of the United States.

WITH A MIXTURE of great surprise and astonishment I have read with attention the sentiments you have submitted to my perusal. Be assured, sir, no occurrence in the course of the war has given me more painful sensations than your information of there being such ideas existing in the army as you have expressed, and I must view with abhorrence and reprehend with severity. For the present the communication of them will rest in my own bosom, unless some further agitation of the matter shall make a disclosure necessary.

I am much at a loss to conceive what part of my conduct could have given encouragement to an address, which to me seems big with the greatest mischiefs that can befall my country. If I am not deceived in the knowledge of myself, you could not have found a person to whom your schemes are more disagreeable. . . . Let me conjure you, then, if you have any regard for your country, concern for yourself or posterity, or respect for me, to banish these thoughts from your mind and never communicate, as from yourself or anyone else, a sentiment of like nature.

His most pressing problem of this period was a threatened revolt of the officers of the army. In March 1783, an anonymous petition was circulated in the camp on the bank of the Hudson calling for a meeting of all officers to demand proper compensation from Congress. To the surprise of the officers, Washington attended the meeting with a prepared speech. The petition, he said, was "addressed more to the feelings and passions than to the reason and judgment of the army."

A few weeks previously Washington had ordered spectacles. After stumbling through the first few paragraphs of his closely written manuscript he took them from his pocket and said, "Gentlemen, you will permit me to put on my spectacles, for I have gone not only gray, but almost blind, in the service of my country." Then he continued:

. . . If my conduct heretofore has not evinced to you that I have been a faithful friend to the army, my declaration of it at this time would be equally unavailing and improper. But as I was among the first who embarked in the cause of our common country—as I have never left your side one moment but when called from you on public duty—as I have been the constant companion and witness of your distresses and not among the last to feel and acknowledge your merits—as I have ever considered my own military reputation as inseparably connected with that of the army—as my heart has ever expanded with joy when I have heard its praises . . . it can *scarcely be supposed,* at this late stage of the war, that I am indifferent to its interests. But how are they to be promoted? The way is plain, says the anonymous addresser. If war continues, remove into the unsettled country; there establish yourselves and leave an ungrateful country to defend itself. But who are they to defend? Our wives, our children, our farms and other property which we leave behind us; or in this state of hostile separation, are we to take the two first . . . to perish in a wilderness, with hunger, cold and nakedness? If peace takes place, never sheathe your swords, says he, until you have obtained full and ample justice. This dreadful alternative, of either deserting our country in the extremest hour of her distress or turning our arms against it . . . has something so shocking in it that humanity revolts at the idea. My God! what can this writer have in view, by recommending such measures? Can he be a friend to the army? Can he be a friend to this country? Rather, is he not an insidious foe? . . . plotting the ruin of both, by sowing the seeds of discord and separation between the civil and military powers of the continent?

After counseling patience and promising the officers that he would use his best efforts in their behalf, he expressed his assurance that "you will, by the dignity of your conduct, afford occasion for posterity to say, when speaking of the glorious example you have exhibited to mankind, "had this day been wanting, the world had never seen the last stage of perfection to which human nature is capable of attaining." Perhaps Winston Churchill had this last phrase of Washington's in mind when he said, with more felicity of phrase, "If the British Empire and its commonwealth lasts for a thousand years, men will still say; 'this was their finest hour.' "

After peace was assured, and while he waited for the British to evacuate New York, Washington addressed a "Circular to the States" expressing his views on the hopeful future of the United States. He commented on his prospective retirement "to pass the remainder of life in a state of undisturbed repose," and then added:

. . . This is the time of their political probation; this is the moment when the eyes of the whole world are turned upon them; this is the moment to establish or ruin their national character forever; this is the favorable moment to give such a tone to our Federal Government as will enable it to answer the ends of its institution. Or this may be the ill-fated moment for relaxing the powers of the Union, annihilating the cement of the Confederation, and exposing us to become the sport of European politics, which may play one state against another to prevent their growing importance and to serve their own interested purposes. For, according to the system of policy the states shall adopt at this moment, they will stand or fall and, by their confirmation or lapse, it is yet to be decided whether the Revolution must ultimately be considered as a blessing or a curse—a blessing or a curse, not to the present age alone, for with our fate will the destiny of unborn millions be involved. . . .

Then he proceeded:

. . . There are four things which I humbly conceive are essential to the well-being, I may even venture to say, to the existence, of the United States as an independent power:

1st. An indissoluble Union of the States under one Federal head.

2nd. A sacred regard to public justice.

3rd. The adoption of a proper peace establishment, and

4th. The prevalence of that pacific and friendly disposition among the people of the United States which will induce them to forget their local prejudices and policies, to make those mutual concessions which are requisite to the general prosperity and, in some instances, to sacrifice their individual advantages to the interest of the community.

These are the pillars on which the glorious fabric of our independency and national character must be supported. Liberty is the basis, and whoever would dare to sap the foundation or overturn the structure, under whatever specious pretexts he may attempt it, will merit the bitterest execration and the severest punishment which can be inflicted by his injured country.

The circular continued to set forth that the honor of the country required that the public debt and the nation's defenders be paid. Then Washington returned to the basic essential for future happiness and security—"an indissoluble union."

. . . It will be part of my duty to assert without reserve, and to insist upon the following positions.

That unless the states will suffer Congress to exercise those prerogatives they are undoubtedly invested with by the Constitution [i.e. Articles of Confederation] everything must very rapidly tend to anarchy and confusion.

That it is indispensable to the happiness of the individual states that there should be lodged somewhere a supreme power to regulate and govern the general concerns of the confederated republic, without which the Union cannot be of long duration . . .

That whatever measures have a tendency to dissolve the union or contribute to violate or lessen the sovereign authority ought to be considered as hostile to the liberty and independency of America, and the authors of them treated accordingly.

And lastly, that unless we can be enabled by the concurrence of the states to participate of the fruits of the Revolution and enjoy the essential benefits of civil society, under a form of government so free and uncorrupted, so happily guarded against the danger of oppression, as has been devised and adopted by the Articles of Confederation, it will be a subject of regret that so much blood and treasure have been lavished to no purpose, that so many sufferings have been encountered without a compensation, and that so many sacrifices have been made in vain.

This circular to the states was promptly dubbed "Washington's Legacy" and received wide acclaim. One editorial hailed it as "dictated by the immediate spirit of God."

On November 25, 1783, Washington led his little army into New York on the heels of the departing British—the first step in a triumphal journey which would end, for him, at Mount Vernon. There was the tearful, emotional farewell to his officers at Fraunces Tavern, then a slow journey to Philadelphia, interrupted with ovations and addresses at New Brunswick and Trenton. In Philadelphia church bells rang and cannon boomed to welcome the new nation's great hero. Washington addressed a message to Congress asking for an audience "to resign the commission I have the honor of holding in their service."

This, too, was a highly emotional occasion. On December 23, Washington was escorted in to the chamber in the State House where Congress was in session. The President of the body addressed him: "Sir, the United States in Congress assembled are prepared to receive your communications." Washington rose, bowed, and started to read his prepared address:

MR. PRESIDENT: The great events on which my resignation depended having at length taken place, I have now the honor of offering my sincere congratulations to Congress and of presenting myself before them to surrender into their hands the trust committed to me and to claim the indulgence of retiring from the service of my country.

Happy in the confirmation of our independence and sovereignty and pleased with the opportunity afforded the United States of becoming a respectable nation, I resign with satisfaction the appointment I accepted with diffidence—a diffidence in my abilities to accomplish so arduous a task, which, however, was superseded by a confidence in the rectitude of our cause, the support of the Supreme Power of the Union, and the patronage of Heaven. . . .

After a few more sentences Washington broke down and could not immediately continue. When he had regained control he concluded, "Having now finished the work assigned me I retire from the great theater of action; and bidding an affectionate farewell to this august body under whose orders I have so long acted, I here offer my commission and take my leave of all the employments of public life." He then drew his commission from his pocket and presented it to the President of Congress. After a brief farewell to every delegate he swung into the saddle and galloped toward home, reaching Mount Vernon on Christmas Eve.

Washington had not realized how badly his financial situation had deteriorated during his absence. Lund had managed as best he could, but while he supervised the home property, rents on other land had not been paid, the products of plantation industries had been paid for in worthless, depreciated currency, and slaves had run off to the British or been sold to pay taxes. At one point Washington had only eighty-six pounds in hard money. When a nephew requested a loan, Washington sadly replied:

YOU VERY MUCH MISTAKE my circumstances when you suppose me in a condition to advance money. I made no money from my estate during the nine years I was absent from it, and brought none home with me. Those who owed me, for the most part, took advantage of the depreciation and paid me off with sixpence in the pound. Those to whom I was indebted I have yet to pay, without other means, if they will not wait, than selling part of my estate.

Washington did not know how to economize. He continued to make improvements on Mount Vernon: redecorating a room in stucco, paving a piazza with flagstones from England; building an icehouse and a greenhouse. And there were the guests. They flocked to Mount Vernon to see the great man, and he could not be inhospitable. It was not unusual for fifteen or twenty to sit down to dinner. In a single year eight tons of pork passed through the smokehouse, and Washington's diary noted that it was eighteen months after he returned before he and Martha first had dinner alone. His home, he said, "may be compared to a well-resorted tavern, as scarcely any strangers who are going from North to South, or from South to North, do not spend a day or two at it."

Added to the chores of farm management and entertainment was a heavy burden of correspondence. In his first few months at home without a secretary Washington wrote more letters in his own hand than at any other period of his life. His voluminous mail included, he said, "Letters (often of an unmeaning nature) from foreigners; inquiries after Dick, Tom and Harry, who *may have been* in some part or at *some time* in the Continental service; . . . introductions; applications for copies of papers; references of a thousand old matters with which I *ought* not to be troubled more than the Grand Mogul but which must receive an answer of some sort."

But Washington was never too busy to be concerned about others whom he considered deserving. When he learned that Thomas Paine was in straightened circumstances he wrote to James Madison, "Can nothing be done in our Assembly for poor Paine? Must the merits and services of *Common Sense* continue to glide down the stream of time, unrewarded by this country? His writings certainly have had a powerful effect on the public mind; ought they not then to meet an adequate return? He is poor! he is chagrined! and almost, if not altogether, in despair of relief." And again to Patrick Henry, "To say what effect the writings of this gentleman have had on our public affairs at the epochas at which they were given to the world would, to a person of your information, be altogether unnecessary; . . . If his services appear in your eyes to merit reward I am persuaded you will endeavor to do justice to them."

Washington's first return to public affairs was in connection with the Society of the Cincinnati, of which he was president general. This association of army officers had been formed, before the army disbanded, to perpetuate their comradeship in peacetime. Before a year was out it was the subject of widespread criticism. Benjamin Franklin feared that it would become "a society of hereditary knights." Washington wrote to Thomas Jefferson, asking his opinion and saying, "People are alarmed, especially in the eastern states. How justly, or how contrary to the avowed principles of the Society and the purity of their motives, I will not declare least it should appear that I wanted to bias your judgment rather than to obtain an opinion." When Jefferson, too, criticized the organization, Washington called a meeting in Philadelphia, saying, "If we cannot convince the people that their fears are ill-founded we should (at least in a degree) yield to them." At this meeting he proposed that the Society change its bylaws to:

STRIKE OUT EVERY WORD, sentence, and clause which has a political tendency.

Discontinue the hereditary part in all its connections, *absolutely,* without any substitution which can be construed into concealment or a change of ground *only;* for this would, in my opinion, increase, rather than allay suspicions.

Admit no more honorary members into the Society.

Reject subscriptions or donations from every person who is not a citizen of the United States.

Place the funds upon such a footing as to remove the jealousies which are entertained on that score . . .

Abolish the General Meetings altogether as unnecessary. . . .

No alterations short of what is here enumerated will, in my opinion, reconcile the Society to the community. Whether these will do it is questionable.

In March 1784 Washington received a letter from Jefferson suggesting that he take the lead in a project for linking the upper waters of the Ohio with the Virginia rivers before New York captured the western trade by opening an easy route to the Hudson. He replied, "My opinion coincides perfectly with yours respecting the practicability of an easy and short communication between the waters of the Ohio and Potomac . . . but I confess to you freely, I have no expectation that the public will adopt the measure." He outlined to his fellow Virginian all of the difficulties he anticipated from the political and public attitude toward such a venture, and then continued that "the immense advantages which this country would derive from the measure" might cause him to modify "that line of conduct with which I meant to glide gently down the stream of life." He then mounted and rode to visit his western lands and survey the western waters.

By the time he returned he had formed a bold, broad plan. "Extend the inland navigation of the eastern waters, communicate them as near as possible (by excellent roads) with those which run to the westward. Open these to the Ohio and such others as extend from the Ohio toward Lake Erie; and we shall not only draw the produce of the western settlers but the fur and peltry trade of the Lakes also to our ports." He wrote to the governor of Virginia:

THE WESTERN SETTLERS (I speak now from my own observation) stand as it were upon a pivot; the touch of a feather would turn them any way. They have looked down the Mississippi until the Spaniards (very impoliticly I think, for themselves) threw difficulties in their way; and they looked that way for no other reason than because they could glide gently down the stream; without considering, perhaps, the fatigues of the voyage back again and the time necessary to perform it in; and because they have no other means of coming to us but by a long land transportation and unimproved roads. These causes have hitherto checked the industry of the present settlers . . . for . . . they have no incitements to labor. But smooth the road once, and make easy the way for them, and then see what an influx of articles will be poured upon us . . . and how amply we shall be compensated for any trouble and expense we may encounter to effect it.

He continued to outline a detailed plan of how the project should be handled, pushed a bill through the Virginia legislature to authorize a stock company and visited Maryland and induced that state to pass a similar bill. Observing Washington's exertions in this matter, James Madison shrewdly commented, "The earnestness with which he espouses the undertaking is hardly to be described, and shows that a mind like his, capable of grand views, and which has long been occupied with them, cannot bear a vacancy." Although this project did not fully materialize, Washington never lost interest in it; and it had some bearing on the location of the nation's capital on the banks of the Potomac.

In 1785 and 1786 Washington worked as his own plantation manager. He had divided his eastern Virginia lands into six separate farms—the Mansion House (Mount Vernon), Dogue, Ferry, Muddy Hole, River and French. Although rheumatism was now bothering him he tried to visit each farm on every weekday, a round of about twenty miles. He was experimenting with "a new course in cropping" which involved crop rotation, the use of fertilizers and the prevention of soil erosion. His return to more prosperous circumstances was slow. He wrote Lund, "My estate for the last eleven years has not been able to make both ends meet. . . . I am not able to pay debts unless I could sell land, which I have publicly advertised without finding bidders." Still he continued to improve Mount Vernon, and sometimes made labor contracts with rather strange stipulations; as with the gardener who was to receive four dollars at Christmas "with which he may be drunk for four days and four nights."

Not all of his problems were weighty ones. One diary entry indicates his interest in a very minor economy:

IN ORDER TO try the difference between burning spermaceti and tallow candles I took one of each, the first weighing 3 oz. 10 p.w. 6 g., and the second 5 oz. 2 p.w., and lighted them at the same instant. The first burnt 8 hours and 21 minutes; when, of the latter, their remained 14 pennyweight—which continued to burn one hour and a quarter longer, making in all 9 hours and 36 minutes. By which it appears (as both burnt without flaring) that, estimating spermaceti candles at 3/ pr. lb., the former is dearer than the latter as 30 is to nearly 13, in others words more than 2¼ dearer.

At about this time Washington became convinced that mules might make better draft animals than horses, and he experimented with breeding some. The king of Spain sent him a fine jackass, and one diary entry reads, "Captain Sullivan, of a ship at Alexandria, agreeable to my request, came here to dinner, to interpret between me and the Spaniard who had the care of the Jack ass sent me. My questions and his answers respecting the Jack are committed to writing." Lafayette proposed to send him jackasses from Malta, and Washington wrote:

YOUR ASSURANCES, my dear Marquis, respecting the male and female asses, are highly pleasing to me. I shall look for them with much expectation and great satisfaction, as a valuable acquisition and important service.

The Jack which I have already received from Spain in appearance is fine; but his late royal master, though past his grand climacteric, cannot be less moved by female allurements than he is; or, when prompted, can proceed with more deliberation and majestic solemnity to the work of procreation.

Increasingly, Washington was becoming concerned with the weakness of the federal government and the need for a more perfect Union of the states. If state jealousies were not subordinated to give Congress more power, he said, the Union would cease to exist. He told Henry Knox ". . . contracted ideas, local pursuits and absurd jealousy are continually leading us from those great and fundamental principles which are characteristic of wise and powerful nations, and without which we are no more than a rope of sand, and shall as easily be broken."

He said, "the Confederation appears to me to be little more than a shadow without substance." And again, "If we are afraid to trust one another under qualified powers there is an end of the Union." He pointed out, "We are either a united people, or we are not. If the former, let us in all matters of general concern act as a nation which has national objects to promote and a national character to support. If we are not, let us no longer act a farce by pretending to it." In one letter to John Jay he said, "I do not conceive we can exist long as a nation without having lodged somewhere a power which will pervade the whole Union in as energetic a manner as the authority of the state governments extends over the several states." And in another letter to Jay, "That it is necessary to revise and amend the Articles of Confederation, I entertain *no* doubt; but what may be the consequences of such an attempt is doubtful. Yet something must be done or the fabric must fall, for it certainly is tottering."

In the fall of 1786 Washington's fears for the Union were aggravated by news of a rebellion in western Massachusetts, led by Captain Davis Shays. He heard that the rebels were demanding "the abolition of debts, the division of property, and the reunion with Great Britain." In Washington's mind this was proof of the need for a stronger federal government. To Henry Lee he wrote:

THEY EXHIBIT a melancholy proof of what our trans-Atlantic foe has predicted; and of another thing perhaps, which is still more to be regretted and is yet more unaccountable—that mankind when left to themselves are unfit for their own government. I am mortified beyond expression when I view the clouds that have spread over the brightest morn that ever dawned upon any country. . . .

You talk, my good sir, of employing influence to appease the present tumults in Massachusetts. I know not where that influence is to be found, and, if attainable, that it would be a proper remedy for the disorders. Influence is no government. Let us have one by which our lives, liberties and properties will be secured; or let us know the worst at once. . . . My humble opinion is that there is a call for decision. Know precisely what the insurgents aim at. If they have *real* grievances, redress them if possible. . . . If they have not, employ the force of government against them at once. . . .

These are my sentiments. Precedents are dangerous things; let the reins of government then be braced and held with a steady hand and every violation of the Constitution be reprehended. If defective, let it be amended—but not suffered to be trampled upon whilst it has an existence.

He encouraged energetic James Madison to inspire the Virginia Assembly to take the lead in advocating changes in the Articles of Confederation which would bring about a stronger federal government. To the young Virginian he wrote:

LET US LOOK to our national character and to things beyond the present period. No morn ever dawned more favorably than ours did; and no day was ever more clouded than the present! Wisdom, and good examples, are necessary at this time to rescue the political machine from the impending storm. Virginia has now an opportunity to set the latter, and has enough of the former, I hope, to take the lead in promoting this great and arduous work. Without some alteration in our political creed the superstructure we have been seven years raising, at the expense of so much blood and treasure, must fall. We are fast verging to anarchy and confusion! . . .

To you I am sure I need not add aught on this subject. The consequences of a lax or inefficient government are too obvious to be dwelt on. Thirteen sovereignties pulling against each other, and all tugging at the federal head, will soon bring ruin on the whole; whereas a liberal and energetic Constitution, well guarded and closely watched to prevent encroachments, might restore us to that degree of respectability and consequence to which we had a fair claim and the brightest prospect of attaining.

Madison's reply called for Washington to assume the leadership:

IN CASE OF civil discord, I have already told you it was seriously my opinion that you could not remain neuter, and that you would be obliged in self-defense to take part on one side or the other, or withdraw from the continent. Your friends are of the same opinion.

On February 21, 1787—the day before Washington's fifty-fifth birthday—Congress voted to call a convention of state delegates in Philadelphia in May "for the sole and express purpose of revising the Articles of Confederation." Virginia appointed Washington to lead her delegation—a move which brought a series of unusual letters from Washington. Should he go—or should he not?

On March 15 he wrote that he would not attend:

HOWEVER DESIROUS I am, and always shall be, to comply with any commands of my country, I do not conceive that I can, with consistent conduct, attend the proposed Convention to be held in Philadelphia in May next. For besides the declaration which I made in a very solemn manner when I was about to retire—of bidding adieu to all public employment—I had, just before the appointment of delegates to this Convention, written and dispatched circular letters to the several state Societies of the Cincinnati informing them of my intention not to attend the General Meeting which was to take place about the same time and at the same city.

On March 28 he wrote that he would attend, reluctantly, if his health permitted, "as my friends, with a degree of solicitude which is unusual, seem to wish for my attendance on this occasion I have come to a resolution to go, if my health will permit . . . for independently of all other considerations, I have of late been so much afflicted with rheumatic complaint in my shoulder that at times I am hardly able to raise my hand to my head, or turn myself in bed."

Aside from his rheumatism—which did not prevent his riding around his farms—and his embarrassment at attending the Convention after refusing to go to the Society of the Cincinnati meeting, Washington's real reason for hesitating was that he doubted that the Convention would be attended by men of stature and that it would accomplish anything. He feared the effect of a failure on his reputation. This he made clear, in confidence, in a letter to Virginia's Governor Edmund Randolph when he finally decided to go:

I VERY MUCH FEAR that all the states will not appear in Convention, and that some of them will come fettered so as to impede rather than accelerate the great object of their convening which, under the peculiar circumstances of my case, would place me in a more disagreeable situation than any other member would stand in. As I have yielded, however, to what appeared to be the earnest wishes of my friends, I will hope for the best.

On May 8, 1787 Washington noted in his diary: "A concise account of my journey to Philadelphia and the maner of spending my time there, and places where, will now follow." The account was very concise, consisting chiefly of a record of where he ate, and with whom. Sessions of the Constitutional Convention were secret and Washington noted that "no minutes of the proceedings has been or will be inserted in this journal." He did record his arrival in Phliadelphia.

AT GRAY'S FERRY the city light horse, commanded by Colonel Miles, met me and escorted me in by the artillery officers who stood arranged and saluted as I passed. . . . being . . . warmly and kindly pressed by Mr. and Mrs. Robert Morris to lodge with them, I did so. . . . Waited on the President [of Pennsylvania], Doctor Franklin, as soon as I got to town. On my arrival, the bells were chimed.

This was but Washington's third meeting with the oldest of the Founding Fathers—Franklin was now eighty-one. They had first met thirty-two years before during the Braddock expedition and again when Franklin visited the General's headquarters at Cambridge in 1775.

Washington was elected President of the Convention, and throughout the summer and early fall he sat quietly in the chair, contributing little but his presence to the proceedings. This was also true, to a lesser extent, of Benjamin Franklin. Hammering out the Constitution was the work of younger delegates. Yet had the two great men not been there it is doubtful that the Convention would have accomplished its purpose.

Washington wrote little about the Convention, for the reason which he gave in a letter to a nephew: "As the proceedings of the Convention are not intended to be made known till the business is finished I can give you no information on this score except that the sentiments of the different members seem to accord more than I expected they would, as far as we have yet gone." A month later he was not so sanguine of success when he wrote to Alexander Hamilton, who had left the Convention:

WHEN I REFER YOU to the state of the councils which prevailed at the period you left this city, and add that they are now, if possible, in a worse train than ever, you will find but little ground on which the hope of a good establishment can be formed. In a word, I *almost* despair of seeing a favorable issue to the proceedings of our Convention, and do therefore repent having had any agency in the business.

The men who oppose a strong and energetic government are, in my opinion, narrow-minded politicians, or are under the influence of local views. The apprehension expressed by them that the *people* will not accede to the form proposed is the *ostensible,* not the *real* cause of the opposition. . . . I am sorry you went away. I wish you were back. The crisis is equally important and alarming, and no opposition under such circumstances should discourage exertions till the signature is fixed.

The only record of the proceedings at the Constitutional Convention is in James Madison's journal. The young Virginian noted that Washington made only one speech. After the Constitution was engrossed, and Franklin had made a motion that it be adopted unanimously, an amendment was proposed to change the basis of representation in the House of Representatives to 30,000 instead of 40,000. Washington spoke in favor of this motion, saying that the larger basis gave "insufficient security for the rights and interests of the people." In deference to Washington the amendment was immediately adopted before Franklin's motion was passed.

Washington sent copies of the Constitution to Jefferson and to Lafayette in France, without an expression of opinion. To the latter he wrote: "It is the production of four months deliberation. It is now a Child of Fortune, to be fostered by some and buffeted by others. What will be the general opinion on, or the reception of, is not for me to decide, nor shall I say anything for or against it." With a copy which he sent to Patrick Henry he commented, "I wish the Constitution which is offered had been made more perfect, but I sincerely believe it is the best that could be obtained at this time; and, as a constitutional door is opened for amendment hereafter, the adoption of it under the present circumstances of the Union is in my opinion desirable."

Perhaps Washington's most important influence on the Constitution came after the Convention. To become effective the document had to be ratified by nine states, and there was strong antifederalist sentiment in several areas. The chief reason given by many for ratifying the Constitution was that Washington and Franklin had signed it. The *Pennsylvania Packet* editorialized, "The arguments, if they be arguments, most insisted upon in favor of the proposed Constitution are that if the plan is not a good one it is impossible that either General Washington or Doctor Franklin would have recommended it." And a Boston paper said, of Washington and Franklin, "The military virtues of the former and the philosophic splendor of the latter will be obscured by the new luster they will acquire as the legislators of an immense continent." James Monroe expressed the prevalent view when he wrote to Thomas Jefferson, "Be assured [General Washington's] influence carried the government."

There were some, said Washington, who would indulge in "traducing and villifying" the members of the Convention on the score that they sought personal gain from a stronger federal government. This did not bother the Virginian. He queried:

AT MY AGE, and in my circumstances, what sinister object or personal emolument had I to seek after in this life? The growing infirmities of age and the increasing love of retirement daily confirm my decided predilection for domestic life: and the great Searcher of human hearts is my witness that I have no wish which aspires beyond the humble and happy lot of living and dying a private citizen on my own farm.

The retirement which he sought would not be a life of ease. There was the ever present need for keeping the wolf from the door. In telling Dr. Craik that he could not pay all that he owed the physician he wrote, "I never felt the want of money so sensibly since I was a boy of fifteen years old as I have done for the last twelve months and probably shall do for twelve months more to come." He put off the sheriff three times when that official came to collect taxes on Mount Vernon and was mortified to receive a polite dunning letter for his church pew rent.

But though he talked of retirement he must have known that it was not to be. By early 1788 the ground swell of "Washington for President" came to the surface throughout the country. He read the *Pennsylvania Packet,* one of the country's most important newspapers, which mentioned him frequently as President-to-be, and never mentioned anyone else. He must have heard the toasts: from New York, "General Washington—may his wisdom and virtue preside in the councils of his country"; from Wilmington, "To Farmer Washington—may he, like a second Connatus, be called from the plow to rule a great people." From Frederick, Maryland, "May the Savior of America gratify the ardent wishes of his countrymen by accepting that post which the voice of mankind has assigned him."

Then there were the letters—sacks of them from his former officers, from political leaders, from common people, and one from Lafayette, who was concerned that the President, under the Constitution, might perpetuate himself in office, although he did not fear this if Washington occupied the position. To this Washington replied:

I CONFESS I DIFFER widely myself from Mr. Jefferson and you as to the necessity or expediency of rotation in that appointment. . . . There cannot, in my judgment, be the least danger that the President will by any practicable intrigue ever be able to continue himself one moment in office, much less perpetuate himself in it; but in the last stage of corrupted morals and political depravity. . . . When a people shall have become incapable of governing themselves and fit for a master, it is of little consequence from what quarter he comes.

And, he continued:

. . . In answer to the observations you make on the probability of my election to the Presidency (knowing me as you do) I need only say that it has no enticing charms and no fascinating allurements for me. However, it might not be decent for me to say I would refuse to accept or even to speak much about an appointment which may never take place: for in so doing, one might possibly incur the application of the moral resulting from that Fable in which the Fox is represented as inveighing against the sourness of the grapes because he could not reach them.

Washington's most lengthy exposition of his thinking, pro and con, on the subject of the Presidency was in a letter to Henry Lee in September 1788:

SHOULD THE CONTINGENCY you suggest take place, and (for argument sake alone let me say it) should my unfeigned reluctance to accept the office be overcome by a deference for the reasons and opinions of my friends; might I not, after the declarations I have made . . . in the judgment of the impartial world and of posterity, be chargeable with levity and inconsistency—if not with rashness and ambition? Nay, farther, would there not even be some apparent foundation for the two former charges? Now justice to myself and tranquillity of conscience require that I should act a part . . . at least capable of vindication. Nor will you conceive me to be too solicitious for reputation. Though I prize, as I ought, the good opinion of my fellow citizens; yet, if I know myself, I would not seek or retain popularity at the expense of one social duty or moral virtue.

While doing what my conscience informed me was right, as it respected my God, my country and myself, I could despise all the party clamor and unjust censure which must be expected from some whose personal enmity might be occasioned by their hostility to the government. I am conscious that I fear alone to give any real occasion for obloquy, and that I do not dread to meet with unmerited reproach. And certain I am whensoever I shall be convinced the good of my country requires my reputation to be put in risk, regard for my own fame will not come in competition with an object of so much magnitude.

If I declined the task, it would lie upon quite another principle. . . . My increasing fondness for agricultural amusements and my growing love of retirement augment and confirm my decided predilection for the character of a private citizen; yet it would be no one of these motives, nor the hazard to which my former reptuation might be exposed, or the terror of encountering new fatigues and troubles that would deter me from an acceptance; but a belief that some other person, who had less pretense and less inclination to be excused, could execute all the duties full as satisfactorily as myself. . . . You will perceive, my dear sir, by what is here observed (and which you will be pleased to consider in the light of a confidential communication) that my inclinations will dispose and decide me to remain as I am unless a clear and insurmountable conviction should be impressed on my mind that some very disagreeable consequences must in all human probability result from the indulgence of my wishes.

In a similar letter to Alexander Hamilton he proposed that if he did accept the appointment—which would be "attended with more diffidence and reluctance than I ever experienced before in my life"—he might do so with the "sole determination of lending whatever assistance might be in my power to promote the public weal, in hopes that at a convenient and early period my services might be dispensed with and that I might be permitted once more to retire, to pass an unclouded evening, after the stormy day of life, in the bosom of domestic tranquillity."

In a letter to General Lincoln, in October 1788, he indicated that he was beginning to accept the inevitable. He first called "Heaven to witness that this very act would be the greatest sacrifice of my personal feelings and wishes that ever I have been called upon to make," and then inferentially endorsed Lincoln's proposal of John Adams for the Vice-Presidency by writing, "From the extent and respectability of Massachusetts it might reasonably be expected, that he [the Vice-President] would be chosen from that state." Without mentioning Adams he said that any true "Federalist" would not be "disagreeable" to him, and added, "I would most certainly treat him with perfect sincerity and the greatest candor in every respect. I would give him my full confidence, and use my utmost endeavors to cooperate with him in promoting and rendering permanent the national prosperity. This should be my great, my only aim, under the fixed and irrevocable resolution of leaving to other hands the helm of the state as soon as my services could possibly with propriety be dispensed with." Three months later Washington made his endorsement of Adams more definite in another letter to Lincoln. "In Maryland and this state it is probable Mr. John Adams will have a considerable number of the votes of the electors. Some of those gentlemen will have been advised that this measure would be entirely agreeable to me and that I considered it to be the only certain way to prevent the election of an antifederalist."

The first announcement that he had been elected President came to Washington in a most casual way. He had asked General Henry Knox to buy some "superfine broadcloth" in New York for a suit for himself and a riding habit for Martha. On February 16, 1789, Knox wrote him, "The cloths have not yet arrived although expected by the first wind. The moment they come to hand I will forward those for you and Mrs. Washington." Then, without even a paragraph break, Knox continued, "It appears by the returns of elections hitherto obtained, which is as far as Maryland southward, that Your Excellency has every vote for President and Mr. John Adams twenty-eight for Vice-President exclusive of New Jersey and Delaware, whose votes for Vice [President] are not known."

On the very day that Congress was supposed to meet first in New York, March 4, 1789, Washington wrote to a wealthy man in Alexandria, "I am inclined to do what I never expected to be reduced to the necessity of doing; that is to borrow money upon interest. Five hundred pounds would enable me to discharge what I owe in Alexandria, etc., and to leave the state (if it shall not be permitted me to remain at home in retirement) without doing this would be exceedingly disagreeable to me." He would have to enter his new role as the nation's Chief Executive on borrowed funds.

Muddy roads prevented a quorum from reaching the national legislature until April 1. It was not until April 14 that Charles Thomson, Secretary of Congress, drew rein at Mount Vernon and delivered this formal notification:

SIR, I have the honor to transmit to Your Excellency the information of your unanimous election to the office of President of the United States of America. Suffer me, sir, to indulge the hope that so auspicious a mark of public confidence will meet your approbation, and be considered as a sure pledge of the affection and support you are to expect from a free and an enlightened people.

I am, sir, with Sentiments of Respect,

Your obedient humble servant

John Langdon.

Washington had an answer already prepared and read it to Thomson:

SIR, I have been long accustomed to entertain so great a respect for the opinion of my fellow citizens that the knowledge of their unanimous suffrages having been given in my favor scarcely leaves me the alternative for an option. Whatever may have been my private feelings and sentiments, I believe I cannot give a greater evidence of my sensibility for the honor they have done me than by accepting the appointment.

I am so much affected by this fresh proof of my country's esteem and confidence that silence can best explain my gratitude—while I realize the arduous nature of the task which is conferred on me, and feel my inability to perform it, I wish there may not be reason for regretting the choice. All I can promise is only that which can be accomplished by an honest zeal.

Upon considering how long time some of the gentlemen of both Houses of Congress have been at New York, how anxiously desirous they must be to proceed to business, and how deeply the public mind appears to be impressed with the necessity of doing it immediately, I cannot find myself at liberty to delay my journey. I shall therefore be in readiness to set out the day after tomorrow.

On April 16, 1789, Washington noted in his diary:

I BADE ADIEU to Mount Vernon, to private life and to domestic felicity, and with a mind oppressed with more anxious and painful sensations than I have words to express set out for New York . . . with the best disposition to render service to my country in obedience to its call, but with less hope of answering its expectations.

CHAPTER IX

THE SMOOTH FIRST TERM

❦

"Almighty God, we make our earnest prayer that Thou wilt keep the United States in Thy holy protection; that Thou wilt incline the hearts of the citizens to cultivate a spirt of subordination and obedience to government; to entertain a brotherly affection and love for one another and for their fellow citizens of the United States at large." So prayed Washington on April 30, 1789. He had just been sworn in as the first President of the United States on a half-enclosed portico before Federal Hall on Wall Street in New York where the United States subtreasury building now stands.

It was the culmination of a hectic and tiring two weeks since he had left Mount Vernon. His trip north had been a triumphal procession, with celebrations, dinners and addresses at each city on the route. The entrance to New York had been made by water, in a festooned barge rowed by twenty-six uniformed harbor pilots. The ships in the harbor were dressed; their cannon crashed salutes; sloops with singers swooped close to the Presidential barge so that he could hear their hymns of praise. He noted in his diary, "The display of boats . . . the decorations of the ships, the roar of cannon, and the loud acclamations of the people . . . filled my mind with sensations as painful (considering the reverse of this scene, which may be the case after all my labors to do good) as they are pleasing."

Five days after his inauguration he wrote:

I GREATLY APPREHEND that my countrymen will expect too much from me. I fear, if the issue of public measures should not correspond with their sanguine expectations, they will turn the extravagant (and I may say undue) praises which they are heaping upon me at this moment, into equally extravagant (though I will fondly hope unmerited) censures. So much is expected, so many untoward circumstances may intervene, in such a new and critical situation that I feel an insuperable diffidence in my own abilities.

Washington's initial problems were broad and manifold. What, exactly, did a President do? What was his relation to Congress? How should he order his personal life? How should he be addressed? This last question, the proper title for a President, became a national issue between the Federalists and the Antifederalists. The majority of the Senate, led by John Adams, wanted to call him "His Highness, the President of the United States of America and Protector of their Liberties." The Lower House would have nought to do with "Highness" and insisted on the simple title, "President of the United States." Washington's only comment on this dispute was that it was

. . . to be lamented [that Adams] and some others have stirred a question which has given rise to so much animadversion, and which I confess has given me much uneasiness lest it should be supposed by some, unacquainted with the facts, that the object they had in view was not displeasing to me. The truth is the question was moved before I arrived, without any privity or knowledge of it on my part, and urged . . . contrary to my opinion; for I foresaw and predicted the reception it has met with and the use that would be made of it by the adversaries of the government.

In organizing his personal life Washington initially decided to neither extend nor accept invitations, although he did make personal appearances. But he was somewhat dubious of the rectitude of this. If he kept himself too remote he might be thought to ape a king and close "the avenues of useful information from the many, and make [himself] more dependent on that of the few." He submitted a list of questions on this subject to John Jay, John Adams, Alexander Hamilton and James Madison, saying, "The President of the United States wishes to avail himself of your sentiments on the following points:

"1st. Whether a line of conduct equally distant from an association with all kinds of company on the one hand and from a total seculsion from society on the other ought to be adopted by him? And, in that case, how is it to be done?" Further, he asked whether it would "tend to prompt impertinent applications and involve disagreeable consequences" if he met all comers at 8:00 A.M. every morning; whether he could ask "six, eight or ten official characters" to dinner "without exciting clamors in the rest of the community?" Whether he could give "about four great entertainments in a year on such great occasions as . . . the Anniversary of the Declaration of Independence . . . the alliance with France . . . the peace with Great Britain . . . the organization of the general government"; and "in what light would his appearance *rarely at tea* parties be considered?"

Based on the replies of his colleagues Washington chose, "that line of conduct which combined public advantage with private convenience and which in my judgment was unexceptionable in itself." This involved holding two levees a week at which he would be available to callers. Of this regime he said that "had I not adopted it, I should have been unable to have attended to *any* sort of business unless I had applied the hours allotted to rest and refreshment. . . ."

The President's house at 3 Cherry Street ran more smoothly after his wife arrived, late in May. Martha firmly believed that a First Lady's place was in the home, and she ran it with a quiet, assured efficiency. As a hostess she was not scintillating; but her warmth and graciousness did much to humanize her dignified and somewhat austere husband. That indefatigable female correspondent of the period, Abigail Adams, left this picture of her:

I TOOK the earliest opportunity . . . to go and pay my respects to Mrs. Washington. She received me with great ease and politeness. She is plain in her dress, but that plainness is the best of every article. . . . Her hair is white, her teeth beautiful, her person rather short than otherwise. . . . Her manners are modest and unassuming, dignified and feminine, not the tincture of hauteur about her. . . . Mrs. Washington is one of those unassuming characters which create love and esteem. A most becoming pleasantness sits upon her countenance and an unaffected deportment which renders her the object of veneration and respect. With all these feelings and sensations I found myself much more deeply impressed than I ever did before their Majesties of Britain.

Martha may have seemed at ease in her position, but she did not relish it. Before the end of the year she wrote:

WITH RESPECT TO MYSELF, I sometimes think the arrangement is not quite as it ought to have been; that I, who had much rather be at home, should occupy a place with which a great many younger and gayer women would be prodigiously pleased. . . . I know too much of the vanity of human affairs to expect felicity from the splendid scenes of public life. I am still determined to be cheerful and to be happy in whatever situation I may be; for I have also learned from experience that the greater part of our happiness or misery depends upon our disposition, and not upon our circumstances.

The inclusion of this letter of Martha's in the papers of her husband may be justified because he might have written it. There was a distinct improvement in the grammar and style of Martha's letters starting in 1787. The reason came to light fairly recently by the discovery, in the Powel Collection at Mount Vernon, of several interesting pairs of letters; one of each pair, unsigned, in the hand of Washington; the other an exact signed copy in Martha's hand. With all that he had to do, the Chief Executive apparently found time to assist his wife in improving her correspondence.

Some aspects of Washington's mode of life gave cause for concern to many who suspected any formal or ceremonial activities as smacking of monarchy. He wanted to make the office of the President "respectable" and he loved display—particularly in his equipage. His large coach was elaborately redecorated and drawn by six matched horses. His mount was a handsome white steed with a leopardskin saddlecloth. When he moved to a larger house on Broadway he renovated and refurnished it at considerable expense. There were fourteen white servants and seven slaves, and the hall was manned by powdered lackeys. Much of this did not sit well with the common people, although Washington was not personally censured. One anonymous writer said that the "Old General" was "being taken over" by the great, and added, "These fine folks would spoil our General if they could. He never was a greater man than when he rode among us with his dusty boots." When Thomas Jefferson arrived to take his place in the Cabinet he was "much alarmed, indeed, at the mimicry I found established of royal forms and ceremonies."

Washington felt that the executive department was distinct from Congress but that the Constitution required him to show proper deference to the legislative branch. They were the lawmakers, and he did not believe that he had the right to interfere or seek to guide their deliberations except in some matter of extreme importance. He wrote that "as the Constitution of the United States, and the laws made under it, must mark the line of my official conduct, I could not justify my taking a single step in any matter which appeared to me to require their [Congress] agency, without its being first obtained."

The new President's most immediate and pressing problem was that of appointments. He was deluged with jobseekers: some strangers, some old friends, some his ex-officers. He refused to be swayed by friendship or nepotism. He answered an application from his old subordinate, General Heath, by writing:

THERE IS, I believe, no part of my administration in which I shall find myself more embarrassed than that of nominating persons to offices. The pretensions will be so numerous, and many of them so nearly equal, that it will require no small degree of discernment and investigation to hit upon the right. I shall, however, in all events have the consolation of reflecting that I entered upon my duty without the restriction of a single engagement and, if I know myself, under no partial influences. I shall leave no means in my power unessayed to find out the most deserving and best qualified persons to fill the several departments which it falls to my lot to supply."

When his nephew, Bushrod Washington, applied for appointment as a District Attorney for Virginia the uncle put him in his place with:

HOWEVER DESERVING you may be of the [office] you have suggested, your standing at the bar would not justify my nomination of you . . . in preference of some of the oldest and most esteemed lawyers . . . in your own state, who are desirous of this appointment.

Then he added:

. . . My political conduct in nominations, even if I was uninfluenced by principle, must be exceedingly circumspect and proof against just criticism, for the eyes of Argus are upon me and no slip will pass unnoticed that can be improved into a supposed partiality for friends or relatives.

Late in August 1789 Washington received word that his mother had died in Fredericksburg, an event which caused him to reflect:

AWFUL AND AFFECTING as the death of a parent is, there is consolation in knowing that Heaven has spared ours to an age beyond which few attain and favored her with the full enjoyment of her mental faculties and as much bodily strength as usually falls to the lot of fourscore. Under these considerations and a hope that she is translated to a happier place, it is the duty of her relatives to yield due submission to the decrees of the Creator.

Washington's relationship with his mother might be described as dutiful and polite. There seemingly was not deep affection for the demanding old woman. Most of Washington's letters to and about her are critical, yet much of the mother was visible in her son in more restrained form. Mary Washington might be described as "grasping." George, particularly in early manhood, was "acquisitive." Mary's persistency was, in George, perseverance—a quality which contributed much to the winning of the Revolution.

When Congress recessed at the end of September 1789, Washington regarded its first session as a success. He wrote Gouverneur Morris:

. . . the national government is organized and, as far as my information goes, to the satisfaction of all parties. . . . Opposition to it is either no more, or hides its head. . . . It is hoped and expected it will take strong root, and that the nonacceding states will very soon become members of the Union. No doubt is entertained of North Carolina, nor would there be of Rhode Island had not the majority of that people bid adieu, long since, to every principle of honor, common sense, and honesty.

The most important act of Washington's first year in office was the appointment of his four heads of departments (they were not yet called Cabinet officers) after Congress had passed the bills formally establishing their functions. His old chief of artillery, Henry Knox, became Secretary of War; his old secretary, Alexander Hamilton, became Secretary of the Treasury. Fellow Virginian Edmund Randolph, was appointed Attorney General. John Jay had been serving as Secretary of Foreign Affairs. He was moved to

Chief Justice of the Supreme Court and Washington unwittingly laid the foundation for much discord (and, incidentally, the two-party political system) by writing to Thomas Jefferson, who was on his way home from France.

IN THE SELECTION of characters to fill the important offices of government in the United States I was naturally led to contemplate the talents and disposition which I knew you to possess and entertain for the service of your country. And without being able to consult your inclination, or to derive any knowledge of your intentions from letters either to myself or to any other of your friends, I was determined, as well by motives of private regard as a conviction of public propriety, to nominate you for the Department of State, which under its present organization involves many of the most interesting objects of the executive authority.

When he had asked his colleagues for advice on his conduct as President, Washington had concluded with the question: "Whether, during the recess of Congress, it would not be advantageous to the interests of the Union for the President to make the tour of the United States, in order to become better acquainted with their principal characters and internal circumstances, as well as to be more accessible to numbers of well-informed persons who might give him useful information and advices on political subjects?" They all advised this, and the President set out on a tour of the northern states on October 15, 1789—carefully avoiding Rhode Island, which was not yet a member of the Union.

Washington devoted thirty-two pages in his diary to a fairly detailed description of his twenty-nine-day tour—where he went, who and what he saw, how he was received. He had eyes for everything. On the first day he recorded, as he moved through Westchester County:

THE ROAD for the greater part, indeed the whole way, was very rough and stony, but the land strong, well covered with grass

Courtesy of the Pennsylvania Academy of the Fine Arts

"The Lansdowne Portrait" of Washington late in life was painted by Gilbert Stuart in Philadelphia in April 1796. It now hangs in the Pennsylvania Academy of the Fine Arts.

and a luxuriant crop of Indian corn intermixed with pompions [pumpkins] which were yet ungathered in the fields. We met four droves of beef cattle for the New York market (about thirty in a drove), some of which were very fine—also a flock of sheep for the same place. We scarcely passed a farmhouse that did not abound in geese. Their cattle seemed to be of a good quality, and their hogs large, but rather long-legged. No dwelling house is seen without a stone or brick chimney, and rarely any without a shingled roof—generally the sides are of shingles also.

He recorded that Westchester farmers had sown wheat and rye sparingly, "on account of the destruction which had of late years been made of that grain by what is called the Hessian fly"; that the harbor of New Haven "is not good for large vessels"; and that "the linen manufacture does not appear to be of so much importance as I had been led to believe." At Wallingford he saw "the white mulberry growing, raised from the seed to feed the silk worm. We also saw samples of "lustring [silk] exceeding good, which had been manufactured from the cocoon raised in this town, and silk thread very fine" and recorded that the "Wollen Manufactory" of Hartford "seems to be going on with spirit. Their broadcloths are not of the first quality, as yet, but they are good. . . . I ordered a suit to be sent to me at New York." He learned that "The chief employment of the people of Marblehead (males) is fishing; about 110 vessels and 800 men and boys are engaged in this business. Their chief export is fish"; and that in Lynn "175,000 pairs of shoes (women's chiefly) have been made in a year by about 400 workmen"; and that "lumber, fish, and potash, with some provisions, composed the principal articles of export" of Portsmouth. He dined at Lexington "and viewed the spot on which the first blood was spilt in the dispute with Great Britain, on the 19th of April, 1775."

Many of his diary entries represented a detailed industrial survey of New England. Of a factory in Boston he wrote:

THEY HAVE MANUFACTURED thirty-two pieces of duck of thirty or forty yards each in a week. . . . They have twenty-eight looms at work, and fourteen girls spinning with both hands, the flax being fastened to their waist. Children (girls) turn the wheels for them, and with this assistance each spinner can turn out fourteen pounds of thread per day when they stick to it; but as they are paid by the piece, or work they do, there is no other restraint upon them but to come at 8 o'clock in the morning, and return at 6 in the evening. They are the daughters of decayed families, and are girls of character—none others are admitted.

Washington's diary gives equal attention, with apparent satisfaction and no particularly apparent modesty, to his reception in various communities; as in Boston, which he entered:

. . . preceded by the town corps, very handsomely dressed, we passed through the citizens classed in their different professions, and under their own banners till we came to the State House; from which across the street an arch was thrown; in the front of which was this inscription—"To the man who unites all hearts"—and on the other—"To Columbia's favorite son." . . . after passing through the arch, and entering the State House at the south end and ascending to the upper floor and returning to a balcony at the north end, three cheers was given by a vast concourse of people who by this time had assembled at the arch—then followed an ode composed in honor of the President and well sung by a band of select singers—after this three cheers—followed by the different professions and mechanics in the order they were drawn up with their colors through a lane of the people which had thronged about the arch under which they passed. The streets, the doors, windows and tops of the houses were crowded with well-dressed ladies and gentlemen.

Washington's regard for punctilio and protocol was pointed up by two incidents in Massachusetts. He refused to review the militia at Cambridge because they were under the control of Governor John Hancock and not of the President. He wrote:

. . . that as I conceived there was an impropriety in my *reviewing* the militia, or seeing them perform maneuvers otherwise than as a private man, I could no more than pass along the line which, if he [the officer commanding] thought proper, might be under arms to receive me at that time."

So much deference was due the governor. But in Boston Washington wrote, immediately after his description of the big reception, "Having engaged yesterday to take an informal dinner with the governor today—but under a full persuasion that he would have waited upon me so soon as I should have arrived—I excused myself upon his not doing it and informing me through his secretary that he was too much indisposed to do it; being resolved to receive the visit. Dined at my lodgings, where the Vice-President [John Adams] favored me with his company." After dinner the lieutenant governor—no less a person than Samuel Adams—called at the tavern "to express the governor's concern that he had not been in a condition to call upon me so soon as I came to town. I informed them in explicit terms that I should not see the governor unless it was at my own lodgings." The next day Hancock sent a note saying that he would like to "pay his respects in half an hour. This would have been done much sooner, had his health in any degree permitted. He now hazards everything as it respects his health, for the desirable purpose." Washington replied somewhat sarcastically:

THE PRESIDENT of the United States presents his best respects to the Governor, and has the honor to inform him that he shall be at home 'till 2 o'clock. The President of the United States need not express the pleasure it will give him to see the Governor; but, at the same time, he most earnestly begs that the Governor will not hazard his health on the occasion.

One of the President's first acts after returning to New York was the issuance of a proclamation which established the last Thursday in November as Thanksgiving Day, although he did not contemplate that it would be a day of feasting. After saying that "both Houses of Congress have by their joint committee requested me to recommend to the people of the United States a day of public thanksgiving and prayer," the Thanksgiving Proclamation continued:

I DO RECOMMEND and assign Thursday the 26th of November next to be devoted by the people of these states to the service of that great and glorious Being, who is the beneficent Author of all the good that was, that is or that will be. That we may then all unite in rendering unto Him our sincere and humble thanks for His kind care and protection of the people of this country previous to their becoming a nation; for the signal and manifold mercies and the favorable interpositions of His Providence which we experienced in the course and conclusion of the late war; for the great degree of tranquillity, union and plenty which we have since enjoyed; for the peaceable and rational manner in which we have been enabled to establish constitutions of government for our safety and happiness . . . for the civil and religious liberty with which we are blessed and the means we have of acquiring and diffusing useful knowledge; and in general for all the great and various favors which He hath been pleased to confer upon us.

And also that we may then unite in most humbly offering our prayers and supplications to the great Lord and Ruler of nations and beseech Him to pardon our national and other transgressions; to enable us all, whether in public or private stations, to perform our several and relative duties properly and punctually; to render our national government a blessing to all the people by constantly being a government of wise, just and constitutional laws, discreetly and faithfully executed and obeyed; to protect and guide all sovereigns and nations (especially such as have shown kindness unto us) and to bless them with good government, peace and concord; to promote the knowledge and practice of true religion and virtue and the increase of science among them and us; and generally to grant unto all mankind such a degree of temporal prosperity as He alone knows to be best.

On January 7, 1790, Washington rode in some state to deliver his first Annual Message to the second session of Congress. In line with his policy of not interfering with the lawmakers, it was a rather innocuous document. He started by commenting on "the present favorable prospects of our public affairs" and "the concord, peace and plenty with which we are blessed." He said, "A free people ought to be not only armed, but disciplined; to which end a uniform and well-digested plan is requisite" and that such a plan should provide for "the comfortable support of the officers and soldiers with a due regard to economy." He reminded Congress that protection against Indian attacks was still necessary and touched on the need for regulations governing naturalization and weights and measures, "the advancement of agriculture, commerce, and manufactures by all proper means," and "due attention to the post office and post roads." He said that "knowledge is in every country the surest basis of public happiness," but was rather vague about how this basis of happiness could be established. "Whether this desirable object will be best promoted by afforing aids to seminaries of learning already established; by the institution of a national university; or by any other expedients will be well worthy of a place in the deliberations of the legislature."

A week later the President presented to Congress, without comment, Alexander Hamilton's plan for putting the United States on its financial feet. Some aspects of this were extremely controversial, particularly the recommendation for "assumption" of the war debts of the several states by the federal government. Some states, particularly Virginia, had paid off part of their debts and saw no reason why they should now contribute to liquidating those of their delinquent sisters. Washington privately disagreed with his fellow Virginians. He wrote:

THE QUESTION of assumption has occupied a great deal of time, and no wonder; for it is certainly a very important one and, under *proper* restrictions, . . . I conceive to be just. The cause in which the expenses of the war was incurred was a common cause. The states, in Congress, declared it so at the beginning and pledged themselves to stand by each other. If, then, some states were harder pressed than others, or from particular or local circumstances contracted heavier debts, it is but reasonable when this fact is ascertained (though it is a sentiment I have not made known here) that an allowance ought to be made them. . . . Had the invaded and hard-pressed states believed the case would have been otherwise, opposition in them would very soon, I believe, have changed to submission and given a different termination to the war."

In May 1790 Washington contracted pneumonia; an attack so severe that both Madison and Jefferson reported that his death was imminent. A few months previously he had undergone an operation for a very painful tumor on his thigh. When he recovered from pneumonia he commented pessimistically that his third illness would probably be his last: "I have already had, within less than a year, two *severe* attacks; the last worse than the first. A third, more than probable, will put me to sleep with my fathers; at what distance this may be I know not. Within the last twelve months I have undergone more and severer sickness than thirty preceding years afflicted me with, put it all together." This might indicate that Washington was superstitious about things coming in threes, although there is no other evidence on this point.

Also in May 1790 Rhode Island at last ratified the Constitution. In congratulating her governor on this happy event Washington wrote:

HAVING NOW ATTAINED the desirable object of uniting under one general government all those states which were originally confederated we have a right to expect, with the blessing of a Divine Providence, that our country will afford us all those domestic enjoyments of which a free people only can boast; and at the same time secure that respectability abroad which she is entitled to by nature and from circumstances. Since the bond of Union is now complete, and we once more consider ourselves as one family, it is much to be hoped that reproaches will cease and prejudices be done away; for we should all remember that we are members of that community upon whose general success depends our particular and individual welfare and, therefore, if we mean to support the liberty and independence which it has cost us so much blood and treasure to establish, we must drive far away the demon of party spirit and local reproach.

Things were running smoothly during the summer of 1790. The President wrote to De Rochambeau:

WE HAVE A GOOD GOVERNMENT in theory and are carrying it pretty happily into practice. In a government which depends so much in its first stages on public opinion, much circumspection is still necessary for those who are engaged in its administration. Fortunately the current of public sentiment runs with us, and all things hitherto seem to succeed according to our wishes. In the meantime population increases, land is cleared, commerce extended, manufactories [multiply] and Heaven smiles upon us with favorable seasons and abundant crops.

In this same letter Washington made one of his rather rare facetious comments, this one on the French Revolution. He wrote:

THE LITTLE ANECDOTE which you recall to mind, my dear Count, of your countrymen at Rhode Island who burnt their mouths with the hot soup, while mine waited leisurely for it to cool, perhaps, when politically applied . . . has not less truth than pleasantry in its resemblance of national characters. But if there shall be no worse consequence resulting from too great eagerness in swallowing something so delightful as liberty than that of suffering a momentary pain or making a ridiculous figure with a scalded mouth, upon the whole it may be said you Frenchmen have come off well considering how immoderately you thirsted for the cup of liberty. And no wonder, as you drank it to the bottom, that some licentiousness should have been mingled with the dregs."

Washington's second Annual Message to Congress continued the theme that all is well:

IN MEETING YOU again I feel much satisfaction in being able to repeat my congratulations on the favorable prospects which continue to distinguish our public affairs. The abundant fruits of another year have blessed our country with plenty and with the means of a flourishing commerce. The progress of public credit is witnessed by a considerable rise of American stock abroad as well as at home, and the revenues alloted for this and other national purposes have been productive beyond the calculations by which they were regulated.

There was nothing of consequence in the message. He told Congress that he had borrowed three million florins from the Dutch; asked them to admit Kentucky to the Union; again reminded them of the need for protection of the frontier from Indians; suggested that, in view of "the disturbed situation in Europe, and particularly the posture of the great maritime powers," Congress might give some thought to a merchant marine. After mentioning the judicial system which had "opened the doors of justice to all descriptions of persons," and the need for regulation of the consular service, he concluded with: "The establishment of the militia, of a mint, of standards of weights and measures, of the post office and post roads are subjects which I presume you will resume, of course, and which are abundantly urged by their own importance."

As soon as Congress adjourned in March 1791, Washington set out on a tour of the southern states to match his previous visit to

New England, first instructing his secretary, Tobias Lear, to "furnish Mrs. Washington with what money she may want and from time to time ask her if she does want, as she is not fond of applying." The trip did not start auspiciously. The roads were bad, as was the weather. A horse went lame and Washington's riding horse "also appeared to be very unwell, his appetite had entirely failed him." A boat on which he had taken passage ran aground at the mouth of the Severn River, and Washington recorded that he layed "all night in my greatcoat and boots in a berth not long enough for me by the head, and much cramped." He finally reached the Potomac, where there was work to be done much to his liking.

During his second year in office the nation's capital had been moved temporarily to Philadelphia, and Congress had approved a permanent capital between Maryland and Virginia on the bank of the Potomac. This decision was the result of the first big political "deal." Jefferson had traded Virginia congressional votes for "assumption" in return for Hamilton's pledge of northern votes for the Potomac site. Washington had no part in the deal, but he still believed that the Potomac would someday be the water route to the west.

When he arrived at the river, federal commissioners, surveyors and the engineer, Major Pierre Charles L'Enfant, were already on the scene; but there was some difficulty about acquiring the land. Every local farmer envisioned his unfertile farm as a priceless lot in the center of the city, and the neighboring towns of Georgetown and Carrollsburg were vying to become the hub of the new town. Washington was well experienced in dealing for land. His diary reports:

FINDING THE INTERESTS of the landholders about Georgetown and those about Carrollsburg much at variance and that their fears and jealousies of each [other] were counteracting the public purposes and might prove injurious to its best interests, whilst if properly managed they might be made to subserve it, I requested them to meet me at six o'clock this afternoon at my lodgings, which they accordingly did.

To this meeting I represented that the contention in which they seemed engaged did not, in my opinion, comport with the public interest or that of their own; that while each party was aiming to obtain the public buildings they might, by placing the matter on a contracted scale, defeat the measure altogether; . . . that neither the offer from Georgetown or Carrollsburg, separately, was adequate to the end of insuring the object; . . . that, instead of contending which of the two should have it they had better . . . make a common cause of it and thereby secure it to the district. Other arguments were used to show the danger which might result from delay and the good effects that might proceed from a Union.

The next day he recorded:

THE PARTIES to whom I addressed myself yesterday evening, having taken the matter into consideration, saw the propriety of my observations; and that whilst they were contending for the shadow they might lose the substance; and therefore mutually agreed and entered into articles to surrender for public purposes one half of the land they severally possessed within bounds which were designated as necessary for the city to stand.

The land was purchased for twenty-five dollars an acre, with the provision that, when it was divided into lots, the original owners should retain title to alternate lots.

In general, Washington's record of the southern tour is rather a dreary one, with such typical entries as:

I HAD NOT, HOWEVER, rode two miles before it began to be stormy and to rain violently which, with some intervals, it continued to do the whole afternoon. The uncomfortableness of it for men and horses would have induced me to put up; but the only inn short of Halifax having no stables in which the horses could be comfortable and no rooms or beds which appeared tolerable—and everything else having a dirty appearance—I was compelled to keep on to Halifax.

And another:

THE WHOLE ROAD from New Burn to Wilmington (except in a few places of small extent) passes through the most barren country I ever beheld, especially in the parts nearest the latter, which is no other than a bed of white sand.

There were some bright spots. As the trip continued, Washington started to notice, and sometimes count, the beautiful women who fawned on him. He recorded that he was visited "by a great number of the most respectable ladies of Charleston—the first honor of the kind I had ever experienced and it was as flattering as it was singular." The next day, "In the evening went to a very elegant dancing assembly at the Exchange, at which were 256 elegantly dressed and handsome ladies." And on the following day he "dined with a very large company at the Governor's and in the evening went to a concert at the exchange at which there were at least 400 ladies the number and appearance of which exceeded anything of the kind I had ever seen."

At Richmond, Washington received a letter from his secretary in which Lear mentioned that Attorney General Randolph was in danger of losing the slaves he had brought to Pennsylvania, as he had to become a citizen of that state to deal with its courts. Washington wrote Lear that his situation was different because his residence in the state was "incidental as an officer of government only. But whether, among people who are in the practice of *enticing* slaves *even* where there is *no* color of law for it, this distinction will avail I know not." He would take no chances. He told his secretary to

. . . take the best advice you can on the subject, and in case it shall be found that any of my slaves may . . . attempt their freedom . . . it is my wish and desire that you would send the whole, or such part of them as Mrs. Washington may not choose to keep, home. For although I do not think they would be benefited by the change, yet the idea of freedom might be too great a temptation for them to resist. At any rate it might, if they conceived they had a right to it, make them insolent in a state of slavery. . . . If upon taking good advice it is found expedient to send them back to Virginia, I wish to have it accomplished under pretext that may deceive both them and the public; and none I think would so effectually do this as Mrs. Washington coming to Virginia next month. . . . This would naturally bring her maid and Austin and Hercules under the idea of coming to *cook* whilst we remained there. . . . I request that these sentiments and this advice may be known to none but yourself and Mrs. Washington.

Washington's third Annual Message to Congress, delivered on October 25, 1791, reported that the affairs of the country were still progressing smoothly. He noted that agriculture was booming: "Numerous as are the Providential blessings which demand our grateful acknowledgments, the abundance with which another year has again rewarded the industry of the husbandman is too important to escape recollection." He told the lawmakers that the stock of the new Bank of the United States had been subscribed for in a single day; advised them of Indians treaties with friendly tribes and offensive operations by Kentucky militia against unfriendly ones. He pointed out that it was "sincerely to be desired that all need of coercion in future may cease." To accomplish this he said that it was necessary that the Indians

. . . should experience the benefits of an impartial dispensation of justice. That the mode of alienating their lands, the main source of discontent and war, should be so defined and regulated as to obviate imposition and, as far as may be practicable, controversy. . . . That commerce with them should be promoted under regulations tending to secure an equitable deportment toward them, and that such rational experiments should be made for imparting to them the blessings of civilization as may from time to time suit their condition. . . . A system corresponding with the mild principles of religion and philanthropy toward an unenlightened race of men, whose happiness materially depends on the conduct of the United States, would be as honorable to the national character as conformable to the dictates of sound policy.

He continued with a few words on taxes, the new capital, the post office and post roads, the militia, the mint, weights and measures, and a provision for the sale of vacant lands of the United States. He mentioned the census of 1790 which, he said, would give Congress "the pleasing assurance that the present population of the United States borders on 4,000,000 persons."

As Washington entered the last full year of his first term there were straws in the wind which indicated that things would not continue to run so smoothly. The feud between Hamilton and Jefferson was well established, and each was getting a hard core of followers which would develop into two political parties. Hamilton had followed his original financial plan with proposals for a national bank and a tax on whiskey. Congress passed both measures, but not without controversy. Washington commented, "In passing the law for higher duties . . . and more especially on the subject of the bank, the line between the southern and eastern interests appeared more strongly marked than could have been wished; the former against and the latter in favor of those measures. But the debates were conducted with temper and candor."

The division on these measures was more than sectional. It went to the roots of the discord between the Jeffersonian Republicans and the Hamiltonian Federalists. Jefferson feared that added power for the federal government was a trend toward monarchy, to combat which he insisted that the central government should have only such powers as were specifically authorized in the Constitution. Nowhere in that document was there authority for the government to form a bank. Whiskey was an agricultural product, largely of western farmers. Jefferson, a stanch agrarian, believed that the tax on it was discriminatory.

Late in August 1792, while at Mount Vernon, Washington took the first step in trying to reconcile his two principal advisers by sending them almost identical letters. To Jefferson he started with reference to Indian and foreign affairs, and then continued:

HOW UNFORTUNATE and how much is it to be regretted . . . that whilst we are encompassed on all sides with avowed enemies and insidious friends . . . internal dissensions should be harrowing and tearing our vitals. The last, to me, is the most serious, the most alarming, and the most afflicting of the two. And without more charity for the opinions and acts of one another in governmental matters or some more infallible criterion by which the truth of speculative opinions, before they have undergone the test of experience, are to be forejudged than has yet fallen to the lot of fallibility, I believe it will be difficult, if not impracticable, to manage the reins of government or to keep the parts of it together: for if, instead of laying our shoulders to the machine after measures are decided on, one pulls this way and another that before the utility of the thing is fairly tried, it must, inevitably, be torn asunder. And, in my opinion the fairest prospect of happiness and prosperity that ever was presented to man will be lost, perhaps forever!

My earnest wish and my fondest hope therefore is that, instead of wounding suspicions and irritable charges, there may be liberal allowances, mutual forbearances, and temporizing yieldings on *all sides*. Under the exercise of these, matters will go on smoothly and, if possible, more prosperously. Without them everything must rub; the wheels of government will clog; our enemies will triumph and, by throwing their weight into the disaffected scale, may accomplish the ruin of the goodly fabric we have been erecting.

I do not mean to apply these observations or this advice to any particular person or character. I have given them in the same general terms to other officers of the government; because the disagreements which have arisen from difference of opinions and the attacks which have been made upon almost all the measures of government, and most of its executive officers, have, for a long time past, filled me with painful sensations, and cannot fail, I think, of producing unhappy consequences at home and abroad.

Jefferson answered with a long letter saying, in effect, that it was all Hamilton's fault—and offering to resign. Hamilton answered with a short letter saying, in effect, that it was all Jefferson's fault—and offering to resign. Washington could not afford to lose either of these great intellects. He continued his fruitless efforts at reconciliation. In reply to Jefferson's letter of self-justification the President wrote:

I DID NOT REQUIRE the evidence of the extracts which you enclosed me to convince me of your attachment to the Constitution of the United States, or of your disposition to promote the general welfare of this country. But I regret, deeply regret, the difference in opinions which have arisen and divided you and another principal officer of the government, and wish, devoutly, there could be an accommodation of them by mutual yieldings.

A measure of this sort would produce harmony and consequent good in our public councils; the contrary will, inevitably, introduce confusion, and serious mischiefs; and for what? Because mankind cannot think alike but would adopt different means to attain the same end; for I will frankly and solemnly declare that I believe the views of both of you are pure and well meant; and that experience alone will decide with respect to the salubrity of the measures which are the subjects of dispute. Why then, when some of the best citizens in the United States, men of discernment . . . are to be found, some on one side and some on the other of the questions which have caused these agitations, should either of you be so tenacious of your opinions as to make no allowances for those of the other?

While this was going on, during the summer and fall of 1792, Washington was looking forward longingly to retirement at the end of his term in the spring of 1793. This was one matter—perhaps the only one—on which Jefferson and Hamilton agreed. They told the President, in no uncertain terms, that his retirement would be a national catastrophe. This view was expressed by others, particularly James Madison, to whom Washington wrote:

I HAVE NOT BEEN UNMINDFUL of the sentiments expressed by you . . . on the contrary I have again and again revolved them with thoughtful anxiety but without being able to dispose my mind to a longer continuation in the office I have now the honor to hold. I therefore still look forward to the fulfillment of my fondest and most ardent wishes to spend the remainder of my days (which I cannot expect will be many) in ease and tranquillity.

Nothing short of conviction that my dereliction of the chair of government (if it should be the desire of the people to continue me in it) would involve the country in serious disputes respecting the Chief Magistrate, and the disagreeable consequences which might result therefrom in the floating and divided opinions which seem to prevail at present, could in any wise induce me to relinquish the determination I have formed.

But although he expressed his views on retirement privately, he made no public announcement and wrote no other letters on the subject. When the electors met, no alternate candidate for the office of Chief Executive was so much as mentioned. When the votes were counted on February 13, 1793, Washington was again the unanimous choice, although Adams was returned by a majority of only 27 votes out of 127. If, when he prepared to start his second term at the age of sixty-one, Washington had a presentiment that the path would not be so smooth as during the first four years, he did not commit his feeling to paper.

CHAPTER X

THE STORMY SECOND TERM

❦

Even Thomas Jefferson, that man of the people with his fear of monarchial pretensions, could have had no objection to the ceremonies which marked the beginning of Washington's second term. On March 4, 1793, the President rode alone in his carriage to the Senate chamber and delivered this short second Inaugural Address.

FELLOW CITIZENS: I am again called upon by the voice of my country to execute the functions of its Chief Magistrate. When the occasion proper for it shall arrive, I shall endeavor to express the high sense I entertain of this distinguished honor and of the confidence which has been reposed in me by the people of United America. Previous to the execution of any official act of the President, the Constitution requires an Oath of Office. This Oath I am now about to take, and in your presence, [so] that, if it shall be found during my administration of the government I have in any instance violated willingly, or knowingly, the injunction thereof, I may (besides incurring Constitutional punishment) be subject to the upbraidings of all who are now witnesses of the present solemn ceremony.

Washington then took the oath of office and went home. Congress adjourned until December.

The President was still smugly satisfied with the smooth and steady progress of national affairs. A few days after his inauguration he wrote:

IF WE ARE PERMITTED to improve without interruption the great advantages which nature and circumstances have placed within our reach, many years will not revolve before we may be ranked, not only among the most respectable, but among the happiest people on this globe. Our advances to these points are more rapid than the most sanguine among us ever predicted. A spirit of improvement displays itself in every quarter and principally in objects of the greatest public utility, such as opening the inland navigation; . . . improving the old roads and making new ones; building bridges and houses; and, in short, pursuing those things which seem eminently calculated to promote the advantage and accomodation of the people at large. Besides these, the enterprises of individuals show at once what are the happy effects of personal exertions in a country where equal laws and equal rights prevail.

Although the affairs of the country were in good order, those of Mount Vernon were not. Another nephew, George Augustine Washington, had replaced Lund as plantation manager. He had been in poor health for some time, and, late in January, Washington wrote him an affectionate letter which indicated that they both knew that his death was imminent. "The will of Heaven," he said, "is not to be controverted or scrutinized by the children of this world. It therefore becomes the creature of it to submit with patience and resignation to the will of the Creator whether it be to prolong or shorten the number of our days. To bless them with health, or afflict them with pain." When his nephew died ten days later Washington replaced him with an English farmer, Anthony Whiting, who needed more detailed and careful instruction than his nephew—although at no time during his Presidency did Washington loosen his grip on the management of his land. In fact, if selections from his papers were taken in terms of the wordage he devoted to various subjects, about half of those during his years in office would be devoted to farming and land management. He spent every Sunday writing on this subject, and some of his letters to Whiting contained nearly three thousand words.

His letters preached economy: "Nothing should be bought which can be made or done without." This was followed by advice on grinding oyster shells instead of buying lime. There were instructions for feeding slaves, crop rotation, handling livestock and the planting of virtually each individual acre. When the President learned that clover seed had not been sown in accordance with his orders, he sternly warned, "When I do give positive directions in any case whatsoever they are not to be dispensed with." But when he learned that Whiting was ill he immediately ordered him not to "expose yourself in the discharge of my business or use greater exertions than strength will bear." He proposed to arrange a medical consultation and, in the meantime, the President prescribed treatment and diet: "Wearing flannel next the skin is the best cure for and preventative of the rheumatism I ever tried. And for your other complaint, which you suppose to be in your lungs, a vegetable and milk diet I should suppose would be proper; avoiding as much as possible animal food."

Another minor but annoying problem was the progress of the Federal City. Washington had turned over the details of the supervision of this to Jefferson, but things had not gone smoothly. Disagreements between L'Enfant and the commissioners had led to the dismissal of the engineer, although not until after his plan for a city of circles with spokelike avenues radiating from them had been adopted. Of the plans submitted for the Capitol building Washington preferred that of an amateur architect, Dr. William Thornton, of which he wrote the District of Columbia commissioners on the day before his inauguration:

GRANDEUR, SIMPLICITY and convenience appear to be well combined in this plan of Doctor Thornton's that I have no doubt of its meeting with that approbation from you which I have given it upon an attentive inspection, and which it has received from all those who have seen it and are considered as judges of such things. How far the expense of such a building as is exhibited by the plan will comport with the funds of the city, you will be the best judges. . . . And to obviate objections that may be raised on this head, it should be considered that the external of the building will be the only *immediate* expense to be incurred. The internal work, and many of the ornamental parts without, may be finished gradually as the means will permit.

In June, Washington was told that professional architects reported Dr. Thornton's plan unsuitable "on the great points of practicability, time and expense." He asked Jefferson to investigate, saying: "It is unlucky that this investigation of Doctor Thornton's plan, and estimate of the cost, had not preceded the adoption of it. . . . It is better, however, to correct the error, though late, than to proceed in a ruinous measure—in the adoption of which I do not hesitate to confess I was governed by the beauty of the exterior and the distribution on the apartments, declaring then, as I do now, that I had no knowledge in the rules or principles of architecture, and was equally unable to count the cost." He reminded Jefferson that time was of the essence: "Nothing can be done to the foundation until a final decision is had, and this decision ought not to be delayed one moment that can be avoided, because time is wasting fast." Washington could not know that the building would still be unfinished when Abraham Lincoln took office.

The first President officiated at the Masonic ceremony of the laying of the cornerstone and personally inserted an engraved silver plate which read, "The southeast corner stone of the Capitol of the United States of America, in the City of Washington, was laid on the 18th day of September, 1793, in the eighteenth year of American Independence, in the first year of the second term of the Presidency of George Washington, whose virtues in the civil administration of his country have been as conspicuous and beneficial as his military valor and prudence have been useful in establishing her liberties." On the day that he laid the cornerstone, George Washington bought four lots in Washington, D.C.

Meanwhile the cauldron of woes which was to beset Washington's second term was brewing in Europe. The French Republic had been proclaimed; war between France and Austria and Prussia was raging; the blood bath of the revolution had brought Louis XVI to the scaffold. All of this posed complex problems in foreign relations for America, but Washington wrote nothing of them. He was concerned for his friend Lafayette, a mild monarchist, who was imprisoned in Austria. He immediately deposited 2310 guilders for Madame Lafayette in Holland and wrote her, "This sum is, I am certain, the least I am indebted for services rendered me by M. de Lafayette, of which I never yet received that account. I could add much, but it is best perhaps that I should say little on this subject."

Washington's situation in regard to Lafayette was delicate. Officially, he could not interfere in the affairs of a friendly nation to help his friend. He wrote Jefferson:

IF IT HAS NOT BEEN DONE in a former letter, it would be agreeable to me that Mr. Morris [Minister to France] be instructed to neglect no favorable opportunity of *expressing* informally the sentiments and wishes of this country respecting the M. de Lafayette. And I pray you to commit to paper, in answer to the enclosed letter from Madame de Lafayette to me, all the consolation I can with propriety give her consistent with my public character and the national policy; circumstanced as things are.

It seemed likely that a more widespread war was brewing in Europe. To David Humphreys, Minister to Portugal, Washington wrote:

ALL OUR LATE ACCOUNTS from Europe hold up the expectation of a general war in that quarter. For the sake of humanity I hope such an event will not take place; but, if it should, I trust that we shall have too just a sense of our own interest to originate any cause that may involve us in it; and I ardently wish we may not be forced into it by the conduct of other nations.

To Gouverneur Morris in Paris he added:

UNWISE SHOULD WE BE in the extreme to involve ourselves in the contests of European nations, where our weight could be but small tho' the loss to ourselves would be certain. I can, however, with truth aver that this country is not guided by such narrow and mistaken policy as will lead it to wish the destruction of any nation, under an idea that our importance will be increased in proportion as that of others is lessened. We should rejoice to see every nation enjoying all the advantages that nature and its circumstances would admit, consistent with civil liberty and the rights of other nations. Upon this ground the prosperity of this country would unfold itself every day, and every day would it be growing in political importance.

In April, Washington, then in Mount Vernon, received word from Jefferson that France and England were at war. He answered that he was leaving for Philadelphia the next day and added:

IT BEHOOVES the Government of this country to use every means in its power to prevent the citizens thereof from embroiling us with either of those powers, by endeavoring to maintain a strict neutrality. I therefore require that you will give the subject mature consideration, that such measures as shall be deemed most likely to effect this desirable purpose may be adopted without delay.

He wrote an almost identical letter to Hamilton, telling him to set down his views so that "I may as soon as I arrive at the seat of the government take such steps . . . as shall be deemed proper and effectual."

There was no possibility that his two principal advisers could agree on what constituted "proper" steps. Jefferson, and all Republicans were ardent Francophiles; Hamilton, and all Federalists, were equally Anglophile. In Jefferson's mind France was a sister republic fighting for its life against a hated monarchy—and, besides, the United States had treaty obligations to help the French. In Hamilton's mind the new French government was a bloodthirsty mob bent on the destruction of all civilized law and order—and, besides, England was the country's best customer.

Immediately upon his return to Philadelphia, Washington submitted a written list of thirteen questions to his Cabinet. The key queries were:

Question I. Shall a proclamation issue for the purpose of preventing interferences of the citizens of the United States in the war between France and Great Britain, etc.? Shall it contain a declaration of neutrality or not? What shall it contain? . . .

Question IV. Are the United States obliged by good faith to consider the treaties hertofore made with France as applying to the present situation of the parties? May they either renounce them or hold them suspended 'till the government of France shall be established? . . .

Question XIII. Is it necessary or advisable to call together the two Houses of Congress with a view to the present posture of European affairs? If it is, what should be the particular object of such a call?

The only question to which the Cabinet gave a unanimous answer was the last. They wanted no special session of Congress. Discussion on the other points led to the first of many subsequent stormy Cabinet sessions. With some sophistry Jefferson maintained that a Neutrality Proclamation would be unconstitutional. A "declaration of neutrality" was a declaration of "no war," and since only Congress could declare war, by inference only Congress could declare "no war." Based on equally specious reasoning Hamilton insisted that the French treaty was void because the government with which it was made no longer existed. He refused to admit Jefferson's premise that treaties apply to nations not to governments.

Washington listened in silence and then decided. He would issue a Neutrality Proclamation. He would not declare the French treaty void. As a sop to Jefferson, the Neutrality Proclamation did not contain the word "neutrality."

WHEREAS IT APPEARS that a state of war exists between Austria, Prussia, Sardinia, Great Britain and the United Netherlands on the one part, and France on the other, and the duty and interest of the United States require that they should with sincerity and good faith adopt and pursue a conduct friendly and impartial toward the belligerent Powers:

I have therefore thought fit by these presents to declare the disposition of the United States to observe the conduct aforesaid toward those powers respectively; and to exhort and warn the citizens of the United States carefully to avoid all acts and proceedings whatsoever which may in any manner tend to contravene such disposition.

And I do hereby also make known, that whosoever of the citizens of the United States shall render himself liable to punishment or forfeiture under the law of nations by committing, aiding or abetting hostilities against any of the said Powers, or by carrying to any of them those articles which are deemed contraband by the modern usage of nations, will not receive the protection of the United States against such punishment of forfeiture; and further, that I have given instructions to those officers to whom it belongs to cause prosecutions to be instituted against all persons who shall, within the cognizance of the Courts of the United States, violate the law of nations with respect to the Powers at war or any of them.

Opinion of the public and press became sharply divided on supporting France or England. Jefferson wrote to James Monroe,

"Parties seem to have taken a very well defined form in this quarter . . . The war has kindled and brought forward the two parties with an ardor which our own interests, merely, could never excite." The Republican press had been critical of the Administration for some time. Now, for the first time, criticism of Washington appeared in print. Leading the attack was Philip Freneau, publisher of the *National Gazette,* whom Jefferson employed as a French translator in the State Department.

Washington claimed that he was above resentment toward personal criticism—and then proceeded to express his resentment:

IN WHAT WILL this abuse terminate? The result, as it respects myself, I care not; for I have a consolation within that no earthly efforts can deprive me of, and that is that neither ambitious nor interested motives have influenced my conduct. The arrows of malevolence, therefore, however barbed and well pointed, never can reach the most vulnerable part of me; though, whilst I am as a mark, they will be continually aimed. The publications in Freneau's and Bache's papers [Note: Benjamin Franklin Bache, the old seer's grandson, was a Republican publisher in Philadelphia] are outrages on common decency; and they progress in that style in proportion as their pieces are treated with contempt and are passed by in silence by those at whom they are aimed.

Jefferson, in the political diary which he called his "Anas" told a different story. He recorded that Washington thought "that I should interpose in some way with Freneau, perhaps withdraw his appointment as translating clerk to my office. But I will not do it. His paper saved our Constitution which was galloping fast into monarchy." The Secretary of State continued that the President "has not with his usual good sense and *sang froid* looked on the efforts and effects of this free press." When Henry Knox showed Washington a particularly vicious blast of Freneau's at a Cabinet meeting, Jefferson reported:

THE PRESIDENT . . . got into one of those passions when he cannot command himself; ran on much on the personal abuse which had been bestowed on him; defied any man on earth to produce one single act of his since he had been in the government which was not done on the purest motives . . . that *by God* he had rather be on his farm than be *made emperor of the world,* and yet they were charging him with wanting to be a king.

Another development at this time that aroused Washington's ire was the formation, by Republicans, of political clubs called Democratic Societies; patterned on the Jacobin Clubs of France. These were pro-French and were openly critical of Administration policy. Washington bitterly resented these popular groups. He wrote Henry Lee:

. . . these societies were instituted by the artful and designing members . . . primarily to sow the seeds of jealousy and distrust among the people of the government, by destroying all confidence in the Administration of it. . . . I early gave it as my opinion to the confidential characters around me, that, if these societies were not counteracted (not by prosecutions, the ready way to make them grow stronger) or did not fall into disesteem . . . they would shake the government to its foundation. . . . I see, under a display of popular and fascinating guises, the most diabolical attempts to destroy the best fabric of human government and happiness that has ever been presented for the acceptance of mankind.

Despite his protests to the contrary, Washington was keenly sensitive to criticism. He condemned the "demon of party spirit," but he was inclined to see this demon in all who expressed disagreement with his Administration. He did not accept organized opposition as a part of political life, and of the Democratic Societies he wrote:

CAN ANYTHING be more absurd, more arrogant, or more pernicious to the peace of society than for self-created bodies, forming themselves into permanent censors, and under the shade of night in a conclave, . . . to declare that this act is unconstitutional, and that this act is pregnant of mischief. . . . Such a stretch of arrogant presumption . . . is not to be reconciled with laudable motives.

When Washington appeared before the Congress on December 3, 1793, to deliver his fifth Annual Message there was a significant change in that body. A majority of the Lower House was Republican. True, the majority was a slim one, but it assured a further growth of the factional strife which Washington so deplored.

His address dealt largely with foreign affairs and started with a justification of the Neutrality Proclamation.

IT SEEMED . . . my duty to admonish our citizens of the consequences of a contraband trade and of hostile acts. Under these impressions . . . the Proclamation was issued. In this posture of affairs, both new and delicate, I resolved to adopt general rules which should conform to the treaties [of 1778] and assert the privileges of the United States. It rests with the wisdom of Congress to correct, improve or enforce this plan of procedure.

He then made recommendations for stronger defense measures, referred to the need for punitive action against the Indians in the Northwest and suggested that newspapers be freed from a transportation tax. He concluded by saying:

. . . Permit me to bring to your remembrance the magnitude of your task. Without an unprejudiced coolness, the welfare of the government may be hazarded. Without harmony, as far as consists with freedom of sentiment, its dignity may be lost.

A few days later Jefferson resigned from the Cabinet. Washington wrote a friendly but rather formal acceptance and added

. . . I cannot suffer you to leave your station, without assuring you that the opinion which I had formed of your integrity and talents, and which dictated your original nomination, has been confirmed by the fullest experience, and that both have been eminently displayed in the discharge of your duties.

Jefferson was replaced as Secretary of State by Attorney General Randolph, whose post was filled by William Bradford. The change left Washington without a strong Republican adviser. Randolph was, at best, a wishy-washy Republican. Although Washington professed no party, he was, in the minds of most Republicans, being taken into the Federalist camp.

The year 1794 brought increased strain and tension. Great Britain was seizing American ships under Orders in Council, which declared cargoes to France and French colonies contraband. At home, pro-French Republicans were rioting in the streets of Philadelphia. Washington, at the urging of Hamilton, had insisted on the recall of the French minister who was responsible for much of this unrest, Edmond Charles Genêt. He then decided to send a special envoy to England in an attempt to reconcile differences with the old enemy. On April 15 he sent this note to John Jay, Chief Justice of the Supreme Court:

DEAR SIR: At as early an hour this morning, as you can make convenient to yourself, I should be glad to see you. At eight o'clock we breakfast. Then, or after, as suits you best, I will expect to have the satisfaction of conversing with you on an interesting subject.

After his breakfast meeting with Jay, Washington sent a message to the Senate: "I have thought proper to nominate, and do hereby nominate, John Jay, as Envoy extraordinary of the United States, to his Britannic Majesty."

Hamilton, as usual, had advice to offer on Jay's mission. The President should, he claimed, instruct Jay to offer compensation for English vessels which had been taken by proscribed French privateers, not merely to express a favorable opinion on the subject. Washington's reply indicated that he still considered the executive subservient to Congress in such matters:

AS CONGRESS, to whom the matter was referred, did not . . . think proper to take up the subject of compensation for British vessels . . . I do not feel disposed to make any further or more pointed declaration . . . on this head. . . . The powers of the Executive of the United States are more definite, and better understood perhaps, than those of almost any other country; and my aim has been, and will continue to be, neither to stretch nor relax from them in any instance whatever unless imperious circumstances should render the measure indispensable.

One principle cause of hostility toward Great Britain was the refusal of that country to relinquish posts in the Northwest that were within the boundaries of the United States, as provided by the Treaty of Paris. Of this Washington wrote to Jay:

THERE DOES NOT REMAIN a doubt in the mind of any well-informed person in this country . . . that all the difficulties we encounter with the Indians, their hostilities, the murders of helpless women and innocent children along our frontiers, results from the conduct of the agents of Great Britain in this country. . . . They are seducing from our alliances . . . tribes that have hitherto been kept in peace and friendship with us . . . whilst they keep in a state of irritation the tribes who are hostile to us. . .

Can it be expected, I ask, so long as these things are known in the United States . . . that there ever will, or can, be any cordiality between the two countries? I answer NO! And I will undertake, without the gift of prophecy, to predict that it will be impossible to keep this country in a state of amity with Great Britain long if the posts are not surrendered. . . . If they want to be in peace with this country, and to enjoy the benefits of its trade . . . to give up the posts is the only road to it. Withholding them, and the consequences we feel at present continuing, war will be inevitable.

During the summer of 1794 trouble at home temporarily eclipsed the storm in Europe. Reports reached Washington of insurrection in western Pennsylvania against the tax on spirits—the Whiskey Rebellion. A federal marshal and a tax collector had been imprisoned by the insurrectionists; the home of one had been burned; one man had been killed.

Whiskey was an important part of the economy of the western farmers. The market price on the coast for their abundant crops of grain would scarcely pay its transportation cost across the rugged mountains; but if the grain was run through a still the produce of a couple of acres could be carried on a single pack horse. Also, whiskey was a medium of exchange in the West. It was entirely wrong, said the Republican farmers, to tax the currency of the barter system.

Washington wrote that the "lawless and outrageous conduct" of the westerners was instigated by

. . . those who have never missed an opportunity by side blows, or otherwise, to aim their shafts at the general government. . . . I consider this insurrection as the first formidable fruit of the Democratic Societies: brought forth I believe too prematurely for their own views, which may contribute to the annihilation of them. . . . If the laws are to be so trampled upon with impunity, and a minority (a small one too) is to dictate to the majority, there is an end put, at one stroke, to republican government; and nothing but anarchy and confusion is to be expected thereafter.

At a Cabinet meeting Hamilton maintained that the rioting was treason and recommended calling out the militias of Pennsylvania, New Jersey, Maryland and Virginia to suppress it by overwhelming force. Washington agreed to have the militias stand by, but, before employing them he issued a proclamation. With many "Whereases" the President proclaimed that "combinations to defeat the execution of the laws . . . existed in some of the western parts of Pennsylvania"; that "said combinations" have "effected their dangerous and criminal purpose . . . by actual violence" and by "circulating vindictive menaces"; that "many persons in the said western parts of Pennsylvania have at length been hardy enough to perpetuate acts which I am advised amount to treason"; and that it was necessary "to take measures for calling forth the militia, in order to suppress the combinations aforesaid, and to cause the laws to be duly executed."

WHEREFORE . . . I, George Washington, President of the United States, do hereby command all persons, being insurgents as aforesaid, and all others whom it may concern, on or before the first day of September next, to disperse and retire peaceably to their respective abodes. And I do moreover warn all persons whomsoever against aiding, abetting or comforting the perpetrators of the aforesaid treasonable acts; and do require all officers and other citizens, according to their respective duties and the laws of the land, to exert their utmost endeavors to prevent and suppress such dangerous proceedings."

While waiting for the proclamation to take effect Washington diverted himself with one of his rather rare letters of advice to his teen-age stepgranddaughter, Elizabeth Parke Custis. The young lady had asked for his picture. Washington complied with her request and then continued with some gratuitous advice on love and marriage.

DO NOT THEN, in your contemplation of the marriage state, look for perfect felicity before you consent to wed. Nor conceive, from the fine tales the poets and lovers of old have told us of the transports of mutual love, that Heaven has taken its abode on earth. Nor do not deceive yourself in supposing that the only means by which these are to be obtained is to drink deep of the cup and revel in an ocean of love.

Love is a mighty pretty thing; but like all other delicious

things it is cloying; and when the first transports of the passion begins to subside (which it assuredly will do) and yield, oftentimes too late, to more sober reflections, it serves to evince that love is too dainty a food to live upon *alone* and ought not to be considered farther than as a necessary ingredient for that matrimonial happiness which results from a combination of causes, none of which are of greater importance than that the object on whom it is placed should possess good sense, good dispositions, and the means of supporting you in the way you have been brought up. . . . Without these, whatever may be your first impressions of the man, they will end in disappointment. For be assured . . . that there is no truth more certain than that all our enjoyments fall short of our expectations; and to none does it apply with more force than to the gratification of the passions.

After issuing his proclamation, Washington had sent commissioners to deal with the insurgents. When he received word that their attempts at conciliation had failed, he gave orders for the militia to move. Fifteen thousand men from four states were to rendezvous at Bedford, Pennsylvania, for the march over the mountains. Washington set out to join them and recorded the trip in his diary.

On September 30, 1794, he wrote, "I left the City of Philadelphia about half-past ten o'clock this forenoon accompanied by Colonel Hamilton . . . and my private secretary." The diary continues to describe his uneventful trip until he arrived at Carlisle on October 6, where he was, for six days, "employed in organizing the several detachments which had come in from different counties of this state, in a very disjointed and loose manner; or rather I ought to have said in urging and assisting General Mifflin to do it; as I no otherwise took the command of the troops to press them forward, and to provide them with necessaries for their march."

While he was so engaged two emissaries of the insurrectionists—

WILLIAM FINDLEY and David Redick deputed by the Committee of Safety (as it is designated) . . . arrived in camp with the resolutions of the said Committee;–and to give information of the state of things in the four western counties of Pennsylvania . . . to see if it would prevent the march of the army into them . . .

The substance of Mr. Findley's communications were as follows; viz.—that the people in the parts where he was best acquainted had seen their folly, and he believed were disposed to submit to the laws; . . . that he thought the distillers would either enter their stills or would put them down; that the civilian authority was beginning to recover its tone, and enumerated some instances of it; that the ignorance and general want of information among the people far exceeded anything he had any conception of; that it was not merely the excise law their opposition was aimed at, but to all law and government and to the officers of government; and that the situation in which he had been, and the life he had led for some time, was such that rather than go through it again he would prefer quitting this scene altogether . . .

Mr. Redick's information was similar to the above. . . . He added that for a long time after the riots commenced, and until lately, the distrust of one another was such that even friends were afraid to communicate their sentiments to each other. . . .

After hearing what both had to say, I briefly told them that it had been the earnest wish of government to bring the people of those counties to a sense of their duty by mild and lenient means . . . but as I considered the support of the laws as an object of the first magnitude . . . nothing short of the most unequivocal *proofs* of absolute submission should retard the march of the army into the western counties.

The emissaries could not give assurance of total submission so Washington proceeded to Bedford where he—

CALLED the Quarter Master General, Adjutant General, Contractor and others of the Staff Department before me . . . at

9 o'clock this morning, in order to fix on the routes of the two columns and their stages. . . . Matters being thus arranged I wrote a farewell address to the army through the Commander-in-Chief—Governor Lee—to be published in orders and, having prepared his instructions and made every arrangement that occurred as necessary, I prepared for my return to Philadelphia in order to meet Congress and to attend to the civil duties of my office.

The end of the Whiskey Rebellion was something of a farce. The 15,000-man army found no enemy across the mountains. The people welcomed them with good-natured derision. Some 150 supposed leaders were arrested and held for civil trial, and those who were convicted were later pardoned. From his corespondence it seems that Washington was more concerned with suppressing the Democratic Societies than he was with collecting a tax on whiskey. Just as Jefferson equated federalism with monarchism; Washington seemed to equate any organized opposition to the Administration with subversion.

Back in Philadelphia he prepared his sixth Annual Message, which dealt largely with the disturbance in western Pennsylvania. It had, he said, "Been fomented by combinations of men who, careless of consequences and disregarding the unerring truth, that those who rouse cannot always appease a civil convulsion, have disseminated, from an ignorance or perversion of facts, suspicions, jealousies and accusations of the whole government." The Senate, where the Federalists still had a majority, promptly adopted an endorsement of his actions, which shared his condemnation of "the proceedings of certain self-created societies." In the House, James Madison drafted a reply to the President's message which did not support him on this point. Madison wrote Jefferson that Washington's censure of the Democratic Societies was "perhaps the greatest error of his political life." Jefferson replied, "The denunciation of the Democratic Societies is one of the extraordinary acts of boldness of which we have seen so many from the faction of monocrats. It is wonderful, indeed, that the President should have permitted himself to be the organ of such an attack on the freedom of discussion."

Both Hamilton and Knox left the Cabinet at the end of 1794. The President assured Knox of "my most perfect persuasion that you have deserved well of your country," and to Hamilton he wrote, "In every relation which you have borne to me I have found that my confidence in your talents, exertions and integrity has been well placed." Knox was replaced with Timothy Pickering and Hamilton with Oliver Wolcott, both Federalists and neither of the stature of his predecessor.

In a brief peaceful period during the opening months of 1795 Washington offered some of his western land for sale, saying, "The number of full-handed emigrants that are pouring into this country from all quarters owing to the disturbed state of Europe, and the quantity of money brought by them and sent over by others to be vested in lands, have given an astonishing start to the price of this article. If therefore I do not sell soon on the terms I have just mentioned I shall raise my price." Regardless of price he had to sell land for, he wrote, "My public allowance, whatever the world may think of it, is inadequate to the expense of living in this city."

He offered to endow partially a national university in a letter to the commissioners of the District of Columbia:

IT HAS ALWAYS BEEN a source of serious reflection and sincere regret with me that the youth of the United States should be sent to foreign countries for the purpose of education. Although there are doubtless many under these circumstances who escape the danger of contracting principles unfriendly to republican government, yet we ought [not] to deprecate the hazard attending ardent and susceptible minds from . . . [being] prepossessed in favor of other political systems before they are capable of appreciating their own.

For this reason, I have greatly wished to see a plan adopted by which the arts, sciences and belles-lettres could be taught in their *fullest* extent; thereby embracing *all* the . . . means of acquiring the liberal knowledge which is necessary to qualify our citizens for the exigencies of public as well as private life; and . . . by assembling the youth from different parts of this rising republic, contributing . . . to the removal of prejudices which might perhaps sometimes arise from local circumstances.

The Federal City, from its centrality and the advantages which in other respects it must have over any other place in the United States, ought to be preferred as a proper site for such a university. And if a plan can be adopted upon a scale as extensive as I have described, and the execution of it shall commence under favorable auspices, in a reasonable time, with a fair prospect of success, I will grant, in perpetuity, fifty shares in the navigation of Potomac River toward the endowment of it.

He sent sixty dollars to a dentist in New York with a covering note which said, "Your last letter, with its accompaniment [sic] came safe to my hands on Tuesday last. The "accompaniment" was probably his false teeth.

And he wrote a most interesting letter on sex to a stepgranddaughter, Eleanor Parke Custis:

MEN AND WOMEN feel the same inclinations to each other *now* that they always have done, and which they will continue to do until there is a new order of things, and you, as others have done, may find, perhaps, that the passions of your sex are easier raised than allayed. Do not therefore boast too soon or too strongly of your insensibility to, or resistance of, its powers. In the composition of the human frame there is a good deal of inflammable matter, however dormant it may lie for a time, and . . . when the torch is put to it, that which is within you may burst into a blaze; for which reason . . . I will read you a lecture drawn from this text.

Love is said to be an involuntary passion, and it is therefore contended that it cannot be resisted. This is true in part only, for like all things else, when nourished and supplied plentifully with aliment it is rapid in its progress; but let these be withdrawn and it may be stifled in its birth or much stinted in its growth. For example, a woman . . . all beautiful and accomplished, will, while her hand and heart are undisposed of, turn the heads and set the circle in which she moves on fire. Let her marry, and what is the consequence? The madness ceases and all is quiet again. Why? Not because there is an diminution in the charms of the lady, but because there is an end of hope. Hence it follows that love may, and therefore ought to, be under the guidance of reason, for although we cannot avoid first impressions, we may assuredly place them under guard. My motives for treating on this subject are to show you, while you remain Eleanor Parke Custis, spinster, and retain the resolution to love with moderation, the propriety of adhering to the latter resolution, at least until you have secured your game.

In March 1795 the "Treaty of Amity, Commerce and Navigation" which John Jay had negotiated with Great Britain finally arrived in Philadelphia. It was a remarkable document of twenty-eight articles—remarkable because only Article Two, which provided for the evacuation by the British of the Northwest posts, was favorable to the United States; all the rest of the treaty was distinctly pro-British.

When the terms of the treaty became known there was a violent reaction against it. Jay was burned in effigy; Hamilton was stoned from the platform when he tried to speak in New York; addresses of protest from cities and counties piled up on the President's desk. Washington wrote Hamilton:

THE CRY AGAINST the treaty is like that against a mad dog and everyone . . . seems engaged in running it down. . . . It has received the most tortured interpretation and . . . the most abominable misrepresentations. . . . The string which is most played on, because it strikes with most force the popular ear, is the violation, as they term it, of our engagements with France, or, in other words, the predilection shown by [the treaty] to Great Britain at the expense of the French nation.

Despite the public outcry and the fact that Britain was still seizing American ships bound for French ports, Washington decided to ratify the treaty. He wrote Secretary of State Randolph, "A conditional ratification . . . may on all fit occasions be spoken of as my determination. . . . My opinion respecting the treaty is the same now that it was: namely, not favorable to it—but that it is better to ratify it than to suffer matters to remain as they are, unsettled." Washington believed that the widespread resistance to the treaty was inspired by Republicans who sought to discredit the Administration. He wrote:

PARTY DISPUTES are now carried to that length, and truth is so enveloped in mist and false representation, that it is extremely difficult to know through what channel to seek it. This difficulty to one who is of no party . . . is exceedingly to be lamented. But such . . . is the turbulence of human passions in party disputes, when victory more than truth is the palm contended for, that "the post of honor is a private station."

By the fall of 1795 Washington was no longer the great hero, *"sans peur et sans reproche."* Editorials in the Republican press—signed, as was the custom of the time, with pseudonyms—were damning him daily. "Pittachus" in the *Aurora* referred to him as "Saint Washington," and said that he was distinguished by "the seclusion of a monk and the supercillious distance of a tyrant." "Valerius" damned the "dark schemes of ambition" and "political degeneracy" of the Chief Executive and branded him a "usurper." Another writer said that Washington was a "frail mortal whose passions and weaknesses are like those of other men," and a fourth said that Americans had "spoiled their President as a too indulgent parent spoils a child."

There is no doubt that these political attacks deeply disturbed Washington, who never did understand politics or approve of the organized opposition of a rival party. In one of his few letters to Jefferson after the latter left the Cabinet Washington wrote:

UNTIL WITHIN THE LAST YEAR or two ago I had no conception that parties would, or even could, go the length I have been witness to; nor did I believe until lately that it was within the bonds of probability—hardly within those of possibility—that while I was using my utmost exertions to establish a national character of our own, independent . . . of every nation of the earth, and wished, by steering a steady course, to preserve this country from the horrors of a desolating war, that I should be accused of being the enemy of one nation and subject to the influence of another; and, to prove it, that every act of my Administration would be tortured and the grossest and most insidious misrepresentations of them be made by giving one side *only* of a subject, and that too in such exaggerated and indecent terms as could scarcely be applied to a Nero, a notorious defaulter, or even to a common pickpocket. But enough of this; I have already gone farther in the expression of my feelings than I intended.

During his last year in office Washington's Cabinet literally fell apart. Randolph resigned under a cloud caused by an accusation from Pickering and Wolcott that he had taken a bribe from France. Attorney General Bradford died. The President was unable to fill the vacancies with men whom he considered capable. John Marshall refused the post of Attorney General, and five men to whom Washington offered the State portfolio turned it down—including the revolutionary patriot Patrick Henry. Washington sought Hamilton's advice, asking, plaintively, "What am I to do for a Secretary of State? I ask frankly, and with solicitude, and shall receive kindly any sentiments you may express on the occasion. . . . What with the nonacceptance of some, the known dereliction of those who are most fit, the exceptionable drawbacks from [of?] others, and a wish (if it were practicable) to make a geographical distribution of the great officers of the Administration, I find the selection of proper characters an arduous duty." When the posts were finally filled by transferring Pickering to State, appointing Dr. James McHenry to War and Charles Lee to Attorney

General, John Adams commented: "The offices are once more filled, but how differently than when Jefferson, Hamilton, Jay, etc., were here."

Still, when Washington appeared before Congress on December 8, 1795, to deliver his seventh Annual Message he maintained a note of high optimism: "I indulge the persuasion that I have never met you at any period when, more than at present, the situation of our public affairs has afforded just cause for mutual congratulation." He told the lawmakers that the Indians were quiet; that he hoped for "a speedy peace" with the Barbary powers and the "restoration of our unfortunate fellow citizens from a grievous captivity"; and that negotiations with Spain were going well. He announced his determination to accept the British treaty, saying, "If, by prudence and moderation on every side, the extinguishment of all the causes of external discord . . . shall be the happy result, how firm and how precious a foundation will have been laid for accelerating, maturing and establishing the prosperity of our country!" He made an appeal for national unity with a hard-hitting bit of salesmanship on America's glowing future.

OUR AGRICULTURE, commerce and manufactures prosper beyond former example. . . . Our population advances with a celerity which, exceeding the most sanguine calculations, proportionally augments our strength and resources and guarantees our future security. . . . With burdens so light as scarcely to be perceived, with resources fully adequate to our present exigencies, with governments founded on genuine principles of rational liberty, and with mild and wholesome laws, is it too much to say that our country exhibits a spectacle of national happiness never surpassed if ever before equaled? Placed in a situation in every way so auspicious, motives of commanding force impel us . . . to unite our efforts to preserve, prolong and improve our immense advantages. To cooperate with you in this desirable work is a fervent and favorite wish of my heart.

After delivering this glowing prediction, Washington seemed to belie his faith in the future by inserting advertisements in papers in several cities. One read:

"TO BE LET AND POSSESSION GIVEN IN AUTUMN. The farms appertaining to the Mount Vernon estate, in Virginia; four in number; adjoining the Mansion House farm. Leases will be given for the term of fourteen years to *real* farmers of *good* reputation, and none others need apply." This advertisement continued to describe the four farms that were available for a yearly rental of one and one-half bushels of wheat per acre of arable land.

Another advertisement offered "FOR SALE: The following Lands, viz., on the Ohio River, in four tracts." This went on to describe the thirteen tracts totaling 41,000 acres of land which was "unquestionably among the most valuable on the Western water," which he would sell to the highest bidder.

Washington sent copies of his advertisement to correspondents in Europe. He hoped to get English or Scotch tenants for his Virginia lands. He expressed his contempt for his Virginia neighbors as farmers by telling each of his European correspondents, "I have very little expectation of accomplishing the renting part of my plan for next year; nor would I attempt it at all with the slovenly farmers of this country if there was a tolerable well grounded hope of getting them from any other where husbandry is better understood and more rationally practiced."

The outstanding event of Washington's last year in office was the most momentous debate that had, to that time, taken place in the House of Representatives. The Senate had approved the Jay treaty by a bare two-thirds vote, but the appropriation to effectuate it must originate in the Lower House. When the House requested all the correspondence and instructions to Jay, Washington refused to deliver these papers, saying.

I TRUST that no part of my conduct has ever indicated a disposition to withhold any information which the Constitution has enjoined upon the President as a duty to give. . . . The nature of foreign negotiations requires caution and their success must often depend on secrecy. . . . A full disclosure of all the measures, demands or eventual concessions, which may have been proposed or contemplated, would be extremely impolitic. . . . To admit, then, a right in the House of Representatives to demand, and to have as a matter of course, all the papers respecting a negotiation with a foreign power, would be to establish a dangerous precedent. . . . It is perfectly clear to my understanding that the assent of the House of Representatives is not necessary to the validity of a treaty. . . . A just regard to the Constitution and to the duty of my office . . . forbids a compliance with your request.

The House debate lasted for two months. Almost every Representative spoke. Finally, the great Federalist orator, Fisher Ames, swayed enough Republicans to bring about a tie vote, which was broken in favor of the treaty by the vote of the Speaker of the House. Washington saw in this debate an attack on the prerogatives of the executive and wrote:

NO CANDID MAN in the least degree acquainted with the progress of this business will believe for a moment that the *ostensible* dispute was about papers; or that the British treaty was a *good* one or a *bad* one; but whether there *should be a treaty at all* without the concurrence of the House of Representatives. Which was striking at once, and boldly too, at the fundamental principles of the Constitution; and if it were established would render the treaty-making power not only a nulity but such an absolute absurdity as to reflect disgrace on the framers of it. For will anyone suppose that they who framed or those who adopted that instrument . . . to give the power to the President and Senate to make treaties . . . would in the same breath place it in the powers of the House of Representatives to fix their veto on them. . . . Every unbiased mind will answer in the negative. Whence the source and what the object of all this struggle is, I submit to my fellow citizens. Charity would lead one to hope that the motives to it have been pure. Suspicions, however, speak a different language; and my tongue, for the present, shall be silent.

As the turbulent congressional session drew to a close in May 1796, Washington wrote Jay a commentary on the political discord which he hated, ending with a firm announcement of his intention to retire:

I AM SURE the mass of citizens in these United States *mean well,* and I firmly believe they will always *act well,* whenever they can obtain a right understanding of matters; but in some parts of the Union, where the sentiments of their delegates and leaders are adverse to the government and great pains are taken to inculcate a belief that their rights are assailed and their liberties endangered, it is not easy to accomplish this; especially, as it is the case invariably, when the inventors and abetters of pernicious measures use infinitely more industry in disseminating the poison than the well-disposed part of the community to furnish the antidote. To this source all our discontents may be traced and from it our embarrassments proceed. . . .

These things do, as you have supposed, fill my mind with much concern and with serious anxiety. Indeed, the trouble and perplexities which they occasion, added to the weight of years which have passed over me, have worn away my mind more than my body and render ease and retirement indispensably necessary to both during the short time I have to stay here. It would be uncandid therefore . . . not to add that nothing short of events [which] might render a retreat dishonorable will prevent the public annunciation of it in time to obviate a waste or misapplication of votes at the election of President and Vice-President of the United States in December next, upon myself.

CHAPTER XI

THE FAREWELL ADDRESS

❦

In the papers of each of the Founding Fathers there is one outstanding piece of writing. This is less true of Benjamin Franklin than of the others because so much of what he wrote is memorable; but his preface to the 1757 *Poor Richard's Almanac,* reprinted as *"The Way to Wealth,"* ran to some thirteen hundred editions—more than any book other than the Bible. Jefferson's great literary contribution was, of course, the Declaration of Independence. Hamilton's most important piece of writing was his financial plan. Madison's was his journal of the proceedings of the Constitutional Convention. Washington's was, unquestionably, the document which has become known as his Farewell Address.

He started thinking about a valedictory message in 1792 when he expected to retire at the end of his first term. At that time he asked James Madsion to "turn your thoughts to a valedictory address from me to the public; expressing in plain and modest terms that, having been honored with the Presidential chair, and to the best of my abilities contributed to the organization and administration of the government . . . I take my leave of them as a public man." He then continued, in very general terms, to suggest what should be in such a message. It should deal with unity; "the only strife among us ought to be who should be foremost in facilitating and finally accomplishing such great and desirable objects; by giving every possible support and cement to the Union." Even at that time he was beginning to resent public criticism. He told Madison "that however necessary it may be to keep a watchful eye over public servants and public measures, yet there ought to be limits to it; for suspicions unfounded, and jealousies too lively, are irritating to honest feelings and oftentimes are productive of more evil than good."

Four years later Madison was a leader in the enemy camp, politically. Washington now sent the rough draft of the address he proposed to issue, which incorporated four paragraphs he had received from Madison, to Alexander Hamilton with the request that he make "such amendments and corrections as to render it as perfect as the formation is susceptible of; curtailed if too verbose and relieved of all tautology not necessary to enforce the ideas in the original or quoted part. My wish is that the whole may appear in a plain style and be handed to the public in an honest, unaffected, simple garb." He wanted to retain the material quoted from Madison, he explained, to show that the message was "known . . . to one or two of those characters who are now strongest and foremost in the opposition to the government, and consequently to the person administering of it contrary to their views." This, he believed, would cause

. . . it more readily to be believed that I could have no view in extending the powers of the executive beyond the limits prescribed by the Constitution; and will serve to lessen, in the public estimation, the pretensions of that party to the pariotic zeal and watchfulness on which they endeavor to build their own consequence at the expense of others. . . . And besides, it may contribute to blunt, if it does not turn aside, some of the shafts which it may be presumed will be aimed at my annunciation of this event; among which conviction of fallen popularity and despair of being re-elected will be leveled at me with dexterity and keenness.

Hamilton prepared a "draft for incorporating," of which he said: "It has been my object to render this act importantly and lastingly useful . . . to embrace such reflections and sentiments as will wear well, progress in approbation with time, and redound to future reputation." Washington's draft had contained much self-justification. Hamilton had eliminated most of this, a change with which Washington agreed when he wrote Hamilton:

I HAVE GIVEN the paper herewith enclosed several serious and attentive readings and prefer it greatly to the other drafts, being more copious on material points; more dignified on the whole; and with less egotism. . . .

When the first draft was made . . . I thought the occasion was fair (as I had latterly been the subject of considerable invective) to say what is there contained of myself; and as the Address was designed in a more especial manner for the yeomanry of this country I conceived it was proper they should be informed of the object of that abuse, the silence with which it had been treated, and the consequences which would naturally flow from such unceasing and virulent attempts to destroy all confidence in the executive part of the government; and that it was best to do it in language that was plain and intelligible to their understandings. The draft now sent comprehends the most if not all these matters; is better expressed; and I am persuaded goes as far as it ought with respect to any personal mention of myself.

Washington's Farewell Address was not an "address" if this word is considered as synonymous with "speech." He did not deliver it orally to an audience. Rather, it was presented to the nation and the world as an editorial in the *American Daily Advertiser.* The account of the first publication of the Address is contained in a letter from David C. Claypoole, the editor of that paper:

A FEW DAYS before the appearance of this highly interesting document in print I received a message from the President . . .

signifying his desire to see me. I waited on him at the appointed time, and found him sitting alone in the drawing room. He received me very kindly and, after I had paid my respects to him, desired me to take a seat near him; then addressing himself to me, said that he had for some time contemplated retiring from public life, and had at length concluded to do so at the end of the (then) present term: that he had some thoughts and reflections on the occasion, which he deemed proper to communicate to the people of the United States, in the form of an Address, and which he wished to appear in the *Daily Advertiser*. . . . He asked me when I could make publication. I answered that the time should be made perfectly convenient to himself, and the following Monday was fixed on; he then said that his secretary would deliver me the copy on the next morning (Friday) and I withdrew. After the proof sheet had been carefully compared with the copy and corrected by myself, I carried two different revises to be examined by the President; who made but few alterations from the original, except in the punctuation, in which he was very minute.

Washington's "minute" concern for punctuation involved sprinkling commas throughout the text in a seemingly arbitrary manner and, although he stressed that it was to be a simple and straightforward statement, the entire 6,000 word message is verbose and to some extent repetitious. Therefore, in the following lengthy excerpt, punctuation has been modernized and some redundant material eliminated.

September 19, 1796

TO THE PEOPLE OF THE UNITED STATES

FRIENDS AND FELLOW-CITIZENS: The period for a new election of a citizen to administer the Executive Government of the United States being not far distant, and the time actually arrived when your thoughts must be employed in designating the perso who is to be clothed with that important trust, it appears to me proper . . . that I should now apprise you of the resolution I have formed to decline being considered among the number of those out of whom a choice is to be made.

I beg you, at the same time, to do me the justice to be assured that . . . in withdrawing the tender of service which silence in my situation might imply, I am influenced by no diminution of zeal for your future interest, no deficiency of grateful respect for your past kindness; but am supported by a full conviction that the step is compatible with both.

Washington continued to say that he had served as President from a sense of duty rather than desire and that he had wanted to retire at the end of his first term but;

the perplexed and critical posture of our affairs with foreign nations, and the unanimous advice of persons entitled to my confidence, impelled me to abandon the idea. I rejoice that the state of your concerns, external as well as internal, no longer renders the pursuit of inclination incompatible with the sentiment of duty or propriety; and am persuaded whatever partiality may be retained for my services, that in the present circumstances of our country you will not disapprove my determination to retire.

The address continued to express Washington's modest belief in "the inferiority of my qualifications" and to reiterate his desire to retire. He acknowledged "that debt of gratitude which I owe my beloved country for the many honors it has conferred upon me." He expressed appreciation for the opportunity to render "services faithful and persevering, though in usefullness unequal to my zeal." He thanked the people for the "constancy of your support," and added the hope that:

Heaven may continue to you the choicest tokens of its beneficence; that your Union and brotherly affection may be perpetual; that the free constitution, which is the work of your hands, may be sacredly maintained; that its administration in every department may be stamped with wisdom and virtue; that, in fine, the happiness of the people of these states, under the auspices of liberty, may be made complete by so careful a preservation and so prudent a use of this blessing as will acquire to them the glory of recommending it to the applause, the affection, and adoption of every nation which is yet a stranger to it.

Here, perhaps, I ought to stop. But a solicitude for your welfare, which cannot end but with my life, and the apprehension of danger natural to that solicitude, urge me on an occasion like the present to offer to your solemn contemplation, and to recommend to your frequent review, some sentiments which are the result of much reflection, of no inconsiderable observation, and which appear to me all important to the permanency of your felicity as a People. These will be offered to you with the more freedom as you can only see in them the disinterested warnings of a parting friend who can possibly have no personal motive to bias his counsel. . .

The first "sentiment" which Washington offered concerned "the unity of government which constitutes you one people." He pointed out that unity "is a main pillar in the edifice of your real independence, the support of your tranquility at home; your peace abroad; of your safety; of your prosperity; of that very liberty which you so highly prize." But, continued the President:

it is easy to foresee that from different causes and from different quarters much pains will be taken, many artifices employed to weaken in your minds the conviction of this truth; as this is the point in your political fortress against which the batteries of internal and external enemies will be most constantly and actively (though often covertly and insidiously) directed, it is of infinite moment that you should properly estimate the immense value of your national Union to your collective and individual happiness.

The address next spelled out the reasons why the people must not be swayed from whole-hearted support of the national union. The first was patriotism:

Citizens by birth or choice of a common country, that country has a right to concentrate your affections. The name of AMERICAN, which belongs to you in your national capacity, must always exalt the just pride of Patriotism more than any appellation derived from local discriminations. With slight shades of dfference you have the same religion, manners, habits and political principles. You have in a common cause fought and triumphed together. The independence and liberty you possess are the work of joint councils, and joint efforts; of common dangers, sufferings and successes.

In pleading for unity, Washington next appealed to self-interest. The sectional differences which would flare into civil war sixty-five years later were already apparent. Washington sought to prove that the interests of the people of every section of the country were best served by co-operation rather than conflict. "The North," he said, "in an unrestrained intercourse with the South, protected by the equal laws of a common government, finds in the productions of the latter great additional resources of maritime and commercial enterprise and precious materials of manufacturing industry. The South in the same intercourse, benefiting by the agency of the North, sees its agriculture grow and its commerce expand." The North, he said, needed the products of the South; the South needed the maritime strength of the North.

This interdependence was equally true of the East and the West:

The East, in like intercourse with the West, already finds, and in the progressive improvement of interior communications by land and water, will more and more find a valuable vent for the commodities which it brings from abroad or manufactures at home. The West derives from the East supplies requisite to its growth and comfort. And what is perhaps of still greater consequence, it must of necessity owe the secure enjoyment of indispensable outlets for its own productions to the weight, influence and the future maritime strength of the Atlantic side of the Union, directed by an indissoluble community of interest as *one nation*. . . .

While then every part of our country thus feels an immediate and particular interest in Union, all the parts combined cannot fail to find in the United mass of means and efforts greater strength, greater resource, proportionably greater security from external danger, a less frequent interruption of their peace by foreign nations. And, what is of inestimable value, they must derive from Union an exemption from those broils and wars between themselves, which so frequently afflict neighboring countries not tied together by the same government; which their own rivalships alone would be sufficient to produce, but which opposite foreign alliances, attachments and intrigues would stimulate and embitter. . . .

These considerations speak a persuasive language to every reflecting and virtuous mind, and exhibit the continuance of the UNION as a primary object of patriotic desire. Is there a doubt whether a common government can embrace so large a sphere? Let experience solve it. . . . there will always be reason to distrust the patriotism of those who in any quarter may endeavor to weaken its bands.

Washington next wrote at length on a favorite theme—the iniquity of parties in politics through which

designing men may endeavor to excite a belief that there is a real difference of local interests and views. One of the expedients of [a] party to acquire influence, within particular districts, is to misrepresent the opinions and aims of other districts. You cannot shield yourselves too much against the jealousies and heart burnings which spring from these misrepresentations. They tend to render alien to each other those who ought to be bound together by fraternal affection.

After pointing out that the people had adopted "a Constitution of Government . . . for the efficacious management of your common concerns," and that it was "the duty of every individual to obey the established government." Washington continued to belabor those who would put party above unity:

All obstructions to the execution of the laws, all combinations and associations, under whatever plausible character, with the real design to direct, control, counteract, or awe the regular deliberation and action of the constituted authorities are destructive of this fundamental principle and of fatal tendency. They serve to organize faction, to give it an artificial and extraordinary force; to put in the place of the delegated will of the nation, the will of a party; often a small but artful and enterprising minority of the community; and, according to the alternate triumphs of different parties, to make the public administration the mirror of the ill-concerted and incongruous projects of faction, rather than the organ of consistent and wholesome plans digested by common councils and modified by mutual interests. However combinations or associations of the above description may now and then answer popular ends, they are likely, in the course of time and things, to become potent engines by which cunning, ambitious and unprincipled men will be enabled to subvert the power of the people, and to usurp for themselves the reins of Government; destroying afterwards the very engines which have lifted them to unjust dominion.

It would seem that the form of government which Washington espoused in his Farewell Address would today be called totalitarian. Certainly it would be called reactionary. He wrote:

Towards the preservation of your Government and the permanency of your present happy state, it is requisite not only that you steadily discountenance irregular oppositions to its acknowledged authority, but also that you resist with care the spirit of innovation upon its principles however specious the pretexts. . . . In all the changes to which you may be invited, remember that time and habit are at least as necessary to fix the true character of Governments as of other human institutions; . . . that facility in changes upon the credit of mere hypotheses and opinion exposes to perpetual change, from the endless variety of hypotheses and opinion. And remember, especially, that for the efficient management of your common interests, in a country so extensive as ours, a Government of as much vigor as is consistent with the perfect security of liberty is indispensable. . . . It is indeed little else than a name, where the Government is too feeble . . . to confine each member of the Society within the limits prescribed by the laws and to maintain all in the secure and tranquil enjoyment of the rights of person and property.

In Washington's mind the division of the people into two or more parties would bring about almost unspeakable evils in government, and the danger was greatest in a democratic Government. The spirit of the party, he said,

is inseparable from our nature, having its root in the strongest passions of the human mind. It exists under different shapes in all governments, more or less stifled, controlled, or repressed; but in those of the popular form it is seen in its greatest rankness and is truly their worst enemy.

The alternate domination of one faction over another, sharpened by the spirit of revenge natural to party dissension, which in different ages and countries has perpetrated the most horrid enormities, is itself a frightful despotism. But this leads at length to a more formal and permanent despotism. The disorders and miseries which result gradually incline the minds of men to seek security and repose in the absolute power of an individual; and sooner or later the chief of some prevailing faction more able or more fortunate than his competitors turns this disposition to the purposes of his own elevation on the ruins of public liberty. . . .

There is an opinion that parties in free countries are useful checks upon the administration of the Government and serve to keep alive the spirit of liberty. This within certain limits is probably true, and in Governments of a monarchical cast patriotism may look with indulgence, if not with favor, upon the spirit of party. But in those of the popular character, in Governments purely elective, it is a spirit not to be encouraged. From their natural tendency it is certain there will always be enough of that spirit for every salutary purpose. . . . A fire not to be quenched; it demands a uniform vigilance to prevent its bursting into a flame, lest instead of warming it should consume.

The President next briefly warned the people of the need for keeping the three departments of government in balance. They all, he said, must "confine themselves within their respective Constitutional spheres; avoiding in the exercises of the powers of one department to encroach upon another." Such encroachment would "create, whatever the form of government, a real despotism." If experience indicated the desirability of a modification of the distribution of powers among the departments:

let it be corrected by an amendment in the way which the Constitution designates. But let there be no change by usurpation; for though this, in one instance, may be the instrument of good, it is the customary weapon by which free governments are destroyed. The precedent must always greatly overbalance in permanent evil any partial or transient benefit which the use can at any time yield.

Religion and morality were the next subjects for consideration in the Address. These were "indispensable supports" of "political prosperity" and:

In vain would that man claim the tribute of patriotism who should labor to subvert these great pillars of human happiness, these finest props of the duties of men and citizens. . . . A volume could not trace all their connections with private and public felicity. Let it simply be asked where is the security for property, for reputation, for life, if the sense of religious obligation *desert* the oaths which are the instruments of investigation in Courts of Justice? . . .

'Tis substantially true, that virtue of morality is a necessary spring of popular government. The rule indeed extends with more or less force to every species of free government. Who that is a sincere friend to it, can look with indifference upon attempts to shake the foundation of the fabric.

There followed two sentences on education:

Promote then as an object of primary importance, institutions for the general diffusion of knowledge. In proportion as the structure of a government gives force to public opinion, it is essential that public opinion should be enlightened.

Next came finance.

As a very important source of strength and security, cherish public credit. One method of preserving it is to use it as sparingly as possible: avoiding occasions of expense by cultivating peace, but remembering also that timely disbursements to prepare for danger frequently prevent much greater disbursements to repel it; avoiding likewise the accumulation of debt, not only by shunning occasions of expense, but by vigorous exertions in time of peace to discharge the debts which unavoidable wars may have occasioned, not ungenerously throwing upon posterity the burden which we ourselves ought to bear.

Of course, added Washington, the people must remember "that towards the payment of debts there must be revenue; that to have revenue there must be taxes; that no taxes can be devised which are not more or less inconvenient and unpleasant."

The next and longest section of the Farewell Address might be called the keystone of United States foreign policy for the next century and a half. Washington started his preachment on foreign relations by writing:

Observe good faith and justice towards all nations. Cultivate peace and harmony with all. Religion and morality enjoin this conduct; and can it be that good policy does not equally enjoin it? It will be worthy of a free, enlightened, and, at no distant period, a great nation, to give to mankind the magnanimous and too novel example of a people always guided by an exalted justice and benevolence.

But "good faith and justice" were about all that the President proposed to give to other nations. Generally, the balance of his advice on foreign relations was to have as little of them as possible. In view of the then current situation with France and Great Britain he developed at some length the danger of; "Inveterate antipathies against particular nations and passionate attachments for others. . . . The nation which indulges towards another an habitual hatred, or an habitual fondness, is in some degree a slave. It is a slave to its animosity or to its affection, either of which is sufficient to lead it astray from its duty and its interest." After spelling out for many paragraphs the evils of both affection and antipathy in foreign affairs, Washington continued with the best known and most often quoted section of the Farewell Address:

The great rule of conduct for us in regard to foreign nations, is in extending our commercial relations [and] to have with them as little *political* connection as possible. So far as we have already formed engagements let them be fulfilled with perfect good faith. Here let us stop.

Europe has a set of primary interests which to us have none, or a very remote, relation. Hence she must be engaged in frequent controversies, the causes of which are essentially foreign to our concerns. Hence therefore it must be unwise in us to implicate ourselves, by artifical ties, in the ordinary vicissitudes of her politics, or the ordinary combinations and collisions of her friendships or enmities.

Our detached and distant situation invites and enables us to pursue a different course. If we remain one people, under an efficient government, the period is not far off when we may defy material injury from external annoyance; when we may take such an attitude as will cause the neutrality we may at any time resolve upon to be scrupulously respected; when belligerent nations, under the impossibility of making acquisitions upon us, will not lightly hazard the giving us provocation; when we may choose peace or war as our interest guided by our justice shall counsel.

Why forego the advantages of so peculiar a situation? Why quit our own to stand upon foreign ground? Why, by interweaving our destiny with that of any part of Europe, entangle our peace and prosperity in the toils of European ambition, rivalship, interest, humor or caprice?

'Tis our true policy to steer clear of permanent alliances with any portion of the foreign world. So far, I mean, as we are now at liberty to do it—for let me not be understood as capable of patronising infidelity to existing engagements (I hold the maxim no less applicable to public than to private affairs, that honesty is always the best policy). I repeat it therefore, let those engagements be observed in their genuine sense. But in my opinion, it is unnecessary and would be unwise to extend them.

Taking care always to keep ourselves, by suitable establishments, on a respectability defensive posture, we may safely trust to temporary alliances for extraordinary emergencies.

In foreign trade Washington advised

an equal and impartial hand: neither seeking nor granting exclusive favors of preferences . . . constantly keeping in view that it is folly in one nation to look for disinterested favors from another. . . . There can be no greater error than to expect or calculate upon real favors from nation to nation. 'Tis an illusion which experience must cure. . . .

The President started the peroration of his Address by writing:

In offering to you, my countrymen, these counsels of an old and affectionate friend, I dare not hope they will make the strong and lasting impression I could wish; that they will control the usual current of the passions, or prevent our nation from running the course which has hitherto marked the Destiny of Nations. But if I may even flatter myself that they may be productive of some partial benefit, some occasional good; that they may now and then recur to moderate the fury of party spirit, to warn against the mischiefs of foreign intrigue, to guard against the impostures of pretended patriotism; this hope will be a full recompence for the solicitude for your welfare, by which they have been dictated.

How far in the discharge of my official duties, I have been guided by the principles which have been delineated, the public records and other evidences of my conduct must witness to you and to the world. To myself, the assurance of my own conscience is that I have at least believed myself to be guided by them.

Washington then digressed in his summation to defend the Neutrality Proclamation, which he had issued, he said, "to gain time to our country to settle and mature its yet recent institutions, and to progress without interruption to . . . command of its fortunes." After this came the final, heartfelt sentences:

Though in reviewing the incidents of my administration I am unconscious of intentional error, I am nevertheless too sensible of my defects not to think it probable that I may have committed many errors. Whatever they may be I fervently beseech the Almighty to avert or mitigate the evils to which they may tend. I shall also carry with me the hope that my country will never cease to view them with indulgence; and that after forty-five years of my life dedicated to its service, with an upright zeal, the faults of incompetent abilities will be consigned to oblivion, as myself must soon be to the Mansions of rest.

Relying on its kindness in this as in other things, and actuated by that fervent love towards it which is so natural to a man who views in it the native soil of himself and his progenitors for several generations; I anticipate with pleasing expectation that retreat in which I promise myself to realize, without alloy, the sweet enjoyment of partaking, in the midst of my fellow citizens, the benign influence of good laws under a free government, the ever favorite object of my heart, and the happy reward, as I trust, of our mutual cares, labors and dangers.

CHAPTER XII

FIRST IN WAR: FIRST IN PEACE

❦

I BEGIN MY DIURNAL COURSE with the sun; that if my hirelings are not in their places at that time I send them messages expressive of my sorrow for their indisposition. Then having put these wheels in motion I examine the state of things further; and the more they are probed, the deeper I find the wounds are which my buildings have sustained by an absence and neglect of eight years. By the time I have accomplished these matters, breakfast . . . is ready. This over, I mount my horse and ride round my farms, which employs me until it is time to dress for dinner, at which I rarely miss seeing strange faces, come, as they say, out of respect to me. Pray, would not the word curiosity answer as well? And how different, this, from having a few social friends at a cheerful board. The usual time of sitting at table; a walk, and tea, brings me within the dawn of candlelight. . . . If not prevented by company I resolve that, as soon as the glimmering taper supplies the place of the great luminary, I will retire to my writing table and acknowledge the letters I have received. But when the lights are brought, I feel tired and disinclined to engage in this work, conceiving that the next night will do as well. The next comes and with it the same causes for postponement.

So wrote Washington in May 1797 when he had been at Mount Vernon for some ten weeks. At long last he was a private person and rashly bragged that "no consideration under Heaven that I can foresee shall again withdraw me from the walks of private life." If Washington could not foresee a situation that might again require his services it was because he did not want to face certain unpleasant facts. When he had said, in his Farewell Address, that "the state of your concerns, external as well as internal" no longer demanded that he stay in harness he was ignoring a rapidly widening rift with France.

The French were displeased by the Jay treaty which, they claimed, violated America's treaty with them. Then Washington had rather arbitrarily recalled Republican James Monroe from Paris and sought to replace him with Federalist Charles Cotesworth Pinckney, whom the French Directory refused to receive. James Madison called Secretary Pickering's instructions to Pinckney "an overt patronage of the British cause" and predicted that "a push will be made" to persuade Washington into war with France.

Washington had written, in the draft of the Farewell Address which he sent to Hamilton, that "so long as we profess to be Neutral let our public conduct, whatever our private affections may be, accord therewith; without suffering partialities on one hand, or prejudices on the other, to control our actions." But there is much in his writings during his last months in office to indicate his adherence to the anti-French prejudice of the Federalists. He was convinced that the French minister was inciting the Republican press in their attacks on him and condemned what he considered French interference in American affairs.

IT IS A FACT well known, for history proves it, that from the restless temper of the French and the policy of that nation, they attempt openly or covertly, by threats or soothing professions, to influence the conduct of most governments. That they have attempted it with us, a little time will show. But finding a neutral conduct had been adopted, and would not be relinquished by those who administered the government, the next step was to try the people; and to work upon them several presses and many scribblers have been employed. . . . This not working as well as was expected, from a supposition that there was too much confidence and perhaps personal regard for the present Chief Magistrate and his politics, the batteries latterly have been leveled at him particularly and personally. And although he is soon to become a private citizen, his opinions are to be knocked down and his character reduced as low as they are capable of sinking it, even by resorting to absolute falsehoods. . . . To what lengths the French Directory will ultimately go is difficult to say; but that they have been led to the present point by our own people, I have no doubt.

By "our own people" he meant the Republicans—particularly those in the Democratic Societies.

He touched on the subject of French relations in his eighth, and last, Annual Message to Congress, saying:

IT IS WITH MUCH PAIN and deep regret I mention that circumstances of a very unwelcome nature have lately occurred. Our trade has suffered and is suffering extensive injuries in the West Indies from the cruisers and agents of the French Republic, and communications have been received from its minister here which indicate the danger of a further disturbance of our commerce by its authority, and which are in some respects far from agreeable. . . . I reserve for a special message a more particular communication on this interesting subject.

As to internal affairs the President's final message said that he found "ample reason for a renewed expression of that gratitude to the Ruler of the Universe which a continued series of prosperity has so often and so justly called forth." The Indians were peaceful; commissioners were busily surveying the boundary line with Canada and would soon do the same for the boundary of Spanish Florida; American prisoners held by the Barbary powers had been released, but Washington suggested "the gradual creation of a navy." He further "proposed to the consideration of Congress the expediency of establishing a national university and also a military academy."

A continuing aggravation down to Washington's last day in office was the Federal City. Wealthy Robert Morris and John Nicholson had bought much land in the new city—and had not paid for it. Washington wrote his friend Morris that unless he paid up, "the workmen must be discharged . . . whilst the buildings will be left, not only in a stagnant state but in a hurtful situation." The architects were arguing over having a dome on the capitol which, said Washington, "in my judgment is a most desirable thing, and what I always expected was part of the original design until otherwise informed in my late visits to the City." He refused to settle the argument, however; "because I have not sufficient knowledge of the subject to judge with precision."

When the commissioners ran out of money and Congress refused them more, the President helped them get a loan from Maryland, and then insisted that they show their confidence in the project by moving to the barren, muddy site. He wrote:

LET ME GIVE IT strongly as my opinion that *all* the offices and *every matter* and *thing* that relates to the city *ought* to be transacted therein; and the persons to whose care they are committed residents. Measures of this sort would form societies in the city, give it eclat, and by increasing the population, contribute not a little to the accommodation of the members who compose the Congress, for it is of little signification to prepare a house for that body to *sit in* unless there are others for their beds and board.

Usually he called the future capital the Federal City or the District of Columbia; but on March 3, 1797, he proudly used its new name in a letter which began, "Three things relative to the City of Washington call for my decision, and this is the last day I have powers to give any."

Another minor aggravation was explained in a letter to Dr. John Greenwood:

SIR: I must again resort to you for assistance. The teeth herewith enclosed have, by degrees, worked loose and, at length, two or three of them have given way altogether. I send them to you to be repaired, if they are susceptible of it . . . nothing must be done to them which will, in the *least* degree, force the lips out more than *now,* as it does this too much already; but if both upper and lower teeth were to incline inward more, it would show the shape of the mouth better, and not be the worse in any other respect.

Washington made no written comment on the election which replaced him with John Adams and the former Vice-President with Thomas Jefferson. In fact, there is no record that he addressed letters of congratulation to either man. His only letter to the incoming President was one in which he expressed "a *strong hope* that you will not withhold merited promotion for Mr. John [Quincy] Adams because he is your son. . . . I give it as my decided opinion that Mr. Adams is the most valuable public character we have abroad, and that he will prove himself to be the ablest of all our diplomatic corps."

The ex-President's first interest after his retirement was the renovation of Mount Vernon, which had been neglected for eight years. He wrote:

I FIND MYSELF in the situation, nearly, of a young beginner, for although I have not houses to build (except one which I must erect for the accommodation and security of my military, civil and private papers which are voluminous, and may be interesting) yet I have not one or scarcely anything else about me that does not require considerable repairs. In a word I am already surrounded by joiners, masons, painters etc., etc., and such is my anxiety to get out of their hands that I have scarcely a room to put a friend into or to set in myself, without the music of hammers, or the odoriferous smell of paint.

He deplored the fact that he was not a better farmer, saying:

IT IS TRUE . . . that to be a cultivator of land has been my favorite amusement; but it is equally true that I have made very little proficiency in acquiring knowledge either in the principles or practice of husbandry. My employments through life have been so diversified, my absences from home have been so frequent, and so long at a time, as to have prevented me from bestowing the attention and from making the experiments which are necessary to establish facts in the science of agriculture. And now, though I may amuse myself in that way for a short time I may remain on this theater, it is too late in the day for *me* to commence a scientific course of experiments.

His plan to lease four of his farms did not materialize because he could not find farmers of "sufficient wealth, responsibility and character" to please him. To William Strickland, an English agriculturist, he wrote that "it is so natural for man to wish to be the *absolute* lord and master of what he holds in occupancy" that the type of men he wanted were looking westward to buy land; and, he added, "Conviction of these things having left little hope of obtaining such tenants as would answer my purposes, I have had it in contemplation ever since my return home to turn my farms to grazing." He went on to say that agriculture in America was "indeed wretched . . . the primary cause of its being so is that instead of improving a *little* ground well we attempt much, and do it ill . . . we ruin the lands that are already cleared, and either cut down more wood if we have it, or emigrate into the western country."

Washington sought a new source of income from the sale of whiskey. His current plantation manager, James Anderson, had some experience in this line and suggested enlarging the distillery.

Washington asked advice on this: "The thing is new to me, in toto; but in a distillery of another kind (molasses) you must have a good general knowledge of its profits, and whether a ready sale of the spirit is to be calculated on from grain (principally to be raised on my own farms)." He gave his manager permission to go ahead with this venture, but he wanted the still to be near Anderson's house or his own rather than near the mill, "for I fear at the mill, idlers (of which, and bad people, there are many around it) under pretense of coming there with grist could not be restrained from visiting the distillery, nor probably from tempting the distiller, nay more, robbing the still, as the mill would always afford a pretext for coming to that place."

Washington wrote some letters at this time which harked back to missives of a generation before. George Washington Parke Custis was now at the College of New Jersey (Princeton) and seemed to be following in the somewhat delinquent footsteps of his father, Jacky Custis, who was now dead. As he had written to the president of Columbia about the father, Washington now wrote to the head of the New Jersey College about the son, referring to the boy's "almost unconquerable disposition to indolence in everything that did not tend to his amusements," in spite of repeated parental "admonition, encouragement or advice."

To the youth himself, Washington wrote:

YOU ARE NOW EXTENDING into that stage of life when good or bad habits are formed; when the mind will be turned to things useful and praiseworthy, or to dissipation and vice. Fix on whichever it may, it will stick by you; for you know it has been said, and truly, "that as the twig is bent so it will grow." This, in a strong point of view, above the propriety of letting your inexperience be directed by maturer advice, and in placing guard upon the avenues which lead to idleness and vice. The latter will approach like a thief, working upon your passions; encouraged, perhaps, by bad examples. . . . This admonition proceeds from the purest affection for you; but I do not mean by it that you are to become a stoic, or to deprive yourself in the intervals of study of any recreations or manly exercise which reason approves.

'Tis well to be on good terms with all your fellow students, and I am pleased to hear you are so, but while a courteous behavior is due to all, select the most deserving only for your friendships. . . . True friendship is a plant of slow growth; to be sincere there must be a congeniality of temper and pursuits. Virtue and vice can not be allied; nor can idleness and industry. . . . Let your judgment always balance well before you decide; and even then, where there is no occasion for expressing an opinion, it is best to be silent, for there is nothing more certain than that it is at all times more easy to make enemies than friends. And besides, to speak evil of anyone, unless there is unequivocal proofs of their deserving it, is an injury for which there is no adequte reparation. For, as Shakespeare says, "He that robs me of my good name enriches not himself, but renders me poor indeed," or words to that effect.

When the lad left college and came to Mount Vernon, his grandfather wrote a set of rules to which the young man was supposed to conform.

SYSTEM in all things should be aimed at; for in execution, it renders everything more easy. . . .

From breakfast until about an hour before dinner . . . I shall expect you will confine yourself to your studies, and diligently attend to them. . . . While the afternoons are short, and but little interval between rising from dinner and assembling for tea, you may employ that time in walking, or any other recreation. . . .

Rise early, that by habit it may become familiar, agreeable, healthy and profitable. It may, for a while, be irksome to do this, but that will wear off; and the practice will produce a rich harvest forever thereafter, whether in public or private walks of life.

Make it an invariable rule to be in place . . . at the usual breakfasting, dining and tea hours. It is not only disagreeable, but it is also very inconvenient for servants to be running here, and there, and they know not where, to summon you to them. . . .

Saturday may be appropriated to riding, to your gun and other proper amusements.

Time disposed of in this manner makes ample provision for exercise and every useful or necessary recreation; at the same time that the hours allotted for study, *if really applied to it* instead of running up and down stairs, and wasted in conversation with anyone who will talk with you, will enable you to make considerable progress in whatever line is marked out for you.

As usual when Washington was at Mount Vernon there was the steady stream of visitors, although he probably exaggerated when he wrote to his former secretary, Tobias Lear:

I AM ALONE at *present,* and shall be glad to see you this evening. Unless someone pops in, unexpectedly, Mrs. Washington and myself will do what I believe has not been done within the last twenty years by us—that is to set down to dinner by ourselves.

Although his pen was not as busy as usual at this time he did compose a missive in May 1798 to an old correspondent. Sally Fairfax, now a widow, had been living in England for twenty-five years. Washington wrote her:

DURING THIS PERIOD so many important events have occurred, and such changes in men and things have taken place, as the compass of a letter would give you but an inadequate idea of. None of which events, however, nor all of them together, have been able to eradicate from my mind the recollection of those happy moments, the happiest in my life, which I have enjoyed in your company.

He continued to tell her of the building of Washington, D.C., and the opening of the Potomac which was making a thriving city of Alexandria, concluding with: "In a word, if this country can steer clear of European politics . . . and be wise and temperate in its government, it bids fair to be one of the greatest and happiest nations in the world."

Private life did not free Washington from vituperation. Thomas Paine wrote an open letter to Washington which was published by Benny Bache. In vicious anger Paine wrote:

THE CHIEF OF THE ARMY became the patron of . . . fraud. Elevated to the chair of the Presidency, you assumed the merit of everything to yourself. . . . You commenced your Presidential career by encouraging and swallowing the grossest adulation, and traveled America, from one end to the other, to put yourself in the way of receiving it. . . . Treacherous in private friendship (for so you have been to me, and that in the day of danger) and a hypocrite in public life, the world will be puzzled to decide whether you are an apostate or an impostor; whether you have abandoned good principles, or whether you ever had any.

Washington did not answer Paine, but when James Monroe wrote a *View of the Conduct of the Executive of the United States,* the ex-President larded a copy of the pamphlet with pungent sentences which sought to answer every criticism of the former envoy to France. Some of Monroe's statements and Washington's comments follow; Monroe's in italics and Washington's in straight-face type.

In the month of May, 1794 I was invited by the President of the United States, through the Secretary of State, to accept the office of minister plenipotentiary to the French Republic.

After several attempts had failed to obtain a more eligible character.

It had been, too, my fortune, in the course of my service to differ from the administration upon many of our most important public measures.

Is this adduced as conclusive evidence that the Administration was in error? . . .

Our affairs with France had fallen into great derangement, and required an immediate and decisive effort to retrieve them.

Did not this derangment proceed from the injurious conduct of the French? . . .

Upon my arrival in Paris . . . I found that the work of alienation and disunion had been carried further than I had before even suspected.

If we had submitted to them without remonstrating, we should still have been their dear friends and allies. . . .

And so it went, page after page—forty-two pages in all. Monroe insisted that the Federalists back home had sabotaged his mission. The Administration had refused to give him a copy of the Jay treaty or advise him of its contents. Washington countered that Monroe was trying to sabotage the Administration. After one statement of Monroe's that he had assured the French that *"the treaty contained nothing improper, or would not be ratified in case it did."* Washington commented:

SOLICITOUS ALWAYS to get hold of the treaty prematurely for the use of the French government, he omits no opportunity of expressing his chagrin for his disappointment, and would have wished to see the Executive of the United States as indiscreetly forward himself in promulgating it, before it had been submitted to the Senate.

When Monroe said that he was not given the reasons for his recall, Washington replied, "His own reflections might have furnished him with these," and added that he had evidence that Monroe was "promoting the views of a party in his own country that were obstructing every measure of the Administration, and by their attachment to France were hurrying it . . . into a war with Great Britain, in order to favor France." Further, said the ex-President:

NEITHER THE CONSTITUTION, the laws, nor usage, render it necessary for the Executive to assign his reasons. . . . If . . . an agent of his appointment is found incompetent, remiss in his duty or pursuing wrong courses, it becomes his indispensable duty to remove him from office; otherwise he would be responsible for the consequences. Such was Mr. Monroe in the estimation of the President upon trial of him.

Perhaps the most ironic statement in Washington's bitter condemnation of the man who would one day proclaim a doctrine of isolationism which became the basis of America's foreign policy was, "If Mr. Monroe should ever fill the Chair of Government he may (and it is presumed he would be well enough disposed) let the French minister frame his speeches."

Relations with France rapidly worsened. At a special session of Congress John Adams delivered a speech which the Republicans called a "war cry." A three-man mission to France was met with demands for payments "under the table" and an apology for Adam's speech. This was the famed "XYZ affair" which led to the ringing toast: "Millions for defense but not one cent for tribute." In May 1798 Hamilton advised his old chief:

YOU OUGHT TO BE AWARE, my dear sir, that in the event of an open rupture with France, the public voice will again call you to command the armies of your country. . . . All your past labor may demand to give it efficacy this further, this very great sacrifice.

To this Washington replied:

I CANNOT MAKE UP my mind, yet, for the expectation of open war; or, in other words, for a formidable invasion by France. I cannot believe, although I think them capable of *anything bad,* that they will attempt to do more than they have done; that when they perceive the spirit and policy of this country rising into resistance . . . they will desist, *even from those practices.* . . . If I did not view things in this light my mind would be infinitely more disquieted than it is. For if a crisis should arrive when a sense of duty, or a call from my country, should become so imperious as to leave me no choice, I should prepare for the relinquishment, and go with as much reluctance from my present peaceful abode as I should do to the tombs of my Ancestors.

On June 26, 1798, Secretary of War McHenry made a semi-official query: "May we flatter ourselves that, in a crisis so awful and important, you will accept the command of all our armies?" Washington replied with a long letter in which he said

. . . there are . . . things highly important for me to ascertain, and settle, before I could give a decided answer to your question.

First. The propriety, in the opinion of the public . . . of my appearing again on a public theater after declaring the sentiments I did in my Valedictory Address. . . . Second. A conviction in my own breast . . . that it is the wish of my country that the military force of it should be committed to my charge. Third. That the army now to be formed should be so appointed as to afford a well-grounded hope of its doing honor to the country, and credit to him who commands it in the field.

He then elaborated at great length on point number three, saying that he must, this time, have a general staff. He summarized his position by writing:

IF THIS COUNTRY should actually be invaded, or such manifestations of a design to do it as cannot be mistaken, I should be ready to render every service in my power to repel it: Provided; . . . That I can have such characters associated with me as will render the turmoils of war, and the burden of the command, as light as the nature of it will admit. For it is well known that the vicissitudes of war are not within the reach of human control; and the chances of adding to are not greater than the hazard of taking from that reputation the partiality of the world has been pleased to confer for past services.

On July 12 Secretary McHenry arrived at Mount Vernon with a letter from President Adams, which said:

MR. MCHENRY, the Secretary of War, will have the honor to wait on you in my behalf, to impart to you a step I have ventured to take, and which I should have been happy to have communicated in person if such a journey had been, at this time, in my power. . . . If it had been in my power to nominate you to be President of the United States, I should have done it with less hesitation and more pleasure.

With this was enclosed a commission as a lieutenant general dated July 4.

For two days the new Commander-in-Chief and the Secretary of War discussed army organization. When McHenry left he had a list, prepared by Washington, of the general officers that the commander wanted. Leading the list was the name of Alexander Hamilton, as ranking major general, followed by Charles Cotesworth Pinckney and Henry Knox, in that order. McHenry also carried a letter from Washington to President Adams accepting the appointment, although it expressed his "earnest wish that the choice had fallen on a man less declined in years and better qualified to encounter the usual vicissitudes of war." The letter continued:

IT WAS NOT POSSIBLE for me to remain ignorant of, or indifferent to, recent transactions. The conduct of the Directory of France toward our country; their insidious hostility to its government; their various practices to withdraw the affections of the people from it; the evident tendency of their arts and those of their agents to countenance and invigorate opposition; their disregard of solemn treaties and the laws of nations; their war upon our defenseless commerce; their treatment of our Minister of Peace, and their demands amounting to tribute, could not fail to excite in me corresponding sentiments with those my countrymen have so generally expressed in their affectionate addresses to you. Believe me, sir, no one can more cordially approve of the wise and prudent measures of your Administration. They ought to inspire universal confidence, and will no doubt, combined with the state of things, call from Congress such laws and means as will enable you to meet the full force and extent of the crisis.

Satisfied, therefore, that you have sincerely wished and endeavored to avert war, and exhausted to the last drop the cup of reconciliation, we can with pure hearts appeal to heaven for the justice of our cause, and may confidently trust the final result to that kind Providence who has heretofore, and so often, signally favored the people of these United States.

Henry Knox wrote a long and bitter protest at being placed below Hamilton and Pinckney—Federalists whose claims to fame were political rather than military and who had been respectively, a colonel and a brevet brigadier in the Revolution. Knox wrote, sadly, that "for more than twenty years I must have been acting under a perfect delusion. Conscious myself of entertaining for you a sincere, active and invariable friendship, I easily believed it was reciprocal. . . . But I find that others, greatly my juniors in rank, have been, upon a scale of comparison, preferred before me."

Washington replied to this with the somewhat confusing statement that "from information I had no cause to distrust, no doubt remained on my mind that Colonel Hamilton was designated second in command and first if I should decline acceptance by the Federal characters of Congress; whence alone anything like a public sentiment relative thereto could be deduced." He then went on to defend the choice of Hamilton as senior major general, saying that "though his services during the war were not rendered in the grade of a general officer, yet his opportunities and experience could not be short of those that did. And adding these to the important trusts reposed in him in various civil walks of life, he will be found, I trust, upon as high ground as most men in the United States." He further pointed out that Hamilton needed the money, "having a large family and no certain dependence but his profession . . . something as nearly adequate as the case would admit ought to be offered to induce his acceptance."

President Adams submitted the names to the Senate but announced that the order of seniority would be Knox, Pinckney and Hamilton. Both he and Knox were from Massachusetts, and the President said that "the five New England States will not patiently submit to the humiliation that has been meditated for them." He added, "There has been too much intrigue in this business both with General Washington and me."

This brought a long letter from Washington to Adams, in which the Commander-in-Chief lectured the President, saying that a condition of his accepting command was that "the general officers and general staff of the Army should not be appointed without my concurrence." He continued:

IN THE ARRANGEMENT made by me with the Secretary of War, the three major generals stood, Hamilton, Pinckney, Knox; and in this order I expected their commissions would have been dated. This, I conceive, must have been the understanding of the Senate, and certainly was the expectation of all those with whom I have conversed. But you have been pleased to order the last to be first, and the first to be last.

In defending the preferment of Hamilton he said:

THAT HE IS AMBITIOUS I shall readily grant, but it is of that laudable kind which prompts a man to excel in whatever he takes in hand. He is enterprising, quick in his perceptions, and his judgment is intuitively great; qualities essential to a military character and therefore I repeat that his loss will be irreparable.

Washington claimed that he did not want to "increase the powers of the Commander-in-Chief, or to lessen those of the President of the United States." He merely wanted to "secure able codajutors in the arduous task I was about to enter upon." But he added:

To ACCOMPLISH IT, required an intimate knowledge of the component parts of the characters among us, in the higher grades of the late army. And I hope (without incurring the charge of presumption) I may add that the opportunities I have had to judge of these, are second to none.

Washington then changed the subject and added:

. . . Lengthy as this letter is, there is another subject, not less interesting to the Commander-in-Chief of the Armies (be him whom he may) than it is important to the United States, which I beg leave to bring respectfully to your view. We are now near the end of September and not a man recruited, nor a battalion officer appointed, that has come to my knowledge. The consequence is, that the spirit and enthusiasm which prevailed a month or two ago and would have produced the *best* men in a short time, is evaporating *fast,* and a month or two hence may induce but few, and those perhaps of the *worst* sort to enlist. Instead, therefore of having the augmented force in a state of preparation, and under a course of discipline, it is now to be *raised* and possibly may not be in existence when the enemy is in the field. We shall have to meet veteran troops inured to conquest with militia or raw recruits; the consequence of which is not difficult to conceive or foretell.

Seeing, perhaps, an implied threat in Washington's reference to the Commander-in-Chief—"be him whom he may"—Adams backed down and dated all three commissions on the same day saying that if there was any controversy over rank it would be decided by the Commander-in-Chief.

Throughout all this Washington was in constant correspondence with Hamilton, who had much to say on all phases of the subject, and with whom Washington invariably agreed. When the former Secretary of the Treasury alleged that McHenry was incompetent, his chief replied:

YOUR OPINION respecting the unfitness of a certain Gentleman for the office he holds accords with mine, and it is to be regretted, sorely, at this time, that these opinions are so well founded. I early discovered after he entered upon the duties of his office that his talents were unequal to great exertions, or deep resources. In truth they were not expected; for the fact is, it was a Hobson's choice. But such is the case, and what is to be done?

Throughout this period Hamilton was Washington's main confidant and adviser. Most of his other principal colleagues of the Revolution and the early days of the Presidency were estranged or unacceptable politically. He no longer sought the advice of Madison. He did not see or correspond with Jefferson after he left office. Randolph had published a "Vindication" of his conduct as Secretary of State in which he accused the President of having "a temper which . . . rapidly catches a prejudice and with difficulty abandons it," and said that Washington's treatment of him was a deadly stroke from the arm of an elevated and reputed patron." Henry Knox, the man who brought the guns from Ticonderoga to arm Dorchester Heights, had said that his belief in Washington's friendship had been "a perfect delusion." Thomas Paine, who had marched across New Jersey with Washington, and James Monroe, who had crossed the Delaware with him, had attacked their old commander bitterly.

The XYZ affair had aroused public indignation toward France and given the Federalists added strength. This made possible the passage of the Alien and Sedition Acts in the summer of 1798. These laws made it a high misdemeanor for citizens to enter into "unlawful combinations to oppose the execution of national laws." This was aimed at the Democratic Societies. Also, it became a crime to publish any "false, scandalous or malicious writing" against the government, the President or Congress. Under this act Republican editors could be—and some were—imprisoned without trial.

Even arch Federalists John Marshall and Alexander Hamilton opposed the Alien and Sedition Acts, the latter saying, "Let us not establish tyranny." But Washington saw merit in these measures which would curb criticism of government. To Patrick Henry he wrote:

AT SUCH A CRISIS as this, when everything dear and valuable to us is assailed; when this party hangs upon the wheels of government as a dead weight, opposing every measure that is calculated for defense and self-preservation; . . . when measures are systematically and pertinaciously pursued which must eventually dissolve the Union or produce coercion; . . . vain will it be to look for peace and happiness, or for the security of liberty or property. . . . And what else can result from the policy of those among us who, by all the means in their power, are driving matters to extremity, if they cannot be counteracted effectually? The views of men can only be known, or guessed at, by their words or actions. Can those of the *leaders* of opposition be mistaken then, if judged by this rule? . . . If their conduct is viewed with indifference; if there is activity and misrepresentation on one side, and supineness on the other, their numbers, accumulated by intriguing . . . will increase, and nothing, short of omniscience, can foretell the consequences.

In November 1798, Washington journeyed to Philadelphia to spend a month discussing military matters. He compiled a list of fourteen questions to be discussed with Generals Hamilton and Pinckney. Some of these were weighty matters, such as:

1st. Is an invasion of the United States, by France, to be apprehended whilst that power continues at war with Great Britain?

2d. In case such an invasion should take place, what part of the United States, in their opinion, is most likely to be first attacked?

3d. Is it probable that the French will, in the way of exchange or by other means, become possessed of the Floridas and Louisiana?

4th. In case of such an event, what, probably, will be the consequences, as they relate to the United States? What measures will be best to counteract them? And can those measures be carried promptly into effect by the Commander-in-Chief of the Armies? Or must they be previously submitted to the War Office? This question, it will be perceived, presupposes a force in existence.

Other of his queries concerned such trifling subjects as, "What had best be the distinctions in dress, in the badges, and other peculiarities, between the Commander-in-Chief and his suit, and the majors general and their aides?"

On his last day in Philadelphia Washington addressed three lengthy letters to Secretary McHenry emphasizing the need for vigor in raising and organizing an army. He pointed out that

. . . nothing is discoverable in the conduct of France which ought to change or relax our measures of defense. . . . Contemplating the possibility of our being driven to unqualified war, it will be wise to anticipate that frequently the most effectual way to defend is to attack. There may be imagined instances of very great moment to the permanent interests of this country which would certainly require a disciplined force. To raise and prepare such a force will always be a work of considerable time; and it ought to be ready for the conjecture whenever it shall arrive.

This was followed by a complete plan of organization for the army—a plan which was so detailed that it provided for "The coats of the musicians to be of the color of the facings of the corps to which they severally belong. The chief musicians to wear two white worsted epaulettes." These letters were Washington's last close contact with military affairs.

Back at Mount Vernon, Washington, on Christmas Day, penned a long letter to Lafayette. After apologizing for not answering the Frenchman's last six letters he advised him not to come to America. He told the Marquis that "no one in the United States would receive you with open arms, or with more ardent affection than I should." But he added that until "the differences between this country and France are adjusted and harmony between the nations is again restored . . . the scenes you would meet with, and the part you would be stimulated to act . . . would be such as to place you in a situation in which no address or human prudence could free you from embarrassment."

The ex-President then outlined his view of the current crisis:

TO GIVE YOU a complete view of the politics and situation of things in this country would far exceed the limits of a letter; and to trace effects to their causes would be a work of time. But the sum of them may be given in a few words, and amounts to this. That a party exists in the United States, formed by a combination of causes, which oppose the government in all its measures, and are determined . . . to change the nature of it, and to subvert the Constitution. To effect this no means which have a tendency to accomplish their purposes are left unessayed. The friends of government who are anxious to maintain its neutrality and to preserve the country in peace and adopt measures to produce these are charged by them as being Monarchists, Aristocrats and infractors of the Constitution . . . They arrogated to themselves (until the eyes of the people began to discover how outrageously they had been treated in the commercial concerns by the Directory of France) . . . the sole merit of being the friends of France, when in fact they had no more regard for that nation than for the Grand Turk, further than their own views were promoted by it. . . .

On the politics of Europe I shall express no opinion, nor make any inquiry who is right or who is wrong. I wish well to all nations and to all men. My politics are plain and simple. I think every nation has a right to establish that form of government under which it conceives it shall live most happy, provided it infracts no right or is not dangerous to others. And that no governments ought to interfere with the internal concerns of another, except for the security of what is due to themselves.

In February 1799 the Federalists, and Washington, were stunned when President Adams announced to Congress, entirely on his own initiative, that he was sending another mission to France in an effort to reconcile differences. He said he had an assurance from Talleyrand that the mission would be received with due respect. Washington wrote a confidential letter to Secretary of State Pickering, saying that he was informed "that there had been no direct overture from the government of France to that of the United States, for a negotiation. On the contrary, that Mr. Talleyrand was playing the same loose and roundabout game he had attempted the year before with our envoys; and which, as in that case, might mean anything, or nothing, as would subserve his purposes best." He continued to outline how he would have handled the matter had he been the Chief Executive:

HAD WE SAID to Mr. Talleyrand . . . we are still, as we always have been, ready to settle by fair negotiation all differences between the two nations upon open, just and honorable terms; and it rests with the Directory . . . if they are equally sincere to come forward in an unequivocal manner, and prove it by their acts. Such conduct would have shown a dignified willingness on our part to negotiate, and would have tested their sincerity, on the other. Under my present view of the subject this would have been the course I should have pursued, keeping equally in view the horrors of war, and the dignity of the government.

During the last months of his life Washington was plagued, as always, by a shortage of cash. In four years he had sold land in the amount of $50,000, but this, with income from crops and rents, had "scarcely been able to keep me afloat." He offered to sell three of his jackasses for "eight hundred pounds of any one, who will take the three."

One problem was that he had too many slaves; but he refused to sell them. He wrote:

IT IS DEMONSTRATIVELY CLEAR that on this estate (Mount Vernon) I have more working Negroes by a full moiety than can be employed to any advantage. . . . To sell the overplus I cannot, because I am principled against this kind of traffic in human species. To hire them out is almost as bad, because they could not be disposed of in families to any advantage, and to disperse the families I have an aversion. What then is to be done? Something must or I shall be ruined.

Yet, at age sixty-eight, he had not changed his liberal and—in connection with his property—extravagant ways. He loaned Tobias Lear $1500 and replied to a nephew who had applied for a loan:

INCONVENIENT as it is to me (and nothing can be more so than it is at this time) to part with what little money I have in the bank of Alexandria; yet, rather than suffer your Negroes to be taken in execution, and sold perhaps at half price, I will answer your draughts to the amount of one thousand dollars, but not one cent beyond; as that sum will take nearly every farthing I have in the bank.

He was building two houses in Washington, D.C., and could not resist the luxury of expensive imported glass.

Washington visited the new capital a month before his death to inspect proudly his newly finished houses, which he described as being "upon a larger scale than any in the vicinity of the Capitol. . . . The houses are three flush stories of brick, besides garret rooms: and in the judgment of those better acquainted in these matters than I am, capable of accommodating between twenty and thirty boarders. The buildings are not costly, but elegantly plain." He offered to rent the houses for $1200 a year which would be, he figured, "seven and a half per cent on the whole cost"; which was very fair, he thought, because it "was but little more than legal and common interest of money, when it is well known that the wear and tear of houses required much more."

During the last year of his life, although he was in perfect health, Washington made several matter-of-fact references to his "declining years," apparently because he was nearing the Biblical "three-score and ten." His "greatest anxiety" was to "leave all these concerns in such a clear and distinct form as that no reproach may attach itself to me when I have taken my departure for the land of spirits." For this purpose he made a will, dated July 9, 1799, which started:

IN THE NAME of God amen: I, George Washington, of Mount Vernon—a citizen of the United States,—and lately President of the same, do make, ordain and declare this instrument, which is written with my own hand and every page thereof subscribed with my name, to be my last Will & Testament, revoking all others.

The only other known will is that which he made and sent to Martha in 1755.

The new will, after directing that all his debts be "speedily and punctually paid" first provided:

TO MY DEARLY BELOVED WIFE Martha Washington I give and bequeath the use, profit and benefit of my whole Estate, real and personal, for the term of her natural life, except such parts thereof as are specifically disposed of hereafter.

He next mentioned his slaves.

UPON THE DECEASE OF MY WIFE, it is my will and desire that all the slaves which I hold in my own right shall receive their freedom. To emancipate them during her life, would, 'tho earnestly wished by me, be attended with such insuperable difficulties on account of their intermixture by marriages with the Dower Negroes, as to excite the most painful sensations, if not disagreeable consequences. . . . And I do hereby expressly forbid the sale or transportation out of the said Commonwealth of any slave I may die possessed of, under any pretense whatsoever.

He left $4000 "towards the support of a Free School . . . for [the] purpose of educating such orphan children, or the children of such other poor and indigent persons as are unable to accomplish it with their own means"; fifty shares of stock in the Potomac Company "towards the endowment of a UNIVERSITY to be established within the limits of the District of Columbia"; and 100 shares in the James River Company to Liberty-Hall Academy—later Washington and Lee University of whose endowment this bequest is still a part.

After referring to the affairs of his deceased brother Samuel and his wife's brother Bartholomew Dandridge, which he had managed, he made numerous other small bequests. The goldheaded crabtree cane which Benjamin Franklin had left him was willed to his only surviving brother, Charles; other canes and spyglasses went to two nephews; items of furniture to Doctors Craik and Stuart; his Bible to Reverend Bryan Fairfax; a pair of "finely wrought steel pistols" to Lafayette; five nephews could each choose a sword with the injunction "not to unsheathe them for the purpose of shedding blood except it be for self-defense, or in defense of their country and its rights, and in the latter case to keep them unsheathed and prefer falling with them in their hands to the relinquishment thereof"; and to Tobias Lear "I give the use of the farm which he now holds . . . free from rent, during his life."

His greatest gift was Mount Vernon. This he left to "My nephew Bushrod Washington and his heirs." This, he explained, was

. . . partly in consideration of an intimation to his deceased father while we were bachelors, and he had kindly undertaken to superintend my estate during my military services in the former war between Great Britain and France, that if I should fall therein, Mount Vernon—then less extensive in domain than at present—should become his property.

He left acreage other than Mount Vernon to grandnephews, to his favorite stepgranddaughter, Nelly, and to his step grandson, George Washington Parke Custis. He then provided that "all the rest and residue of the estate . . . not disposed of in manner aforesaid" should be sold, divided into twenty-three equal parts and distributed to nephews, grandnephews and other remote relations. Although he had no children of his own, George Washington had a tremendous number of "kinfolk." He closed his will by saying that "all disputes (if unhappily any should arise) shall be decided by three impartial and intelligent men, known for their probity and good understanding; two to be chosen by the disputants—each having the choice of one—and the third by those two."

In the final two months of his life Washington continued to be critical of President Adams' international policy, although he hoped for the best. He expressed his views, in confidence, to three stanch Federalists who were now opposed to Adams. Of the peace mission to France he wrote to Hamilton:

THIS BUSINESS seems to have commenced in an evil hour, and under unfavorable auspices; and I wish mischief may not tread in all its steps, and be the final result of the measure. . . . But I have the same reliance on Providence which you express, and trust that matters will *end well,* however unfavorable they may appear at present.

In a similar vein he wrote to Secretary Pickering:

AS MEN will view the same things in different lights, I would fain hope that the President has caught the true one; and that good will come from the mission which is about to depart. These are my wishes, and no one is more ardent in them; but I see nothing in the present aspect of European affairs on which to build them.

And to Secretary of War McHenry he wrote:

I HAVE, for some time past, viewed the political concerns of the United States with an anxious and painful eye. They appear to me to be moving by hasty strides to some awful crisis; but in what they will result, that Being who sees, foresees, and directs all things alone can tell. The vessel is afloat, or very nearly so, and considering myself as a passenger only, I shall trust to the mariners whose duty it is to watch to steer it into a safe port.

On the morning of December 12, 1799, Washington mounted, as was his custom, to visit his farms. The weather was alternate rain and snow, through which he rode for some five hours. "In the evening," Lear later recorded, "he appeared as well as usual." Next morning it was still snowing, and he penned a brief note to plantation manager James Anderson enclosing a copy of an overall farm plan which he had prepared and ending with a complaint about a cattle pen.

SUCH A PEN as I saw yesterday at Union farm would, if the cattle were kept in it one week, destroy the whole of them. They would be infinitely more comfortable in this, or any other weather in the open fields; Dogue Run farm pen may be in the same condition. It did not occur to me as I passed through the yard of the barn to look into it.

This is the last known letter that he wrote. Before he went to bed he recorded in his diary:

MORNING snowing and abt. 3 inches deep. Wind at No. Et., and Mer. at 30. contg. snowing till 1 o'clock, and abt. 4 it became perfectly clear. Wind in the same place but not hard. Mer. 28 at night.

These are probably the last words that he wrote.

The old General had a sore throat when he went to bed and, about 3:00 A.M., he woke Martha to say that he was ill; but he forbade her to get up in the cold room. At daybreak Lear sent for Dr. Craik and, at Washington's request, an overseer, Rawlins, to come and bleed him. When Dr. Craik, who was in his seventies, failed to arrive by nine o'clock, Martha asked Lear to send for a Dr. Brown. After Craik arrived he sent for a third young doctor, Elisha Cullen Dick. The three medical men diagnosed the illness as "inflammatory quinsy" and applied the crude remedies of the day, including four bleedings that took over eighty ounces of blood.

Throughout the day Washington breathed with great difficulty and writhed on his bed during the long afternoon. Toward evening Dr. Craik suggested that he try to sit up in bed and Washington said, "I feel myself going. I thank you for your attention. You had better not take any more trouble about me but let me go off quietly. I cannot last long." About 10.00 P.M. Lear saw that Washington was trying to speak and leaned close to hear him whisper, "I am just going. Have me decently buried, and do not let my body be put into the vault in less than two days after I am dead." Lear merely nodded and Washington added, "Do you understand me?" Lear replied, "Yes, sir," and the General said, 'Tis well." These were his last words. A few minutes later he withdrew his hand from Lear's and tried to take his own pulse. His hand dropped to the covers. Dr. Craik and Lear leaned over the still form. Martha, from the foot of the bed, asked, "Is he gone?" Lear nodded. " 'Tis well," said Martha, "All is now over, I have no more trials to pass through. I shall soon follow him."

Servants galloped from Mount Vernon with the sad news, and one went to Alexandria to order a coffin and a shroud. On December 17 the body was laid out in the "new room" in a black-lined casket and on the eighteenth moved to the portico where neighbors and crowds from Alexandria filed past. That afternoon a procession filed to the family vault. There was no one of national prominence in it; there had not been time for relatives or friends to arrive from a distance. The casket was carried by four lieutenants of Virginia militia, followed by neighbors, officials from Alexandria and a large delegation of Masons from that city and Washington, D.C. As the bier was placed at the opening of the tomb a schooner in the river fired minute guns. A minister read the Episcopal Order of Burial, and the Masonic Grand Master performed the rights of that order. As the casket was placed in the sepulcher the eleven cannon of the Alexandria militia fired a last salute.

Between Washington's death and what would have been his sixty-ninth birthday 303 eulogies were preached in 185 cities and towns throughout the country extolling the great man. The most famous was delivered by Henry Lee in Philadelphia on December 26, which Congress had designated as a national day of mourning.

FIRST IN WAR, first in peace and first in the hearts of his countrymen, he was second to none in the humble and endearing scenes of private life. Pious, just, humane, temperate and sincere—uniform, dignified and commanding—his example was as edifying to all around him as were the effects of that example lasting. . . . Correct throughout, vice shuddered in his presence and virtue always felt his fostering hand. The purity of his private character gave effulgence to his public virtues. . . . Such was the man for whom our nation mourns.

Douglas Southall Freeman, Washington's most capable biographer, in seeking to explain in simple terms the reason for his subject's greatness, used the expression, "He always walked in a straight line." This, he knew, was a quotation from a self-analysis which Washington had penned to Bryan Fairfax in the last year of his life:

THE FAVORABLE SENTIMENTS which others, you say, have been pleased to express respecting me cannot but be pleasing to a mind who always walked on a straight line, and endeavored as far as human frailties, and perhaps strong passions, would enable him, to discharge the relative duties to his Maker and fellow men, without seeking any indirect or left handed attempts to acquire popularity.

INDEX

❦